NEW AGE ASTROLOGY

Is this really the Age of Aquarius? Certainly astrology has gone through some major changes over the past few years and those of you who have been attending workshops and conferences have seen these changes reflected in the topics discussed.

In this book, editor Joan McEvers has brought together some of the best astrologers in the forefront of new thought in the astrological world. More people are becoming interested in using astrology as a tool in their daily living, growth and understanding of themselves and the world. The astrologers in this book are dedicating themselves to the continuation of astrology's evolution.

Spiritual or metaphysical astrology is nothing new. However, the acceptance of it as something important for students and professionals to understand is growing. There are so many new avenues for the astrologer or person interested in astrology to pursue. Included in this first time anthology of the best in the field are some of the latest in new approaches to astrology.

These new approaches include some old techniques brought up to date, new ideas on participatory and experiential astrology and other such radical concepts. This is truly a book of the future.

Read and enjoy. Practice and understand. Use the techniques for yourself and have a better understanding of the new wave of astrology—far from the stuffiness of the old methods.

Joan McEvers

Author of *12 Times 12*, and co-author with Marion D. March of the highly acclaimed teaching series *The Only Way to . . . Learn Astrology*, as well as *Astrology: Old Theme, New Thoughts*, Joan McEvers is a practicing astrologer in Coeur d'Alene, Idaho.

Born and raised in Chicago where she majored in art and worked as a model and illustrator for an art studio, she moved to the Los Angeles area in 1948, and continued her professional career in the sales field. This is where she met her husband, Dean and raised her four children.

Joan started her serious study of astrology in 1965, studying on her own until 1969, when she took classes with Ruth Hale Oliver. Joan has achieved an international reputation as a teacher and lecturer, speaking for many groups in the U.S. and Canada. A professional member of AFA and an AFAN coordinator, she has had articles published in several national astrological magazines.

In 1975, Joan and Marion founded Aquarius Workshops, Inc., with Joan as President. She also helped establish its quarterly publication *Aspects* which is widely recognized for the wealth of astrological information in each issue.

Her latest individual effort is *12 Times 12*, which came out in a revised and updated version in 1984. In this book, each of the 144 possible Sun/Ascendant combinations is discussed in detail. Every description includes information about personality, appearance, health, likely vocational areas, interest and attitudes. Also in 1984, the latest March/McEvers book *Astrology: Old Theme, New Thoughts* was published. This is a collection of concepts, ideas and lectures on various avenues of astrology and is being well received by the public.

Volume IV of *The Only Way* series is in the works. The working title is *Looking Ahead* and it deals with all kinds of progressions and forecasting. Joan also has a two-hour video *Simplified Horary Astrology*. When she isn't busy teaching, lecturing, writing or counseling clients, Joan keeps occupied with quilting and playing bridge.

THE NEW WORLD ASTROLOGY SERIES

This series is designed to give all people who are interested and involved in astrology the latest information on a variety of subjects. Llewellyn has given much thought to the prevailing trends and to the topics that would be most important to our readers.

Future books will include such topics as financial astrology, locational astrology, electional and mundane astrology, astrology and past lives, and many other subjects of interest to a wide range of people. This project has evolved because of the lack of information on these subjects and because we wanted to offer our readers the viewpoints of the best experts in each field in one volume.

This first book, edited by leading astrologer Joan McEvers, is just the beginning. We anticipate publishing approximately six books per year on varying topics and updating previous editions when new material becomes available. This is the first in a series like this and we know that it will fill a gap in your astrological library. We look only for the best writers and article topics when planning the new books and appreciate any feedback from our readers on subjects you would like to see covered.

Llewellyn's New World Astrology Series will be a welcome addition to the novice, student and professional alike. It will provide introductory as well as advanced information on all of the topics listed above—and more.

Enjoy, and feel free to write to Llewellyn with your suggestions or comments.

Llewellyn's New World Astrology Series

SPIRITUAL, METAPHYSICAL & NEW TRENDS IN MODERN ASTROLOGY

Edited by
Joan McEvers

1988
Llewellyn Publications
St. Paul, Minnesota 55164-0383, U.S.A.

International Standard Book Number: 0-87542-380-9
Library of Congress Catalog Number: 88-6760

First Edition, 1988
First Printing, 1988
Second Printing, 1988

Library of Congress Cataloging-in-Publication Data
Spiritual, metaphysical & new trends in modern astrology.

(Llewellyn's New world astrology series)
1. Astrology. I. McEvers, Joan. II. Title:
Spiritual, metaphysical, and new trends in modern astrology.
III. Series.
BF1708.1.S67   1988   133.5   88-6760
ISBN 0-87542-380-9

Cover Painting: David Egge
Book Design: Terry Buske

Produced by Llewellyn Publications
Typography and Art property of Chester-Kent, Inc.

Published by
LLEWELLYN PUBLICATIONS
A Division of Chester-Kent, Inc.
P.O. Box 64383
St. Paul, MN 55164-0383, U.S.A.

Printed in the United States of America

Contents

INTRODUCTION

In recent decades the media has referred to this period in time as the *"Age of Aquarius."* I prefer to refer to it as the *"Age of Astrology."* At last, astrology is coming of age in this century. In the past, the general attitude of most people has been, "Oh, do you *believe* in astrology?" acting as though you had two heads or a communicable disease. I have never felt that astrology should be viewed as a belief system, any more than the average person views electricity as a belief system.

If you ask the average person if they believe in electricity, they look either baffled or aghast. I hasten to explain that astrology, like electricity, rather than being a belief system is a *tool* to be used for enlightenment. Both can turn on a light when properly applied. Each, when incorrectly used, can be detrimental to the user.

Just as electrical current is set up as a conductor of energy potential, so the horoscope can act as a conductor of potential for the individual. We use electricity in many forms and guises; to provide power and light, for mechanical energy, to better our lives. It is used to both heat and cool our environment, to operate the media, to run the presses, the TV sets, to cook our meals, etc. Yet, unbridled electricity can be devastating, as when a power plant blows up or an electrical fire damages a home.

The same principle applies to astrology. It can be used detrimentally—to coerce as well as to misguide others, to worship as some kind of occult power. A few practitioners tie it to witchcraft. It is easy to see why, in the past, and still unfortunately sometimes in the present, astrology has gained a rather tarnished reputation.

1

2 / Spiritual, Metaphysical & New Trends in Modern Astrology

In the sixties, seventies and eighties, astrology is enjoying a renaissance. It is growing and changing, as does all of life. The client or student who is only interested in what the future holds is being replaced by those who want to know more about their spiritual or karmic links with other people and the world around them. Some of the questions being asked are: "How may I better tune in to my *real goals* in life and work out my true destiny? What is my purpose here in this lifetime?"

In the past their questions mostly reflected concern for the material future, i.e. "What is happening next year? Will I change jobs? Will Joe and I marry?" Now more of those who seek out the astrologer are open to suggestions about how they may better approach their lives by understanding the metaphysical or spiritual directions indicated in their horoscope. And this is the right time for these concerns because great minds are addressing the various opportunities available through this art/science.

More and more members of the general public are using astrological tools to better understand their own presence in this lifetime. Fewer and fewer people frown at those who find the answers they are seeking through a practical application of astrology. But, many people, especially those uninitiated in the way of astrology, are afraid of what can be seen in a horoscope. They read the daily forecasts in the local newspapers or magazines, little realizing that these are generalities based on solar charts; that they suggest that there are only twelve types of people in the world. How many people, who when discovering that you are an astrologer say, "Oh I would never want to have my chart done. I do not want to know when I will die or have an accident. I don't want you to tell me that I will never marry, or that I cannot have children, or that I am about to lose a loved one." The astrologer *cannot* tell when and how a person will die; cannot necessarily tell if you will marry or have children; or see that you are in danger of losing your mother, father, partner or child. But popular misconception enhances the myth that the astrologer is all-knowing, all-seeing.

An astrological chart is not something to be feared. It is based upon mathematical formula, not hocus-pocus. This empirical craft has proven its validity over the centuries. The horoscope, set up for the correct date, time and place of birth, can help you to learn about yourself in relationship to the universe and its inhabitants. Is this bad? Of course not. But when it is presented in the guise of witchcraft, voodoo or fortunetelling, it is understandable why people are put off, shy away and accuse astrologers of trying to foist a *belief* system on them.

The astrological chart is one of the greatest tools in the universe. From it, properly beheld, the accomplished astrologer can discover both positive and negative potentials, good and bad traits, personality, character, career direction, intellectual capacity, romantic and sexual inclinations. Besides all this, relationships of all kinds can be examined . . . marriage, sibling, friendship, parental, co-workers, those in authority.

Your needs, emotions, energy level, philosophical outlook, greatest strengths and weaknesses can be determined from your horoscope, as well as your visions, fantasies, goals, aims, hopes, aspirations and talents. Astrology contributes to a more positive way to organize and live your life.

The Horoscope as a Road Map

You would not think of starting an automobile trip from Utica, New York to Bakersfield, California without referring to a road map. I liken the horoscope to a road map. It shows you all the possible routes you can take, but it *in no way*, says you *must* take one or another. If on the above auto trip, you decide to go through Pittsburgh and Chicago, before heading south, nothing can prevent you from changing your mind and perhaps going through Tennessee and Missouri on your way west.

It is the same with your horoscope. The potential road map is outlined, but *it is your choice* that you take the learning avenues and detours in your life. On your automobile trip, you may encounter a road washout, which necessitates detouring and choosing an alternate route. So it is with your chart and your life. You may start in one particular career, decide you are not comfortable there and choose to go in another direction.

Planets, Signs, Houses and Aspects

In astrology, the planets symbolize the energies available to you; the signs signify the way you can use the energy; the houses suggest the arena where the energy is displayed. Jupiter traditionally has to do with expansion. If Jupiter is in Cancer, the feelings of expansion can be nurturing and caring. With Jupiter in the 7th House, its energy may well be expressed in dealing with others, either on a partnership or public level, or both.

Another example is Mars in Virgo in the 11th House. Used negatively, this can connote critical (Virgo) energy (Mars) directed at friends (11th House), representing the person who cannot understand why no one likes them. Used positively, on the other hand, this can be the placement of someone who, with unerring attention to detail (Virgo) puts tremendous energy (Mars) into community affairs (11th House). Logically, anyone who has this placement will use it both ways at different times. It would be wonderful if we all used the many options in our charts positively all the time. But this rarely happens. At least, not from my experience. We are human and as human beings, we experience negative as well as positive feelings and often give voice and action to them. So it is with the symbology of the horoscope: the patterns may be expressed both by positive and negative action.

Another facet to be considered is aspects. In the above example, if Mars trined the Sun, popular astrological views suggest that the energy between the two planets would flow smoothly. If, on the other hand, Mars squared the Sun, it may connote that there are challenges to be met where these two planets are concerned. My feeling is that the trine does not diminish the likelihood of using the energy in a negative way. In fact, it may seem easier for the person to do just that. Just as there is no guarantee that a square always means difficulty or negative behavior.

There are as many views of aspects and how they are used in the chart, as there are astrologers. My view is that an easy, flowing aspect (trine, sextile) or a challenging stressful aspect (square, opposition, inconjunct) or the neutral conjunction do nothing more than combine the energy of the planets involved. The individual has the choice of how to use these aspects, flowing or challenging, to learn—to understand. To paraphrase Jawaharial Nehru: The horoscope is like a game of cards. The hand that is dealt you represents determinism. The way you play it is free will.

Making Choices

The competent astrologer will discuss the potentials in the horoscope with the client, pointing out various ways the energy can be used, considering progressions and transits applying at the time of the consultation. The person has the choice of how to use the energy generated. There are myriad ramifications in the use of the planetary picture as depicted in the horoscope. Free will is ever present.

How does astrology explain negative and misused energy? This is a question often asked by "believers" as well as scoffers. It is not an easy question to answer, and perhaps assumes a belief in an afterlife. The only answer I am able to come up with is . . . *choice*. We all make choices as we live life. Sometimes we opt for a positive path, sometimes for the negative. Sometimes our choice is conscious, sometimes not. Most of us, who are trying to live by the Golden Rule try to make consciously *good* choices. But often the good choice, as we see it, turns out to be a bad choice through no fault of our own.

Perhaps someone with a negative turn of mind consciously makes bad choices. The astrological chart shows *both* the positive and negative potential. Most astrologers tend to point out the most positive use of the cosmic energies . . . assuming that their listeners are trying to make the best of their potentials. No astrologer wants to influence a client negatively. But, the choice is always up to the individual.

You may well ask, "Doesn't heredity and environment have something to do with the choices we make?" My answer has to be, "Certainly." Your background influences your behavior. So do your surroundings. This does not imply that if your antecedents came over on the Mayflower, or if you were born into the lap of luxury, you will always make the right choices. But, if you were brought up to play by the rules, to honor others, to be honest and true to your own beliefs, chances are you tend to a positive use of the energy depicted in your horoscope.

On the other hand, if your upbringing and background left a lot to be desired, it does not necessarily imply that you will tend to use the energy negatively. Many factors enter into chart analysis. It is necessary for the astrologer to consider your relationship to your parents, your need to rebel or be different, your capacity to deal with, and your attitude toward, authority.

As any competent astrologer knows, the chart of a criminal and that of the upholder of the law are often similar. Why does one choose to use the chart in negative fashion and the other opt to use it more positively? It may very well depend upon heredity and background. But, just as often, we see the case of the "well brought-up" person opting to take the negative path. Again, these actions relate to choice. Much depends upon your spiritual values . . . even your past lives. These are some of the subjects addressed in this book.

New Directions

Aware people realize that this is a period when astrology is opening new doors. Astrology's future is bright. Now and in the future, we may hope to see it used by large personnel departments, in vocational schools to help people choose the proper work fields, in our educational systems to help guide students in their choice of studies. A careful perusal of an individual horoscope can help a person to relocate to maximize health and work potentials.

This book, *Spiritual, Metaphysical and New Trends in Modern Astrology*, is the first in a projected series which will present different astrological opinions and approaches to the reader. Some of the topics to be considered in future volumes of the series, will be relationships, financial, relocational, mundane and event oriented astrology. Each one will present a valid approach to an ancient and revered technique. The selection of authors will be wide-ranging, bringing you, the reader, the opportunity to find out what professional astrologers envision for the future of astrology.

Since astrology is practiced all over the world (except in some remote places in Africa and New Guinea), another book may look at how other cultures view astrology . . . the Mayan, Chinese and Indian, for example. We sincerely hope that this series of books will open new doors for you and make you aware of the many new directions astrology is taking.

When Llewellyn Publications called and asked me to select ten authors to write this book on various spiritual, metaphysical and new trends in astrology, I was delighted at the prospect of a work that would address the many facets of this intriguing subject. The astrologers for this undertaking were carefully chosen from among the many professionals practicing today. Since the publishers are fully cognizant of the many directions astrology is taking, it was suggested that I seek writers who are pioneering, experimental and devising new avenues. Part of my choice was to select those whose views reflected the metaphysical, spiritual and esoteric. I'm sure that you, the reader, will appreciate the varying concepts presented here.

The authors of *Spiritual, Metaphysical and New Trends in Modern Astrology* are from the United States and Canada. There are seven women and three men. California is well represented with six authors—one from Texas, another from Vermont, one from Washington and one is a transplanted American living in France—an eclectic group, I'm sure you will agree.

Many astrologers feel that your past lives can shed light on the current one and you will find their concepts presented here. Others feel that you can alter the way you deal with your planetary energy by physically acting out or dramatizing the planets in your chart.

What is offered here encompasses spiritual, metaphysical and participatory approaches. You may already be familiar with the authors whose works are included, but the segments in this book are mostly all new material. These writers look at astrology from an esoteric, experiential aspect and while you may not always agree with their viewpoints, it is recommended that you read what they have to say with an open mind. Try some of the techniques they explain, and if the particular method appeals to you, you may wish to incorporate it into your astrological work.

You may be intrigued by the participatory approaches of **Angel Thompson** and **Jeff Jawer**. Jeff has long been

demonstrating the *Astrodrama* way of looking at the chart—
acting out the principles represented by the elements,
qualities, planets, signs, houses and aspects. The methods
he presents are simple but well thought out concepts for
better understanding how to use the energy embodied in
the horoscope. Angel uses ritual as well as role playing in
her *transformational* method of investigating the horoscope. She suggests that by acting out the chart, a person is
better able to understand various ways of dealing with life.
She and Jeff both suggest ways to make astrology a living
experience.

Shirley Lyons Meier explains the Carl Payne Tobey
Shadow chart. Tobey called it the Secondary Chart. This is
not to be confused with secondary progressions. Instead, it
is a chart based on Arabic point calculations researched by
Tobey just prior to his death. Though this is an ancient
approach, he pioneered a new system resulting in a different Ascendant—providing a "second" chart. Meier has
made some changes and brought us a new concept to consider. It is a technique well worth examining, as it offers
new insights into the natal horoscope.

Gray Keen elucidates his perception of the real meaning of astrology. He analyzes the connections between Eastern and Western astrological methods, melding them into a
cohesive whole that embodies the best of both. He presents
his conclusions as to where astrology is heading in the
future. His comments on needed legislation are informed
and thought provoking.

Kimberly McSherry addresses the feminine mystique
from an astrological viewpoint. She describes the need for
recognizing, understanding and accepting the feminine/
receptive side of life in tomorrow's world. Kimberly discusses the *"way of the egg"* as opposed to the *"way of the
sperm"* and awakens concepts not usually remarked upon in
astrological literature. Her explanation of intercepted and

retrograde planets is provocative. Her analysis of how the Nodes work in the chart is intriguing as well as enlightening.

Philip Sedgwick explains the galactic center and black holes and how they relate to planetary placements in the horoscope. He joins astrological giants Theodore Landscheidt, Michael Erlewine and Charles Harvey in examining the universe *beyond* our solar system. Sedgwick feels that these are areas for exploration for future thinking astrologers and he is very convincing in his delineations of these new (to many of us) concepts.

Isabel Hickey, Alan Leo and Alice Bailey were some of the pioneering astrologers who made us aware of the esoteric side of the horoscope, the side that relates to the inner, spiritual being. If we wish to apply these principles in the new age astrology is heading into, we can well heed the words of the next four authors.

Myrna Lofthus outlines a method for exploring the horoscope from a *spiritual standpoint*. She discusses how past life activities, shown in the chart, enlighten us and offer avenues of behavior in this lifetime. She touches on the interrelationship of the Sun, Moon and Ascendant, spiritual explanation of the signs, interceptions and the Nodes in setting forth her concepts of possible earlier incarnations. She also explores in depth how the configurations work and evolve from one lifetime to another.

Kathleen Burt interprets the *spiritual* meanings of the signs including their rulers and applies this interpretation to those who counsel and advise others. She offers a delineation of these esoteric links between signs and planets, especially as they relate to the Ascendant. Her interpretation of how the esoteric rulers pertain to the whole chart is most illuminating.

Marion D. March views the meanings of the astrological *glyphs* and you are sure to be impressed by the importance of drawing these symbols correctly. She explains how each stroke of each glyph has symbolic meaning on the spiritual, esoteric level. March also discusses the significance of elements, qualities and houses in the esoteric chart.

Donna Van Toen simplifies the writings of Alice Bailey and presents these concepts in *today's language* in a way that everyone can understand and apply. She analyzes each sign esoterically and considers the esoteric rulers from Bailey's viewpoint. For those of us who have never been able to cope with Bailey's complicated writing, Van Toen's clarification will be greatly appreciated.

I sincerely hope that every reader will find something in this book to enrich their knowledge, to pique their curiosity and to enhance their application of new and renewed astrological techniques.

—Joan McEvers
Coeur d'Alene, Idaho
December, 1987

Gray Keen

Born in Ohio, Keen was a teenage drummer with big bands. His first newspaper employment was as a part-time feature writer and cub reporter at age 15. He studied law and criminology and worked for three years in law enforcement but gravitated back to the writing field. His journalism career spanned 25 years and included positions as editor, publisher, radio news director, talk show host and television news director and anchor. Married, he is the father of eight children.

Gray became interested in astrology at age 11 by reading Lord Francis Bacon. He has practiced astrology in the Bay Area for seven years including corporate personnel work, service to professional counselors and client consulting. He also operates an astrological computer service.

A long time member of NCGR, Gray has also served a one year term as vice president of Professional Astrologers Incorporated. He studied Hindu astrology with Professor K. P. Singh of India, and has been initiated in Kriya Yoga by Swami Hariharananda Giri.

He has written articles for *Today's Astrologer* and *Geocosmic News*.

PERSPECTIVE:
THE ETHEREAL CONCLUSION

Where is astrology going? And who is driving the bus that's taking us there?

If you embrace the idea that astrology and astrologers are all just nifty and that there's no aberration or difficulty in its Western world practice, then you haven't been paying attention. Historically, astrologers are noted for failing, *collectively*, to resolve their problems, so this should alert any reasonably sane person to the probability that there must be something out of focus with astrologers *individually*.

There's no one in charge of the tent flap at the astrology circus so anyone can get in for a couple of paperbacks, drop the magic word "astrologer," and shake hands with the mass of wide-eyed romantics who are hopeful that this time they have found the right astrologer. The author and publisher don't mind—they know they're satisfying a cogent need. And, no one can honestly quarrel with the would-be astrologer because we were all at one time beginners, *unless* we recognize that this situation can be likened to handing a child a loaded gun. For any unregulated activity operates much in the same way as does turning a large pen of rabbits loose on the prairie; each rabbit will clamor in haste to find his own tuft of grass.

The would-be astrologer, to further prepare, might join astrological organizations, receive the publications, attend the conferences, read the latest books, and feel completely confident that all this is sufficient to qualify him as a progressive astrologer.

But it has not been all positive, for he encounters those who laugh at astrology, telling him that any person who would seek out an astrologer lacks a real grip on the stairway handrail of life. He is constantly reminded of the failures and shortcomings of the daily newspaper astrology columns and the occasionally embarrassing appearances of astrologers on television.

It was the latter part of 1985 that he heard about a woman in Europe who, in speaking to her daughter in America by telephone, voiced concern about her morning newspaper headline that read: "American Scientists Disprove Validity of Astrology." While angry as well as gleeful astronomers, materialistic scientists, opportunistic entrepreneurs and religious bigots seemed to take turns with their contrived attacks, the student became aware that part of the world was at war with astrologers. He watched with anticipation but the astrological community stood silent at each confrontation—unwilling or unable to fight—lending credence to the possibility that astrologers might indeed be less than credible. For any endeavor that could not stand before the bright light of challenge automatically earned the stigma of distrust and suspicion.

The student is driven to the role of devil's advocate and begins to sense that esoteric words such as, for example, *arcane, occult, magick, esoteric,* and *astral* are partly responsible for creating a credibility gap with intellectuals. The general public, he soon learns, sees astrologers as disturbed persons who have their eyes closed, head in the clouds and feet that never quite touch the ground. One day, in looking back, he discovers something he'd overlooked—that many astrologers in the Twentieth Century still refer to their clients as "natives," inferring that astrology has failed to mature to adulthood while reflecting the pomposity that could turn off more than the American Indian it insults.

The deluge of techniques, concepts and challenges he has heard and read renders the student dormant with confusion as he is left to mull over the unanswered, the ambiguous, the contradictions, the misguided statements.

He asks himself, "Where is the real astrology?"

Because of doubt, disillusion and embarrassment, the student eventually drifts away from his interest in astrology.

There can be little contest with the condition that astrology in the Western world engenders a breed of ostrich mentalities that default to traditional cliches to serve as personal public relation departments. Perhaps you will recognize some of these popular ones:

"That person simply has not studied astrology as long as I have, so I refuse to debate."

"I accept the Biblical reference and 'turn the other cheek'."

"My faith is in the stars."

"God will take care of me."

"No one will mess with me. I'm an ordained minister and besides, I have a degree in mud wrestling."

Sadly, some of these rebuffs smack of similarity with the rantings of fundamentalist religionists—such as the well-known Texas incident in which an evangelist held a rattlesnake above his head and shouted:

"God will not let this serpent harm me!" . . . whereupon, the rattlesnake bit the evangelist, killing him instantly.

As you walk along a trail in the dense forest, you can see the path only a short distance ahead and a short distance behind you. Since your mind is consumed with the immediacy of the environment which you cannot see, you are less concerned about the path you have traveled. Thus, you are oblivious of the giant anaconda poised precariously on the low hanging limb above your head. A large poisonous spider drops unnoticed onto the back of your jacket. The small oozing spot of ground you nearly slip into . . . is quicksand.

This planet Earth scenario seems to parallel the many astrologers who walk through the forest of life, tuning out much except their own thoughts and the path before their eyes.

There is nothing quite comparable to the astrological profession today. Drivers of cars, trucks, motorcycles, motorhomes, planes and ships at sea—all must have an operator's license. To be a beautician, a physician, a masseuse, a retailer—anyone who provides a service for money—you must have a business license to be lawful. But how many astrologers regard themselves as legitimate business professionals and go to city hall in search of their credibility? Does this not reveal a lack of concern for recognition of the correlation between "lawful" and "legitimate?"

Of course, you are anxious to interject that astrology is "outlawed"—denied by many legal jurisdictions throughout the country. But if the laws are not changed, they will remain, right? Then who will change them? Dentists, chiropractors, accountants, midwives?

Perhaps religious zealots . . . if astrologers don't become aware of what surrounds them, shuck their antipathy and get their message across!

RECTIFYING THE ARCHAIC

In the fall of 1981, Joan Morland and Caroline McVey, of Chula Vista, California, sought local changes. They encouraged their city council to delete the word "astrology" from the paragraph prohibiting the practice of palmistry, mediumship, psychism, fortunetelling and other similar endeavors. Throughout our nation, laws of prohibition lump astrology with all of the above persuasions because our laws were adopted from England many years ago. They have stood as originally enacted largely because a local effort necessary to obliterate them—such as in Chula Vista and Atlanta, Georgia—has failed to materialize sufficiently.

In an effort to discover the parallel conditions existing in the metro area south of Chula Vista, I recently called the business license department in San Diego.

The clerk in charge of the office said:

"All right . . . this license would be under the category of 'fortunetelling?' "

"No," I told her, "astrology is a system of scientific calculation. The interpretations that derive from this are based on traditional empirical references that have established their validity through centuries of time."

"Oh," she replied, "so it has a scientific basis. Well, then I would have to research this under 'science'."

. . . an insight into the bureaucratic modus operandi.

I recall a visit to a friend's house some years ago—the home of a counselor who was seeking her final degree in clinical psychology. On one of the upper corners of her large bathroom mirror was the neatly lettered message, "Responsibility for self begins here."

This suggests the analogy that many astrologers might not be psychologically 'potty-trained.' It is a certainty however, that a large segment of astrologers are still living the carry-over from physician/astrologer Nostradamus who was forced by public and legal concerns to obscure his mystical practice. One would have hoped that the practice of perpetual secrecy would have ended with the success of the Evangeline Adams case in December 1914, for such a posture of indifferent lethargy is counter-productive to any ethical progress.

However, the National Council for Geocosmic Research has successfully published directories with names, addresses and phone numbers of its members—bringing through openness an image of deserved respectability to astrologers. This represents a major step in dissolving the veil of obscurity that allows astrologers to step into the light of reality.

For if astrologers are to function legitimately as prescriptionists for the human condition—to help folks deal with the real as well as the spiritual world—then it can hardly be questioned that the astrologer should be cognizant of, and dedicated to, a strong sense of reality.

Reality, within the bounds of this article, comes in two fabrics—one, the astrologer's personal sense of reality, and two, the reality of astrology.

In the first instance, we must ask:

"What is the would-be astrologer bringing to the profession?

. . . for ultimately, this is the determinant of what the astrologer can bring to the client."

The second condition calls for the question: *"What is astrology?*

The public doesn't know. Many clients believe it is a mixture of Sun sign, a Moon, a rising sign, psychism, fortune-telling, metaphysics, tarot, numerology, channeling, etc.

Western astrology does not have a norm, of sorts, but it can hardly be disputed that there are nearly as many varied practices as there are practitioners! Surgeons have only one way of removing an appendix, but if some contemporary astrologer's techniques were translated into surgical procedures, it is likely that many patients would die. In my experience, I have seen too many astrologers instinctualize a chart and while pretending to be Auntie Mame, supplement their readings with headlines from their pet handbook and an assumed channel from outer space! Astrology, adulterated by individualized variations, becomes a nameless, unclassified persuasion known only to its practitioner.

In any discussion of astrology, one should do so from a purist point of view, otherwise, astrology has no distinct identity.

This is not to say that astrology needs no extensions, no addendums, for astrology is beyond question a fundamental stepping stone to universal truths. But its augmentation and natural extensions reside in traditional disciplines such as psychology, philosophy, religion, history and sociology. Anything less can make the astrology project a toy of someone's fertile fantasies, or an exercise in egocentricity.

Perhaps the most practical solution to Western astrology's quandary during its interim period of development could be realized through the initiation of a proper educational curriculum that could stand the test of antagonists bent on its exclusion. The courses could incorporate at least one major and the remainder in minors among the following: mathematics (with the necessary emphasis on geometry, algebra and trigonometry), Eastern philosophy, religious history, psychology, sociology and classical astrology or cosmobiology or Hindu astrology. These basics would not only ground a person in technical competency, but acquiring a major in one of the humanities would legitimize the astrologer as a legal, professional counselor. Most importantly, *it would circumvent the effects of all existing negative legislation.*

Although we recommend legitimizing what we have, that is only a first step. Where we fail is in recognition and management of the second step—the spiritual knowledge —the step beyond the scientific, the mechanical, the empirical memorization.

Permit another scenario to better illustrate.

When the new astrologer reaches a point of perception —a sudden awesome insight like a large wave engulfing him on a beach—when the chart has talked, giving him a conclusive truth—he knows he has seen beyond himself. As the hair prickles his neck and coldness runs his back, he knows he has stepped across a divide that separates the material from the mental or unknown world—the discovery of an unseen latent power that has been looming in existence for eons of time.

Depending upon this new astrologer's intellect,

philosophy, environmental upbringing, morality, imagination, he will attempt to develop some form of association with this unseen magical power that resides within, around and above the horoscope he holds in his hand. He might be practical, straightforward and without bias in seeking the power source which he instinctively recognizes as an extension of the omnipotent—a thing that came before man and is larger than his own ego.

But this leads him to religion and he is biased against formal religious dogma that seems to be more and more represented by red-neck fundamentalists and born again people.

Whether he skirts the obvious and continues to search for answers, it is most likely that he will, in his future astrological work, attempt to translate his discovery of the unseen power into some kind of spiritual resolve which he can impart to his clients.

He will come to some kind of *ethereal conclusion*. But the ethereal conclusion is where Western astrology begins to disintegrate—that point when strange unsymmetrical bandaids are applied to the picture puzzle to close its gaps. The paralysis arises because there are no clear-cut road maps available in our culture. It is easy to empathize with the infatuation that the intellectually curious find in the mystique and vagaries of the spiritual world. But astrology did not come from K-Mart; it is not some glorified, sophisticated type of crossword puzzle. Astrology was and is an integral part of not just philosophy but also religion. It might have been obscured by deletions from the Christian religious texts, but it has not been disturbed or excluded from Buddhism, Taoism, Judaism or Yoga.

THE SPIRITUAL PATH

The frantic search for that illusive next step will take the student in any number of possible directions. He will listen to others. Frustrated, he might conclude his spiritual search by identifying himself as a "spiritual astrologer," or "psychic astrologer," or simply adapt an uncharted form of metaphysical practice. Unfortunately, many parvenues also choose these identities because it can aggrandize their posture and bring in clients. Labels are free even to the inept. The worst possible solution the student could make would be to gravitate to some kind of pseudo-religious cult.

In the United States, "spiritual" belongs to the religious observances even though it hangs as a cryptic metaphor without a sense of its real significance. This is because, for the most part, our contemporary religious culture is an anemic, socially oriented, once-in-a-while placater of the conscience. Basic Christianity has been all but lost because of the dissolution of many of its texts and its fragmentation into more than 225 denominations. Of that number, 186 are Protestant[1]—whatever that represents of today's runaway growth of fundamentalist inventions. (Many fundamentalist religions do not report their statistics to bonafide data centers.)

Whatever humanitarian or spiritual knowledge original Christianity embraced that has been lost, at least today we are taught bigotry and prejudice by many of our local religions—to suspect and denounce foreign knowledge. Yet Christianity evolved 2,000 years after Buddhism and Judaism had prevailed as the major world religions. Since Eastern philosophy is recognized as the root origin of our knowledge, it is significant that all three of the aforementioned religions embraced astrology as a part of their philosophy. However, the understanding and utilization of this ancient knowledge is so profound that its strengths are only vaguely perceived in the West.

But the distinction between Western and Eastern spirituality is quite simplistic. Wherever spirituality dominates in some Third World countries and Eastern nations, it is because its adherents possess little in the way of material goods. Thus, their minds and eyes are not captured by the seduction of material acquisitions, and so, they must seek their human comfortability elsewhere. As with us, their comfortability comes from a sense of personal security. But in contrast to our "I" oriented society, they accept the condition that they are of dismally low and insignificant station, and tend to instinctualize that there must be something greater and more powerful than they are.

In this country, our minds are dominated by money, possessions, the clock and sexuality. Comforts of this kind turn off man's desperate need to reach further for profound or greater truths. In general, our religions are carefully practiced to tolerate if not embrace our modern attitudes and way of life, and therefore they are not well-structured or intended to encourage our intellectual understanding of the infinite. This can only help to promote our spiritual laziness.

By contrast, Eastern religious worship is designed for man's celebration and recognition of a philosophy that nurtures man's being, his relationship to—and the nature of—the world outside. Astrology has therefore remained valid through ages in the Eastern world because it is interrelated and intertwined with the philosophy of man's existence. Since Western religions expound philosophy through black and white historical accounts, their practical usefulness seems to end where Eastern religion and philosophy begins.

There is no intent to condemn spiritual astrologers who belong to the Christian faith, but instead, it is a call to investigate the greater enlightenment and perceptions available from Eastern culture. Those who have confronted the proverbial brick wall especially have a way over it—a way to proceed—to experience the thousands of years of learning and resultant wisdom of the saints, the seers, the thinkers.

Why should an American astrologer self-satisfied with his format and doing well, bother to make major alterations?

No society known to historians ever reached the plateau of affluence achieved in North America. Such an environment seems to produce apathy, egocentricity, a sense of self-righteousness, and ultimately, as any political science student can tell you, anarchy. Anarchy, a condition of runaway independence and self-motivation, is the acid that corrupts, erodes and eventually destroys democracy. Interestingly, anarchy is always generated and stimulated, history reveals, during the lack of a prevailing, strong moral leadership.

The world is presently sadly lacking in inspiring, honest and humane leadership. From Stalin and Hitler to today's Khomeini and a multitude of similar power leaders who rule by the gun, their own brand of dogma, strength through intimidation and threats and death, they have displaced spiritual rulers. From Buddha to Mahatma Gandhi, the spiritual leaders have led their masses with ideas, awareness of self, the marvel of the mind, and without slaughtering their own. Since astrology is of a spiritual derivation, astrologers must exist, operate, comply and adjudicate in this violent world climate.

Indeed, the core strength of the survival of Eastern beliefs, whether they be Chinese, Tibetan, Hindu, has been due to the profound spiritual agreement and unity among its disciples. Cohesiveness seems to insure survival.

My own astrological work has grown more complex in step with the disparities of the times. The disintegration of the family structure, the wavering uncertainties of economic stability, terrorism, the reason for prolonging personal existence, the constant threat of the outbreak of war, the loss of self-esteem, the search for identity, the fear that arises from corrupt politicians, aloneness, and survival are more and more the client concerns. No longer is the work predominantly about Saturn returns.

To dispel some common myths, it should be recognized that ancient Chinese Confucianism is not a religion but a code of conduct *emphasizing humanitarian ideals*. Chinese Taoism, although a religion and a philosophy, is characterized by *a positive attitude toward the occult and the metaphysical*. ("Tao" means "the way.") Tibetan and Indian Buddhism is a system of thought and ethics that emphasizes *the nature of reality and knowledge, human existence, ethics, psychology and logic*. ("Buddhi" means "intellect" in Sanskrit, but the philosophy is more accurately described as "self-awareness.") There are 13 basic stages of comprehension and enlightenment in the Tibetan Buddhist philosophy[2]—philosophy that promotes the higher evolvement of man.

AN EASTERN VIEW

The exact origin of astrology—its primary role in early religion, philosophy and astronomy lost in the mists of ancient history—is a more than 5,000 year old practice in India. Hindu (Indian) astrology, known little in this country, is finding devotees because it has survived ages of successful use. Significantly, its interpretive structure is based on the insights, knowledge, experience and philosophy of ancient sages and seers. This gives Hindu astrology a foundation and basis of hierarchical profoundness—a structural greatness lacking in our own culture.

For example, the Yogis of the East have said that the end of the Twentieth Century would be the age of insanity. Consider the rampant terrorism through kidnapping and death, the fear of tampered goods on the shelf at your local drug store or supermarket, the shooting of motorists on the highway, children's Halloween treats impregnated with razor blades and poison, the sexual entrapment and murder of small children . . .

Life might not be tolerable without the wealth of

optimists with whom we have the pleasure of sharing the perennial philosophy, "Next year it will be all better." However, our perspectives are so insignificant, so lacking in depth and distance that it should be quite apparent that Eastern knowledge embodies such an awesome quality of predeliction as to overshadow our anemic efforts.

From the Tibetan Vajrayana, the "Crystal Mirror," Volume VII:

"The Bhadrakalpa is one in an endless succession of mahakalpas, great aeons that have continued in sequence since beginningless time. According to most accounts, a mahakalpa consists of four immeasureable kalpas. These in turn contain eighty lesser aeons, variable in length, known as antara kalpas—twenty of creation, twenty of stability, twenty of decay and twenty of emptiness. At present we have reached the kaliyuga, the final stage within an antara kalpa of decay. Our lifespan has decreased from eighty thousand years to one hundred, and it will sink to ten years before the cycle renews itself in emptiness and rebirth. In some traditions a kalpa is exactly 4.32 billion years in length, and the present kaliyuga began in 31.02 B.C."[3]

For the purpose of correlating cycles predicted by ancient seers, we can look also to the Mayan calendar and the Great Cycle that began in 3113 B.C. and ends in 2012 A.D. To attempt to briefly describe the complex work of Dr. Jose Arguelles—the innovator of the Harmonic Convergence celebration August 16 and 17, 1987 and the author of an investigative report on the Mayan culture—would be next to impossible. In *The Mayan Factor*, Arguelles writes: "Plato and Jung called the resonant structures 'archetypes,' form-constants that exist in and define a field of consciousness that transcends both time and the individual." Arguelles 'embroiders' James Lovelock's theory "that the Earth is indeed a conscious, evolving entity" by referring to it as "the intelligence structure of the planet considered as a living organism." Arguelles relates the "galactic beam" concept of the Mayans as a "harmonic resonance" that essentially interrelates the planet, humans and the outer universe. He refers to the galactic beam period as signifying "the transformation of terrestrial intelligence." It would be less than fair to quickly pass over Arguelles' concepts without noting this reference: "Unlike Western science, which bases itself on an investigation of matter—hence scientific materialism —Mayan science bases itself on mind as the foundation of the universe . . . "[4] . . . a worthy concept for the materialistic astrologer to ponder.

From the *Autobiography of a Yogi* by Parmahansa Yogananda, there is a disagreement in the exact timing of the cycles referred to by the ancient sages. Yogananda writes: "Sri Yukteswar discovered the mathematical application of a 24,000 year equinotical cycle to our present age. The cycle is divided into an Ascending Arc and a Descending Arc, each of 12,000 years. Within each arc fall four *Yugas* or Ages, called *Kali, Dwapara, Treta* and *Satya*, corresponding to the Greek ideas of Iron, Bronze, Silver and Golden ages.

"My guru determined by various calculations that the last *Kali Yuga* or Iron Age, of the Ascending Arc, started about A.D. 500. The Iron Age, 1200 years in duration, is a span of materialism; it ended about A.D. 1700. That year ushered in *Dwapara Yuga*, a 2400 year period of electrical and atomi-energy developments: the age of telegraphy, radio, airplanes and other space-annihilators."

However, a publisher's footnote to the above, contends:

"The Hindu scriptures place the present world-age as occurring within the *Kali Yuga* of a much longer universal cycle than the simple 24,000 year equinotical cycle with which Sri Yukteswar was concerned. The universal cycle of the scriptures is 4,300,560,000 years in extent, and measures out a Day of Creation. This vast figure is based on the relationship between the length of the solar year and a multiple of pi (3.1416, the ratio of the circumference to the diameter of a circle).

"The life span for the whole universe, according to the ancient seers, is 314,159,000,000,000 solar years, or 'One Age of Brahma.'

"The Hindu scriptures declare that an earth such as ours is dissolved for one of two reasons: the inhabitants as a whole become either completely good or completely evil. The world mind thus generates a power that releases the captive atoms held together as an earth."[5]

WHERE WE ARE

By presenting the negative view of our astrological and spiritual community, it is hoped that this will more readily lend importance to and interest in, Eastern wisdom. It is worth repeating that the Eastern spiritual strengths are in great part due to the perpetuation of not simply the worship of dead saints and philosophers, but the continued presence of strong and powerful living leaders! Those who practice astrology, philosophy and religious ceremony are thereby unified and strengthened. But to find a spiritual leader today in this hemisphere, one must apparently choose from Billy Graham, Jerry Falwell, Oral Roberts, Pat Robertson or the Bakkers. If this is a satisfactory level for you, be reminded of a bumper sticker that I saw recently that read: *It was a moral majority that killed Christ!*

Our dilemma has not gone unnoticed. For approximately the past 20 years, Buddhist lamas and Yogi descendants of ancient lineage have been sent to visit this country. Indeed, a small number have remained here.

But the path of self-realization and awareness is perhaps the most difficult, dedicated endeavor man can undertake.

Obviously, it cannot be for everyone. A 120 volume set of Tibetan Buddhist Scriptures recently published by Dharma Publishing Company of Berkeley, California, is not in English, but other Buddhist texts in English are available. Perhaps the best recommendation to enable the curious to acquire insight into Eastern thought and perception *through Yoga* would be to read a copy of *Autobiography of a Yogi* by Parmahansa Yogananda, which is available in paperback.

For whenever you're feeling cocksure and complacent with regard to your own understanding and knowledge, be reminded that no one is justified in ever relinquishing their status as a student—or for accepting anything as is without implementing a challenging evaluation.

Many of the great spiritual leaders of the East as well as of the Vatican have also been great astrologers. Astrologers in the Western Hemisphere, therefore, would seem to have their foot in the door to the Western world's spiritual leadership, since there is a vacancy at the top.

But first, one must rise to the occasion.

Notes

1. *Statistical Abstract of the United States,* 107th Edition, published by U.S. Bureau of Census.
2. *Jewell Ornament of Liberation* by Gam po pa, published by Shambhala Publications (1986 paperback edition).
3. Permission to quote from the *Crystal Mirror* granted by Dharma Publishing, Berkeley, California.
4. Permission to quote from *The Mayan Factor* by Dr. Jose Arguelles granted by the publisher Bear & Company, Santa Fe, N.M.
5. Permission to quote from *Autobiography of a Yogi* by Parmahansa Yogananda (Eleventh edition, eighth paper bound printing, 1985) granted by the publisher Self-Realization Fellowship, Los Angeles, California.

Marion D. March

Marion was born in Nuremberg, Germany and raised in Switzerland where she was educated. In 1941 she moved to the U.S. and pursued an acting career. While working in Switzerland for the American Foreign Service, she met her future husband, Nico. They have two children.

A professional astrologer since 1970, Marion has a large clientele in Los Angeles and in Europe, speaks five languages, has lectured all over the world, and been on the faculties of AFA, ISAR, and SWAC, the International Kongress and UAC/86. She was coordinator for UAC/86, the United Astrology Congress.

In 1975 she and Joan McEvers founded Aquarius Workshops, an astrology school headquartered in Los Angeles. Their magazine, *Aspects*, has worldwide distribution, and Aquarius Workshops is an active school and forum for astrological speakers.

With McEvers she has co-authored the very successful series *The Only Way To . . . Learn Astrology*, used in astrology schools all over the world. *The Only Way To . . . Learn About Tomorrow* will be out in Spring, 1988. *Astrology: Old Theme, New Thoughts* is also a best seller.

30

SOME INSIGHTS
INTO ESOTERIC ASTROLOGY

INTRODUCTION

There are two totally different approaches to astrology: one is based on age-old knowledge, personal experience, logic and often psychological insights. The humanistic or mundane astrologer can prove a theory time and time again. Saturn in the 1st house of the natal chart will elicit such questions as, "Were you rather shy in your youth? or quite a mature and serious youngster? or forced to go to work early?" The answer from the client will confirm the astrologer's knowledge. Perhaps Uranus is transiting the 7th house and when the client returns the following year, newly divorced, he'll be duly impressed because you, the astrologer, had warned of such a potential.

The mundane astrologer might see war or strife for a country; the financial one could predict the rise and fall of the stock market; the horary astrologer may locate a lost object—all matters easily checked for accuracy.

But our subject is *Esoteric Astrology*. Can anyone prove or disprove that we have lived before? That we choose our parents or partners or living conditions in order to fulfill our Karma? Can anyone prove that there is a God, that spiritual evolvement can be the final answer to the riddle of life? The obvious answer is *no*.

The next question is then: Do we always need proof of everything? Doesn't even the most exacting scientist start with a theory that may or may not be proven? Is the theory of "God," the "Oneness of the Universe," "As Above, So Below" any different than the "Theory of Relativity" or the "Great Bang" or gravity or sound waves or any other great theory?

What we will discuss here is not proven fact, but a series of rather widely accepted theories—theories that seem the same in the far East, in the near West, in the deep South or cold North; theories that seem to intuitively deliver the same answers through the ages, from different corners of the world, from people of totally different backgrounds and diverse educational levels.

According to the dictionary, the word *Esoteric* really means: "designed for or understood by the specially initiated alone" or "knowledge that is restricted to a small group." Maybe we should coin a different word, one that would explain what we mean. Something like *"Ectoterric"*—"ecto" meaning "out" and "terric" or "terra" meaning "earth," therefore signifying beyond this earth, or past our limited five senses.

What you will learn in the next few pages is just a small part of a lengthy subject, much too complex to fit into the allotted space. In my many years of dealing with Esoteric Astrology, I have found that there are myriad ways to reach a higher spiritual or philosophical understanding of life, to grow and evolve. Each person has to find this path in his or her own manner; what appeals to one may not appeal to another. What opens one person's inner eyes may be meaningless to the next one. There is no right or wrong, just that which is right or wrong for *you*.

The same principle applies when trying to use a different interpretation of your astrological chart. Esoteric Astrology has but one purpose, to help you, through your horoscope, discover why you are here and what your role may be while on this planet. This is quite a task and deserves more than one approach. I urge you to try the different methods offered here and any others you may find through books or teachers, and then work with the one or two that seem to give you what you are looking for.

Will any or all of this new knowledge help you? I hope so. It will certainly show you new ways to find a different path and give you a better understanding of astrology per se. There are people who march to a different drummer, who do not respond to their horoscopes in the ordinary way. They may already be on a more evolved path. If you are a professional astrologer and have such clients, with new insight you will be able to make their charts come alive.

Alice Bailey, for example, noted that as people evolve, they change their emphasis from the emotional lunar qualities to the "divine ego" represented by the Sun. Any person not subject to the emotional ups and downs of the Moon, but working through the radiance of the Sun, would obviously not respond to an ordinary chart interpretation. But even less evolved human beings benefit from some spiritual enlightenment, some philosophy of life that can nurture and sustain them. Esoteric Astrology may open a door or add a new vista.

Those of you who do not believe in Karma may find that your own religion, theories of genes, heredity, the ancestral past as well as the immediate environmental past, morals and mores you were raised with, all played a major role in forming your beliefs of why you are here and how you want to live or die. Just substitute your own vocabulary for any words I may use that do not appeal to you, and you too can profit by finding answers for your role on earth as viewed through the esoteric lens.

For those who do believe in Karma, it is self-evident that in order to understand who you are and where you should go, you first need to know who you were and whence you came. All existence in this universe is cyclic and continuous. The rain falls and forms bodies of water, the water evaporates and forms clouds, which in turn produce water in the form of rain—a continuous cycle. By the same token, the soul or divine ego, or Godhead, or Atman or whatever name you may give it, is also continuous, and like water, will just assume different forms again and again. (According to some religions, the human soul is such that it can stop the cycle at certain stages of evolvement and become one with the "universe" or "Almighty"—but that is another subject.)

Some people consider the new form we take a type of evolution. In other words, whatever evolvement we have reached before determines the form we take the next time around. Whatever experience we did not as yet have we try to seek in the next experience. That, by the way, is the real meaning of the word Karma. Cause and effect, action and reaction. Karma is never punitive, it is neither good nor bad, but only a means to accomplish an educational end, a way of learning what has, as yet, not been learned and benefiting by that which is already known.

I wish to thank Isabel Hickey, Dane Rudhyar, Alan Leo, Alan Oken, Zip Dobyns and Irma Norman, who have given me astrological insights into this field; but, also incorporated in these lines are some ideas and thoughts inspired by such thinkers as Thomas Aquinas, Camille Flammarion, Jacob Boehme, Aldous Huxley, Romain Rolland, Meister Eckhart, Ralph Waldo Emerson, Christopher Isherwood, Karl Jung, Hermann Hesse, Swami Prabhavananda, Vivekananda, Ramakrishna and such books as the Bhagavad Gita and the Upanishads.

SYMBOLIC MEANINGS OF THE GLYPHS

Each stroke of the astrological glyphs has a meaning. As you learn to interpret these strokes, you will gain new insights into the deeper meaning of the planets and signs of the zodiac.

The vertical line | is designated as the line of destiny or intellect. The horizontal line ___ is considered material or physical when at the bottom of a glyph, metaphysical when at the top. When the vertical and horizontal lines meet, they form the cross of matter + . All straight lines are considered intellectual, clear thinking and unemotional.

○ This is the circle of infinity or spirit, while the half circle or crescent ◡ depicts the soul force or consciousness. The not quite completed crescent pouring out toward the right is considered extroverted ⌒ , pouring to the left or within ⌐ is introverted. All curved lines, whether half or complete circles, are considered replete with feeling, responsive and emotional.

If you understand the meaning of these lines and circles, you will have no problem interpreting all the astrological glyphs.

SIGNS

♈ *Aries*—is represented by two not quite completed crescents arising from the straight line of intellect at the bottom. As the crescents move upward in a pouring out motion, they become like a fountain gushing forth the waters of consciousness. Thus Aries starts as an unemotional thinker (straight line), but continues as an emotional extrovert (pouring out to the right) ready to try everything on one hand, but remembering life as an introvert (Pisces) not so long ago, as the crescent pours within on the other side. Much of Aries' brass and bravura is to cover up this inner insecurity.

♉ *Taurus*—The circle of spirit below is supporting the soul force (crescent) above; you could also say it depicts the circle of the Sun supporting (illuminating) the crescent of the Moon. There are no straight lines; the symbol is all-feeling. The Moon always symbolizes the mother and growth.

Thus the total glyph represents fertility.

♊ *Gemini*—"Two pillars of wisdom tied together" are actually two lines of destiny connected by two horizontal or physical lines. The dual lines of mentality or intellect are linked by the physical on the lower level and the metaphysical on the higher level; therefore Gemini can bring the high plane to the lower, and vice versa. There are no curves here; this symbol is detached and cerebral.

♋ *Cancer*—The two circles, or spiritual force, are on the inside of the symbol, so Cancer begins and ends on a spiritual level. Again we have the combination of the solar circle and the lunar crescent, depicting mother and fertility. Also observe the position of the symbol; it shows the acts of taking and giving, within a totally protective design. No straight lines in this glyph either; like Taurus, Cancer is a responsive, emotive and sympathetic sign. In one of the old symbolic interpretations, this glyph denotes the merger of the male sperm with the female ovum, the actual act of fertilization.

♌ *Leo*—The small circle starts on the earth line, pushes way up and then curves down below the earth or physical line. Divine love and power are brought to earth. Again, this glyph is all emotion, all curves.

It also symbolically shows the vein (the small circle) leading to the coronary chamber (large curve) and the artery that pumps the blood through the system (downflow curve).

Leo becomes the center through which all energy must flow and from which all life force emanates.

♍ *Virgo*—The three straight lines represent three levels of consciousness; the conscious, the subconscious, and the superconscious. The third line of the superconscious curves slightly upward, in an outpouring motion, but is held back by the last line which turns totally inward and ends below the horizon. Thus, despite its three levels of consciousness,

Virgo becomes introvertive and materialistic (the symbol ends below the earth line). The coils of energy are kept from being released by the last stroke, which denotes a locked door. This can help you understand why Virgo and the 6th House are so involved with hard work and service—the constant effort to open that closed door, again and again.

The old symbolic interpretation also depicts the untouched vagina, the three coils representing the ovaries and uterus and the closed loop denoting the intact hymen.

≏ *Libra*—The lower line describes the physical, the upper the metaphysical. The crescent in the metaphysical line points upward, symbolizing pure and divine justice. The higher nature of Libra is objective and unattached to matter. The two lines never touch, but Libra is not only mental (straight lines); the feeling curves of the lunar crescent are an important part of this sign.

The other description of this glyph is the Sun sinking beneath the horizon; night will dominate. Libra is the border between night and day.

♏ *Scorpio*—Again, three lines symbolize three levels of consciousness, but Scorpio's consciousness works differently from Virgo's. Line one represents the lower mind, imbued with animal desire (Scorpion); line two depicts the higher mind trying to evolve (the eagle); and line three incorporates the regenerative ability (the phoenix). The last stroke of the symbol is an upward curve, but instead of pouring out, it ends in a barb, a pointed carrier holding it back and imbuing it with earthly desire.

This is also considered the symbol for the concentrated tension in the male sexual organ, as well as the tail of the scorpion raised in order to inflict death on its chosen victim.

♐ *Sagittarius*—The lower part of the shaft connotes the animal nature of this symbol, likened to the centaur, half-horse, half-man. The upper part portrays the arrow shooting into the sky. The line dividing the shaft indicates duality or indecisiveness as to how or where to aim the great physical and mental powers. At its highest, the symbol characterizes aspirations released by the soul, its target: infinity. At its lowest Sagittarius does not really aim its arrow, and the barb at the end of the shaft holds it back to indulge in simple human desires.

♑ *Capricorn*—The line of intellect moves down into the realm of realism and materiality, then rises and at its highest level forms the circle of spirit; but the crescent of consciousness flows downward and below the earth level it ends by swinging inward, into self-consciousness. Please note that this intricate glyph is the only one of the zodiacal signs that incorporates the straight line, the crescent and the full circle.

Some foreign countries use this slightly different glyph. It is drawn by starting at the top, thus the first horizontal line is metaphysical, merging into the crescent of consciousness which flows downward into the circle of spirit, but ending with the line of matter, pointing inward into self-consciousness. The symbol tells very much the same story, only in different words. Capricorn hails from a higher source and comes down to earth and matter in order to look within, and into the past. This particular symbol does not seem to represent the sea goat.

♒ *Aquarius*—This glyph consists of all angular lines which denote pure electrical impulses and magnetism. The lower physical and upper metaphysical lines both end by pointing upward, yet they never touch, indicating total detachment. There are no curves in this glyph; the waves portrayed here are those of electricity, not water.

This symbol also mirrors the original glyph for water, "aqua" being the Latin word for water. But the water poured out is supposed to symbolize the water of consciousness.

The glyph also shows the four ways of conveyance—the first by foot, the second by animal, the third by mechanical ability, and the fourth unfinished upward stroke illustrating the ultimate form, not as yet perfected—telepathy or brain waves.

♓ *Pisces*—The two crescents of consciousness are back to back, tied by the horizontal line of matter. This line is in the middle, wavering between physical and metaphysical. The emotional forces of the two crescents, imbued with the compassionate quality of pouring out and pouring within, are also being pulled in two directions, forward and backward illustrating the proverbial story of the two fish trying to swim in different directions.

The glyph is also interpreted as the crescent of the finite consciousness, of man versus the infinite consciousness of the universe, the middle line describing earth where the two forces meet, thus depicting the struggle between body and soul.

PLANETS

⊙ *Sun*—This is the perfect shape, without beginning or end, the symbol of infinity. The dot inside can be interpreted as the inner light, or as the opening from which manifestation is born out of the unmanifested—namely man. Thus man is totally embedded in the spiritual circle of eternity.

☽ *Moon*—The two crescents of consciousness, or soul force, are linked on the lower or earth level and on the higher or spiritual level. The glyph is all curves, very emotional, and being only a semi-circle, it lives in the reflective light of the infinite Sun. The symbol is turned back, facing itself, as it carries in it our past.

⊕ *Earth*—The glyph for Earth is very easy to interpret. It is the cross of matter within the circle of infinity, or matter encased in spirit.

☿ *Mercury*—The circle of spirit rises over the cross of matter, topped off by the crescent of consciousness. The line of destiny or intellect struggles upward to be manifested in spiritual awareness.

How the awareness is manifested will depend on which sign of the zodiac Mercury occupies. In sympathetic, emotional Cancer, for example, Mercury could enter the path to spirituality through what the Vedas calls Bhakti Yoga, the path of love, while Mercury in Gemini could begin the quest through Jnana Yoga, the path of the intellect.

♀ *Venus*—The ancient form of this glyph hails from the Egyptian ankh ♀ or ansata, signifying the giver of life. Again we see the spiritual circle of infinity above the cross of matter, matter trying to reach up to infinity.

But Venus has another side; the glyph also represents the mirror held by the goddess Venus—the mirror which reflects our own attitudes and values. It can be the mirror of vanity and pleasure, or love and affection, again depending to a great extent on the sign Venus is placed in, as well as its aspects.

♂ *Mars*—The circle of spirituality is at the lowest point of the glyph, the straight line is slanted upward, striving or driving to reach higher, yet ending in the barb of desire.

This upward line ending in a barb also symbolizes the concentrated sexual energy of the penis (as it did with Scorpio's glyph). In other words, Mars starts in spirit and tries to reach high, but is often held back by the animalistic instincts of desire and penetration.

♂ There is an old glyph for Mars, which looks like an upside-down Venus. The circle of spirituality is still at the bottom, but instead of a shaft with a barb, this symbol has the cross of matter rising above the circle, denoting at its highest, matter created out of the primal energy of spirit, and at its lowest level, the material values outweighing the spiritual ones.

♃ *Jupiter*—The crescent of consciousness is higher than the cross of matter. The glyph starts on an earthly plane and struggles upward to new awareness, but the crescent faces backward and inward, and depending upon what is found within, can become enlightened or self-oriented and self-indulgent.

♄ *Saturn*—The cross of matter is the most elevated part of this glyph, Saturn representing matter in its purest sense. The crescent of consciousness curves first downward and inward, but ends with an upward and outward projection. Even on the most concrete level of earth, we first have to look at ourselves within, before we can reach out to others and finally reach up to evolve. It is important to draw this glyph correctly, because with the last stroke ending in an upward curve, Saturn represents the positive teacher. If it ends turned inward, Saturn can symbolize the denier imposing limitations.

♅ *Uranus*—The glyph used in the United States and England, originally ♓ , was meant to portray the letter H for Uranus' discoverer, Sir William Hershel. But there is deep symbolic meaning in even the most innocent designs. One glyph is all straight lines, pure intellect without emotion. The cross of matter in the center rises from the circle of infinity, below the earth line from our deepest subconscious, flanked on each side by lines of destiny or abstract intellect.

The other popular design with curved lines resembling Pisces describes the crescents of finite and infinite consciousness, joined by the line of manifestation or earth, all resting on the line of destiny born out of the circle of infinity. Though this symbol is much used, the straight-lined glyph better describes the known qualities of Uranus.

♦ In many parts of Europe a third glyph is employed which looks like an upright Mars or the Sun with a barb on top. The circle of infinity, including man, is at the bottom of the glyph, which does not start below the earthline as the previous two symbols do. The barb of desire stops the short line of intellect from truly developing or taking off. This glyph, in my opinion, does not depict many of the Uranian characteristics.

ψ *Neptune*—The crescent or soul force is pierced by the cross of matter, resulting in a symbol which looks like a three pronged fork. Each prong denotes an aspect of human consciousness, all to be purified by Neptune's divine waters. The emotional crescent of the soul is divided by the physical aspects of life, again showing the struggle between body and soul, so well symbolized by the glyph for Pisces.

Some people try to make a very pretty design and draw Neptune's glyph to look like a trident, barbs and all. If you understand the meaning of the barbs so far, you know that they do not belong at the end of Neptune's crescent.

P *Pluto*—There are so many symbols for Pluto, I hardly know where to start. In the United States, we mainly use two of them. One is another innocent accident (as with Uranus), combining the letters P and L to honor Pluto's discoverer, Percival Lowell. But even this "accident" takes on symbolic meaning, describing well the object in question. That is the beautiful mystery of life showing the inner harmony of man with the universe. The glyph starts on the physical line of matter, merging into the line of destiny and at its highest, the crescent of consciousness, turned back and facing itself, looking inward, deep and probing into its dark depth.

♀ The other glyph originally called "Minerva" by Isabel Hickey, has the crescent of consciousness above linked to the cross of matter below; hovering over it all is the circle of spirit. On its least evolved level, spirit would descend through the soul force to manifest as matter; on its highest level matter would rise through the soul force to regenerate as spirit, to be reborn.

⅄ Here are six other symbols for Pluto ♇ as used throughout the world. ♃ By now you know so much about glyph interpretation ♉ that you can have fun delineating them. ⊖ Maybe you will like one better ☽ than the one you're using now and you can make it your own.

AN ESOTERIC VIEW OF THE QUALITIES, ELEMENTS AND HOUSES

To truly understand an esoteric approach to astrology as well as the role you play in it, you have to understand the very basic meaning of the planets, signs, houses, qualities and elements, because in astrology every part taken apart is also part of the whole. The 1st house is not only the 1st house, it is also Aries, Mars, Cardinal, Fire and Angular. In esoteric astrology, even more than in a natal interpretation (if that is possible), it is very important *never to lose sight of the entire picture.*

THE QUALITIES

Cardinal stands for activity and *creation* and represents the doer of the zodiac. **Fixed** embodies solidarity and *preservation.* **Mutable** depicts interrelation and *transmutation.* The word transmutation needs to be understood in its proper context. Everything is born "creation," lives "preservation" and dies; but death is only a change in the form of energy. The energy itself never dies. Form and matter are mortal; essence is immortal. Thus death and destruction, the commonly used words, really become a form of "transmutation."

THE ELEMENTS

Fire is a force that "reaches out;" it represents spiritual rebirth as well as the growth potential in all its implications.

Aries reaches out right now, to today, to this moment; *Leo* reaches out to tomorrow, and *Sagittarius* reaches out toward a distant future.

Earth is the land we live on—the physical, concrete reality as visualized by our five senses. *Taurus'* vision is realistic, but in a sensual, tactile and often artistic way. *Virgo's* reality is practical and down-to-earth, but imbued with enough mental orientation (remember the straight lines of the glyph) that it likes to analyze rather than just feel. *Capricorn's* concept is expedient and business-like, disciplined and responsible, but all actions are colored by its background, upbringing and past experience. The material needs and urges are conditioned by what has gone before.

Air represents the atmosphere and gasses that surround us, but it also describes the ether which fills all space and is part of the entire universe. It is non-material, yet has properties of its own; it is directly responsible for all physical and chemical activity, and is the sole vehicle of all electric and magnetic fields for forms of energy known to mankind. What other functions this universal medium may possess are yet to be discovered.

Therefore *Air* is yesterday, today and tomorrow—the element of the mind in all its ramifications. *Gemini's* mind can and wants to look at everything past, present, and future, and then in a detached, unemotional manner communicate its learning to everyone (remember all those straight lines in Gemini's glyph). *Libra's* mentality is more complex—able to comprehend tomorrow. Libra needs to experience today before deciding about the future, and feels the need to weigh other people's reactions before committing one way or the other. *Aquarius* (again only straight lines in the glyph, no emotions involved) cannot only understand the future, but mentally discovers the future. Without a future to reach for, Aquarius resents the present.

Water constitutes 70% of a person's body and therefore can easily outweigh the other elements. It is also the primary element of the past, the absorption of that which was, whether ideas digested and submerged as memories or subconscious habit patterns. The glyphs of all three water signs are pure curves, circles and crescents, each seeking spiritual enlightenment, but so imbued with instincts, intuition and sensitivities that, just like water, they embrace all, knowing no barriers and rarely using mind or reason.

This element can best be understood when relating it to the three properties of *Water*—namely, in its liquid form, as frozen ice, or vaporous as gas or steam. *Cancer*, of course, relates to the liquid form of water. Since our bodies are 70% water, Cancer equates to our physical properties, such as heredity, the absorption of the genes, and the genetic background. The collected thoughts or acquired habits are united with the genetic heredity through our parents. Cancer represents the home we choose for ourselves.

Scorpio is embodied in frozen water, fixed in its subconscious pattern, deeply rooted in its feelings. It shows our potential for really coming to grips with ourselves. Scorpio represents the buried layers of the past, frozen into place, back through many lifetimes.

Pisces emotions are closest to the surface. Vapors and gases evaporate quickly; the subconscious can swiftly absorb and shed that which bothers it. Pisces' problems stem from the life previously lived, and as such find it fairly easy to resolve once they decide whether they want to live here on earth or have themselves nailed on the cross in order to return to another dimension. (See notes on the glyph.)

THE HOUSES

If you translate this concept into houses, you realize that the 4th, 8th and 12th, *the houses of endings*, have assimilated the past, have soaked up memories, feelings and emotions, each in its own way relating back to the qualities and elements. When interpreting the 4th House, remember the Cancer glyph and its self-protective design, but also visualize the Moon and realize that the two crescents meet on the lower earth home, and on the higher, true giving level.

The 8th House not only parallels Scorpio and its frozen water, but also reflects some of Pluto's symbols. Transformation, ascribed to the 8th House, does not come easily; this is a Succedent House, relating to a Fixed sign which as such believes in preserving the status quo. But the phoenix beckons and after heart wrenching digging in the depths of its icy waters, far reaching changes can be made.

The description used for Pisces goes double for the 12th House. The potential recollection of the immediate past can be its crowning glory by opening an easy path to the subconscious, thus guiding the soul to its true purpose this time around. But this same recollection can also be its self-undoing, wishing to go "back home", not being willing to fight the realistic battles of earth with its five limited senses. When in that mode, the 12th House can feel put upon or victimized and become its own worst enemy by closing the door to the self (1st House).

The 3rd, 7th and 11th, the *houses of relationships*, depict detached, abstract and mental approaches. The 3rd House does it alone; the 7th House with someone and the 11th House for someone. The 3rd House expresses according to its early environment, the 7th according to its relation with one other and the 11th according to the needs of the group.

The *houses of substance*—the 2nd, 6th and 10th—like to look for accomplishments in the here and now. The 2nd House (Succedent Earth) will try to preserve that which exists and build on that base. The 6th House (Cadent Earth) wants to transmute or change that which is, into something more practical, more understandable, more usable.

The 10th House (Angular Earth) will work to create for itself a secure base from which to climb the ladder to success. Once this material success is reached, the 10th can become one of the most evolved houses. After all, it is the highest point in the chart, representing the culmination of all that can be achieved and the consequences of the past. The Cardinality of the 10th House describes someone who is not afraid to work for achievement, and the Earth element, once it overcomes its material drive, can see reality in its total dimension. Many of our great philosophers, saints, sages and seers have predominantly Earth charts or planets in the Substance houses.

The 1st, 5th and 9th, or *houses of life* reach out to the future with great zest, self-confidence and enthusiasm. The 1st House, being Angular and Cardinal, cares mostly about today; but give a 1st House planet a direction in which to head and without a moment's hesitation, the task will be accomplished with vim and vigor . . . though maybe a bit differently than you intended, since Aries' sense of pioneering is ever present in the 1st House.

The 5th House is concerned with the immediate future; but being Succedent, the approach has to be based on something that already exists, something that is tried and true. Then the Leo quality will take over and embellish, embroider and dramatically present everything in a new light. Point a 5th House planet in a higher direction and it will give itself to that goal with total heart and dedication.

The 9th House lives for tomorrow; the glyph for Sagittarius depicts the arrow shooting for the stars. But remember that even that lofty symbol has a divided shaft and the lower part embodies the beast part of the centaur. The aspirations can reach infinity or be held back to the human desires of the earth plane. The 9th House ideas and ideals can be restricted to the missionary who sees only one side of everything and in his zeal spends his energies forcing everyone to see it his way —or to the truly spiritual person who knows that truth and enlightenment are within, to be found in his own superconscious (9th House) mind.

To summarize: the 4th, 8th, 10th and 12th Houses represent the *past patterns* we brought with us. The 4th, 8th and 12th because they are Water Houses; the 10th because it is Saturn ruled.

The 1st, 2nd, 3rd, 6th and 7th are the houses of the *present*, the *here and now*. The 2nd and 6th are earthly now, the 3rd and 7th are the airy here and the 1st is the fiery present.

The 5th, 9th and 11th are the houses of *the future*. The 5th and 9th are the fiery outreach toward times to come and the 11th looks for the yet to be, the unknown tomorrow and ever after.

There is not enough room in this article to go into the many facets of esoteric astrology, but to give you a brief synopsis:

In my teachings I spend quite a bit of time interpreting the esoteric meaning of the planets, paying particular attention to the Moon and its Nodes. Venus, Saturn, Neptune, Pluto and the Midheaven. Each in its own way can give you new awareness.

To really understand the chart on a more philosophical or spiritual level, a new approach to aspects is helpful. I use the major ones, namely the conjunction, sextile, square, trine and opposition. Of particular importance is the quincunx (inconjunct) which assumes a different meaning when looked at esoterically. So does the quintile, an aspect I rarely use in my everyday practice.

The same applies to some of the Arabian Parts, especially the Part of Fortune (Ascendant plus Moon minus Sun), Part of Spirit (Ascendant plus Sun minus Moon) and the Web (Ascendant plus Neptune minus Sun). These Parts can help you understand where you came from, where you could benefit by going, and even where you may be trapped in between.

Another important phase, especially for those who believe in Karma, is a deeper comprehension of the meaning of retrograde planets as well as intercepted signs. In my many years of teaching this subject, I have found that the houses that carry the same sign on the cusp twice are nearly more important than the houses that hold the interception!

For another glimpse as to why we possibly are here and where we might go in order to fulfill our role this time around, there is a "Karmic Wheel" based on the midpoint of the Sun and Moon. In a woman's chart calculate the midpoint from the Moon to the Sun. In a man's chart from the Sun to the Moon. This midpoint becomes your esoteric Ascendant; all other cusps are based on that Ascendant. By placing your natal planets in this new wheel you can get a different perception of your role in this life.

Each house tells its own story. Very helpful to understanding all your relationships is the 7th House where you can find karmic affinities or burdens with others. Figuring from the 7th to the 8th House cusps, what planet(s) does your mate, son, daughter, mother, father, lover, friend bring to you?

For those readers who like to explore new realms, I recommend a look at your heliocentric chart. But don't put it on the same wheel with your geocentric horoscope. Instead perceive it as an imprint on the ethers of space seen in its universal meaning rather than the restricted or limited view of an earth oriented world.

I hope this glimpse into the esoteric world will encourage you to look deeper and further.

Kimberly McSherry

A student of the metaphysical sciences since 1970, Kimberly McSherry's diverse educational background includes degrees in the fields of Education, Psychology and the Humanities. She is a certified Gestalt therapist and a lecturer of national recognition. She is currently working in Houston, Texas, as a private consultant combining therapy and the metaphysical sciences and teaching classes in astrology.

Her resume includes teaching High School English, giving college astrology courses, writing articles, lecturing and speaking at various conferences.

Kim has a B.S. in Education from Kent University, an M.A. in Humanities from State University of N.Y. at Buffalo, and a M.Ed. Psych. from the University of Houston.

She is currently studying native Indians while traveling with Thunder Woman. Befitting her Cancer Moon, she loves to cook, sew and do crafts. Kimberly is writing a book, the working title of which is *The Transformative Power of Astrology*. It incorporates some of the themes expressed here.

THE FEMININE ELEMENT
OF ASTROLOGY:
REFRAMING THE DARKNESS

There is a point in consciousness, a point beyond space and time, called, for lack of a better word, God. The pathway from here to there is a spiral moving out in a circular motion from a singular, focused point called *center*. The spiral is broadening in scope with each rotation, expanding ever outward, opening to ever higher levels of awareness. The movement toward this place is called *evolution-growth-progress.*

If you begin at this point in consciousness called God and travel in any direction as far as you can go before your travel becomes a returning, you will reach another point in consciousness, equally unfathomable and profound, which for lack of a better word, is called Goddess. The pathway to this place called Goddess is exactly the same spiral, only the direction one must travel to get there is the opposite. This movement from the all-encompassing, broadest spectrum of the spiral toward the singular, most focused point of center is an inward, backward and downward movement. The movement toward this place in consciousness is also called evolution-growth-progress. Movement in either direction —out from center or inward toward it—describes two different pathways which can be utilized to expand awareness or grow in consciousness—two possible directions for getting to exactly the same place.

I believe that in a long ago time, before the Greeks laid down the laws and rules of astrology now governing Western thought, before the Druids established the underlying

51

attitudes currently prevailing in Western consciousness, before the Aryan invasions which destroyed the matriarchal cults, there existed a much deeper awareness, a total acceptance and an equal value for these two points in consciousness called God and Goddess.

Perhaps at one time in ancient history, the totally and purely objective fact of the spiral was understood—that motion/movement in any direction, from any point, equals growth and eventual evolution. But somewhere along the way, we thinking humans began to separate and divide from the union of the spiral. We created concepts of good and evil, and the chasm between God and Goddess grew, creating a split in consciousness. So we stopped seeing that the two are really one, mutually dependent and necessary to the existence of the other. We created two diametrically opposing forces and the struggles which ensued between them have continued throughout history to this very day. Perhaps what the symbol of Armageddon is really about is a point in the evolution of mankind where we are confronted with the choice to either break the spiral spectrum completely, which will surely result in the destruction of life on the planet as we know it, or to close the chasm we have created, reunite the spectrum in conscious awareness and return to an understanding of union between polarities which the spiral represents.

Astrology, like all universal languages, is subject to the interpretation and definitions of the culture using it. I have discovered that many of the concepts and principles in astrology which relate to the Goddess-end of the spiral of consciousness are invalid, based on the fears and prejudices which often revolve around a misunderstood thing. In a culture which places such a tremendous emphasis and high regard on Light, the visible and obvious, energy projected outward and external realities, it is only logical that the elements of Dark, the unconscious, invisible and sometimes unknowable realities, be repressed and denied. And a thing repressed and denied can only become manifest in reality in its most negative form, serving only to perpetuate the myth and drive the demons even deeper into oblivion. Oblivion is that black, scary place where things that go bump in the night tend to take on diabolic proportions.

My experience of this current transit of Pluto through Scorpio is a re-emergence in memory of that long ago time when these two points in the spiral called God and Goddess sat upon equal thrones in consciousness—a time when each was equally valued for the natural gifts it bestowed, and each was equally feared and held in awe of the horrific ramifications incurred for the misuse of these gifts. The wrath of Kali is surely no more horrifying than the wrath of the angry Hebrew God, Jehovah. Yet the face of Kali and her cross-cultural counterparts somehow grew darker, more evil and fearful.

As Pluto moves deeper into Scorpio, we become more painfully aware of the negative ramifications of this prolonged imbalance. The need to transform and heal all conditions of society and collective attitudes which support and perpetuate the imbalance is mounting to a critical point. Armageddon is upon us and in us right now! All humans now alive on the planet are engaged in mortal combat in their own way, in their own world. But I don't think the battle is about overcoming some dark and sinister evil force out there somewhere. I think the battle is about overcoming the belief that there is one! And I believe that to win this battle, and enter a new age called Aquarius, we must ultimately return to that point in truth when we knew and lived in the Way of the Spectrum, a state of mind where we can once again view the world and each experience in terms of:

> This isn't good.
> This isn't bad.
> This just is . . . and I wonder what it is about!?

In order to reflect awareness (or more accurately, revived memory) astrology must look long and hard at the definitions and concepts laid down so long ago, at a time and by a culture whose value system powerfully reflected a one-sided preference. Some of these concepts, those which I believe to be feminine in nature, are in dramatic need of reconceptualization. Feminine concepts in astrology are those which deal with inner-directed reality, and which demand that understanding and insight be directed toward the center. These include such concepts as retrograde motion, intercepted signs and planets, void-of-course Moon, lunar phase in general, the South Node of the Moon, the Water element and its rulers.

The definitions we use and the attitudes we perpetuate about these concepts are based on a world-view reflecting a high regard for the masculine side of the spectrum of consciousness and the pathway used to achieve it (i.e. action, direct motion expressed outward from center, external reality which can be seen and verified, projection and movement toward a future potential aspiration). The definitions we use are therefore subject to the same kind of misunderstanding and ignorance which shrouds the feminine side of the spectrum in general. Please understand that the words masculine and feminine are *not* about men and women, in this context. Both sexes have supported this imbalance for thousands of years and both sexes are subject to equal degrees of suffering for this imbalance. The issue presented here is about an outer-directed way of expressing energy vs. an inner-directed way. My belief is that the result (i.e. consciousness) is exactly the same, regardless of which path one chooses. But for those men and women who most naturally favor the latter way, there are no healthy models available to accurately reflect the more positive side of this preference.

Like most astrologers, I have for many years been

learning the concepts, definitions and rules of this science/ art, ingesting them whole and anchoring them firmly into my memory banks, trying desperately to merge with them so that they could become me. I tried to make them fit my experience of self and life, when in fact, they did not. Then one day, around Saturn return time, I think, I developed a serious case of astrological indigestion. I decided to go back to square one and chew on some of those principles I had swallowed whole. This process will no doubt provide me with jaw exercise for the rest of my life. I encourage all astrologers to start chewing, to start forgetting what we think we know and start watching for the truth like our ancient astrological forefathers did in the past. By observing and testing those taken for granted, locked in steel truths, one may come to discover that they only work when forced, or when reality can be twisted around a bit to make them work.

As a teacher of astrology, I have had the opportunity to watch hundreds of students go through the process of reacting to the negative treatment given these feminine concepts in the majority of the books on the subject. They read the descriptions and come into class aghast at their wretched fate—to have 12th House planets, or Venus retrograde, or a void-of-course Moon at birth. They want to have the South Node removed and woe be the one with Saturn aspects. Cancer, Scorpio or Pisces placements guarantee a weakness of character which will no doubt result in some kind of institutionalization, or at least misery, suffering and anti-social behavior. What could they possibly have done in another lifetime to deserve such punishment this time around? I have seen whole lives change with the gleeful proclamation, "My birthtime was wrong! My Sun moved out of the interception!" And thus the process of reframing begins . . .

To explore and seek awareness in and of the feminine

mode is not quite like the kind of learning that we as a culture have been taught and grown accustomed to. To go outside of self in search of knowledge, to read other people's words and seek the opinion of experts—this is only part of the learning process. The model for the other part of learning hardly exists, cannot be taught but only discovered, and is rarely supported by the culture or verified by those significant others out there. Outer space is vast, limitless and unfathomable. We send out probes to seek and gather data.

The counterpart is inner space, equally vast and limitless. Data is not actively sought, but received and allowed in a moment of readiness. Probes can become lost, be redirected or dissolve and disappear. The aspect of learning which goes on in inner space is mysterious and nebulous. It has to do with the individual nature of a person and is much like the magical process of gestation which goes on in the womb. There is no external coach involved telling the fetus what it should do next—no outside opinions. It simply knows and instinctually responds to its own readiness. The process is honored as it occurs, and surrender to it is easy because there is no choice. One cannot tell a tree how to grow. Oaks do not waste time trying to be elms. And no two trees grow at exactly the same rate or in exactly the same way. Yet each tree is perfect and perfectly attuned to its own nature.

Much of our experience of the world is based on some external force telling us how we are supposed to define reality. So many oaks trying to crease a sense of oakness in so many elms. Each individual already knows how to grow. The place of knowing lies deep within the core essence of inner space. People born with a preponderance for the feminine path of evolution are people who must find and ultimately be content with living in inner space. Their reality must be personally defined and they must learn to honor it privately without much validation from the outer world.

Perceptions are deepened when one lives mostly in inner space, and the ability to project one's knowing must be consciously developed it it is to be had at all. Learning is a much more passive process than for those born without these conditions. It demands a willingness to understand and surrender to the natural rhythm of one's own nature, which sometimes commands us to stop when everyone else seems to be going. Learning is an experience rather than an active choice/pursuit. And learning is everywhere, if one is able to allow the symbiosis required—the pulling in of data, the merging with it and the acceptance of the transformation which results . . . no judgment.

In keeping with my Scorpio nature, I have divided the world into two ways of being. There is the *way of the sperm* and there is the *way of the egg*. They are both essential to life and each is necessary in its proper time. The sperm way of experiencing the world is the most natural way for those with a proclivity for the masculine end of the spectrum of consciousness. The egg way of experiencing the world is reflected by those with a natrual preference for the feminine end. We are each a composite of both. The goal is to get them in balance and develop the ability to operate in the mode required by any given circumstance. Sometimes success can only be achieved when one is willing to be in the way of the egg; sometimes the sperm is the only option. One task of a lifetime is to learn which one works best when. Another task is to recognize one's preference and find ways to develop and strengthen that one which is lacking in nature. The third and hardest task is to honor both as necessary and essential to the process of actualization, i.e. becoming a whole person.

By nature those who tend toward the way of the sperm are very similar in approach to the sperm part of creation in the human reproductive system. They are active, self-propelled and initiatory about life and in their pursuit of growth/awareness. They go out, often in a rush of enthusiasm (abundant energy) and in great numbers with one objective in mind—to seek and conquer that thing which will guarantee continuance. Some deeply unconscious motivation instills in them the knowing that survival depends upon reaching their goal. The competition is experienced as overwhelming. Only the fastest, the strongest and the best will reach the mark. So they struggle against all odds, swim hard against the current and fight ferociously ever outward, ever upward toward the goal. Striving is an essential element in whatever reality they create. There is a kind of reckless and carefree abandon available in the knowledge that they are in constant production and there are millions more where they came from. There is also a quiet desperation inherent in the realization of the limitations of their brief existence.

The way of the egg is vastly different, even opposite in nature, and very similar to the egg part of creation in the human reproductive system. Deeply ingrained in the psychic structure of egg consciousness is the awareness of its limitation. There are only so many to be produced in a given lifetime and when they are gone, they are gone. This knowing fosters a necessary sense of conservation and caution. The egg is pushed from its safe, secure environment, usually alone and with no self-propelling ability, is forced to trust the fates for safe passage. It is guided and urged along its path by outside forces. It can only go where it is taken. But what is lacking in locomotion is made up for with self-containment. There is no choice but to surrender to the motion and have faith that those forces in control of its fate know what they are doing. Perhaps deep within the consciousness there is also the knowing that its survival/continuance depends upon something from outside itself for ignition. So just once it will allow penetration. Then the shield goes up and a big red *keep out* sign is posted against all other possible interlopers. It absorbs and merges within itself that which has entered so that each can continue. The result is Life, and ultimate manifestation of a form that is both and neither, greater than the sum of its parts.

The cultural models for both of these ways of being are in a process of transition right now. What follows is a brief summary of some of the astrological principles which I feel call for egg consciousness, as well as some suggestions for a more positive approach to defining them. This is not meant to indicate that those principles invested more in sperm consciousness are less important or less in need of reframing. But to work on one end of the spectrum is, in truth, to work on both. That is the way of polarity. This is simply my truth as I have come to understand it thus far. Being big with egg consciousness, I am aware that I am still being pulled ever deeper into awareness, but the insights presented here have made it easier to enjoy the ride. Participation in the process makes one that much more trusting of it. If this helps to validate the experience of one other egg on the planet, then I am fulfilled.

RETROGRADES AND INTERCEPTIONS

Retrograde planets and those which are intercepted in the birth chart operate most effectively through the modality of egg consciousness. The psychic urges represented by these planets are shielded within a protective casing, much like the egg following fertilization. It is not that direct action (projection) of the planetary energy cannot be expressed. What is more important in the psychic structure of the individual is the invisible process which goes on prior to the externalization of energy. It is as if the person was "born pregnant" in regard to the archetype represented by that retrograde planet. The greatest mastery possible is the potential of that force, but mastery depends upon one's ability for focus within a confined area of concentration.

This mysterious inner processing information is the gift of the retrograde. External stimuli which apply or are destined to activate the particular planet are absorbed into the psychic structure and "carried" to full term. The experience must travel to a personal, subjective place where it can merge with all other experiences collected thus far in the life of the individual. I believe that when a retrograde is involved, the repository of experience transcends time and space as we know it to include cellular memory of all past lifetimes. The individual must become one with the stimulus, blend it accordingly with all other experience and finally, come to an understanding of it in relation to all things. There is a deepening of the idea (input) which goes beyond the limitations of its physical reality, a total "groking" which incorporates all levels of acknowledgement—mental, emotional, physical and spiritual—of the thing being translated.

When a planet is retrograde or intercepted, it is more frightening to make mistakes with the energy or psychic urge (action) represented by the planet. The subjectivity which imbues the operation of the planet makes it difficult to trust the initial impressions regarding "needs" of the planet involved. Direct expression is more carefully planned and calculated before execution. Resultant action reflects this caution, possessing a greater depth, a more total understanding and accuracy which, in the long run, compensates for the speedier reaction and abundance of outflow more evident when the planet is in direct motion. The process of the retrograde/interception involves absorption, merging, blending and universalizing before a reaction to the input can manifest in outer reality. The older people grow, the greater value they can place on the wisdom and perfect execution, which is the potential gift of the planet.

The external expression of the process or psychic urge represented by each planet is slow to manifest. In youth this can pose a problem, not because a retrograde/interception is bad but because we live in a culture which values speedy process, i.e. fast foods, fast relief, fast results. So **Mercury retrograde or intercepted** slows down and deepens one's ability to process and communicate information. As input is analyzed in regard to personal experience and memory, it must go through a longer process, travel to center and back out again. Of course the end result rarely looks the same as that of other people. Sometimes the original input is so dramatically altered that one cannot even discern what it was. Often the end result reflects an originality and unique-ness which is nothing short of genius.

The reason Mercury retrograde by transit is such a "bug-a-boo" is because most people are not used to taking the time to totally experience information and process it in relation to the bigger picture at hand. Our thinking is so programmed as to be automatic. Mercury retrograde affords one the opportunity to slow down and pay much greater attention to the processes of daily routine and life. It is a wonderful time to reprogram some of those underlying assumptions which are not creating a reality conducive to happiness. What is called for when this transit occurs is that more time be taken and greater caution used in reading those contracts that are not supposed to be signed. Check and double check the address on that envelope which is not supposed to be mailed and pray that the mailman has a natal retrograde Mercury. Pay closer attention to the plan-ning of those future events which are not supposed to be planned at this time. Honor the process, observe the assump-tions and grow in greater wisdom from the opportunity a Mercury retrograde. Then one need not suffer the terrible consequences so often attributed to this transit.

Venus retrograde or intercepted slows down and deepens one's ability to experience the bonding process, to recognize and attract that which complements one's own natural way of being in the world. It is not that one is unable to create successful and meaningful relationships, but that the process required to do so takes time, patience and discrimination. The object of the desired bonding must go through many tests and trials to insure a proper fit. The person with Venus retrograde tends not to assume permanence and so continually works to maintain a balanced flow between self and the desired object. The ultimate potential is the ability to form lasting relationships which are not taken for granted, and a value system which will withstand any circumstance perpetrated by external forces.

Mars retrograde or intercepted slows down and deepens one's instinctual need/ability to define oneself and take action to insure survival. Action is more carefully planned; all options and possible consequences are analyzed. The gift is instinct tempered with conscious awareness which operates in perfect synchronicity. The ultimate potential is an identity which cannot be shaken and the ability to experience a total merging with another. When one is firmly anchored in the self there is no fear of being lost in the merging, which makes real union possible. There is also the potential gift of a finely tuned instinctual nature which is capable of immediately assessing the totality of a dangerous situation—to recognize the danger, analyze the possibilities and act to insure survival all in a moment of whole awareness. When Mars is invested with egg consciousness, action and defense blend together to appear as one process. Mars retrograde seems to be much more aligned with the Scorpio side of rulership than with Aries. If it ever comes down to a moment of annihilation of life on this planet, what will be left when the dust clears are the Scorpios, those with Mars retrograde, and of course, the cockroaches.

Jupiter retrograde or intercepted slows down and deepens the ability to grow and expand in consciousness. The individual has a greater sensitivity to all the possibilities and therefore a greater discrimination in choosing which to pursue. These people are less subject to public opinion and less likely to jump into the latest growth fad. They are much more discriminating concerning choice of teachers or bodies of knowledge worth investigating. Careful and cautious expansion yields lasting results.

Saturn retrograde or intercepted slows down and deepens the ability to establish and maintain solid structural systems in both the personal and outer world. Saturn is the creator of form and the forms created by one with Saturn retrograde or intercepted are unshakeable. There is heightened sensitivity to the possibility of error, so every base is covered thoroughly before the end result ever emerges into physical manifestation. The authority must ultimately live within the individual, so this placement increases the ability to own one's personal responsibility for the reality which is created. Personal structures are tested and retested so as to become firmly anchored in the inner world. There is an innate appreciation for the limits inherent in living in a society and a heightened social consciousness which ultimately enables one to facilitate change within a system in a non-threatening and acceptable way.

Uranus retrograde or intercepted slows down and deepens the ability to individualize and express one's uniqueness to the outer world. This placement increases the sensitivity of social reaction to change, thereby increasing the ability to facilitate change in more subtle, less threatening ways. Uranus, with patience, learns to work within the existing system and make needed reforms much more palatable. There is also a deeper investment in one's own right to individuality and the ability to remove self and support from a system which refuses to make those necessary reforms. Uranus retrograde or intercepted is not afraid to go it alone and sometimes going it alone is what the situation demands.

Neptune retrograde or intercepted slows down and

deepens the ability to accept and surrender to the ebb and flow of universal rhythms. There is a greater sensitivity to other dimensional possibilities and it becomes an essential part of the perceptual base to automatically take into consideration the larger picture operating at any given time. A true understanding of the "I am God" principle is more readily available to this placement of Neptune. It is much easier to surrender the little self and participate more lovingly and willingly in the impersonal life. The more hopeless the circumstance, the more valuable and appreciated Neptune retrograde becomes. These people are much more conscious of the need to create a space in life through which they can experience a total devotion to service. If a specific area is consciously created, then the other areas need not reflect the sacrifice so often demanded of Neptune.

Pluto retrograde or intercepted slows down and deepens the ability to understand and experience merging and to be transformed by it. There is an increased sensitivity to issues of power and its abusive potential and a much deeper understanding of the spiritual side of sexuality. An intuitive understanding of all that is considered to be Dark is available to this placement of Pluto. With acceptance of the Darkness, they can become some of the most powerful transformers of social conditions on the planet. These people are born with a profound awareness of occult principles. Somehow in the life the potential mastery of those principles unfolds. The result is not always pleasant, but most often necessary to some kind of needed evolutionary change.

It is not by accident that the outer planets travel retrograde as often as they travel direct. They represent a kind of consciousness which extends beyond the personal, a collective awareness or attunement with the universal principles underlying the existence of all things in all time. The fact that they are retrograde as often as they are direct is perhaps a statement of the equality granted both modes of growth by universal forces. The recent discovery of these planets, coinciding with the dawning of a new age, is in my opinion, a symbol of readiness for a collective world view which accepts and honors both egg and sperm conscious-ness as equally valuable pathways of evolution. It is like the act of breathing. Which is more important? The taking in of air or its eventual release?

VOID-OF-COURSE

The traditional descriptions of the void-of-course Moon are filled with what not to do as well as difficulties created by the period of the void. Taking action, beginning new projects, and making decisions are absolute "no-nos," It is always described as a time of "not tos." Little attention is paid to the positive potential of the period. The v/c Moon has made its last aspect and is now in a state of much needed rest. The Moon gives form to a potential creation and anchors emotional commitment to its support/nurturance. It pro-vides the egg within energy which can take form and ulti-mately manifest. That takes energy and hard work. Time for integration and adjustment to the new condition is required.

There are just as many "shoulds" which need to be considered during a v/c Moon. It is a valuable and impor-tant time of gestation and processing, a time to gently and quietly integrate and become one with the new awarenesses and commitments conceived during the previous, more active phase of the Moon's transit. This invisible and mys-terious process of gestation which occurs within the womb is a perfect analogy for the necessary process in conscious-ness provided and available to us when the Moon is void.

Tremendous care must be taken by a woman carrying that energy during that time. She can choose to focus on all of the things she cannot do, or she can choose to make pregnancy a priority and honor the "shoulds" of the time. There is increasing evidence that the end result, a human being, reflects the attitude adopted by its mother. The same is true of a void Moon. One can choose to devote time and energy to the processes facilitated by the period, ie. contemplation, completion, assessment and evaluation, and simply checking into the self to see how one feels about the current state of affairs in the personal life. These processes are as important and valuable as those more appropriate during the more active lunar phase. In fact, emotional health, balance and stability depend on one's ability to "check out" and recharge. The v/c Moon is not the problem. Cultural attitude about productive use of time is.

In American Indian tradition, there are many rules and taboos concerning "Moontime," the point in a woman's menstrual cycle when the blood is flowing. The period during a void-of-course Moon is much like this point in a woman's cycle in terms of the energies at work. The traditions have been distorted through the years and are now translated into isolation, separation and a forced ostracizing from all ongoing ceremony and ritual. Women during this time are required to remain in a Moon Lodge and are told that they are engaged in their own ceremony, which is so powerful so as to disrupt the flow of any other ceremony in progress. Much lip service is given to honoring the time, but no one can remember how that was done, or what specific functions were designated to be performed solely by the women in the Moon Lodge. The result is much resentment and a feeling of "unclean woman," hardly a healthy state of mind within which to honor one's own ceremony.

Many cultures share in this treatment of menstrual blood. Jewish boys are taught that to make love to a woman during this time results in her having complete and total power over him. Hindu tradition supports the taboo, placing horrific ramifications on such contact, as well. Some traditions teach that women during this time can drain the life essence of a man foolish enough to risk sexual contact. These attitudes reflect the same treatment given the v/c Moon. Like most superstitions, there is some truth and validity at the base of such beliefs, the original intentions of which have been dramatically distorted and perverted through the years.

The original intention of these traditions revolved around the honoring of a very sacred process, understood and revered in an earlier time. Woman's natural cycle was a symbol of the universal ebb and flow of energy. The time of the bleeding was a cleansing of the body, much like the process that Mother Earth engages in during autumn every year. This cleansing was in necessary preparation for the next round of fertility and renewal. The time of flow was also a time of mourning for the death of the lost child which had not been conceived during the past cycle. It was a time of honoring with proper ritual and ceremony, that phase of the life cycle called death, without which there could be no life.

Pluto currently transiting through Scorpio brings back into conscious awareness the significance of this critical phase. *How we end things is as important as how we begin them.* In ancient times women were not forced into isolation and made to feel as if their presence was disruptive to the mainstream of the community. They were responsible for mourning the dead and facilitating their peaceful passage to the other side. They created healing totems and made prayers for the sick and needy. They rested, integrating and evaluating the progress of and for the entire community. This work was so important that they were relieved of the burdens of the daily responsibilities of functional maintainence and child care in order to devote complete energy to Moon Lodge activity. These traditions have been lost to us, but the memories are being revived. With revival comes a deeper appreciation of these magical processes in consciousness symbolized by this process in woman and most appropriately engaged in during the quiet, resting time of Luna.

The void-of-course Moon is a time to focus on the quality of the endings in life. It is for completion, the tying up of loose ends, saying good-bye to the thoughts and experiences which have no hope of growing or adding to one's personal evolution, and a time to properly mourn their passing. It is a time to engage in the internal process of integration, to absorb and become one with that which is necessary to the growth of the individual, and to release that which must be released in order to grow. It need not be a negative time, complete with limitation and restriction, if used as it is meant to be used, and valued for its special process in consciousness. The v/c Moon is the invisible part of the creative process without which no end product can take form. The prerequisite to creation is that invisible process which no one ever sees—the imaging, ruminating, assessing and formulating of the dream. We forget that every act of creation begins with that dream, born of imagination or the process of healing pain and anguish in one's life. The v/c Moon is a time for creating a fertile, clear space from which the dream can emerge.

THE NODAL AXIS

The South Node of the chart is another one of those concepts which suffers from negative interpretation and for which few positive models can be found. It is called *a point of addiction*, to be avoided at all cost. To be working through the South Node is considered a weakness. South Node conjunctions to personal planets, or to another in synastry, are nothing but bad news or something to do with difficult karmic connections. Rarely is the South Node presented in terms of what it is good for, or a positive way to work with this point. If it is allowed to exist in thought, then there must be some useful purpose for the thing. The Gods don't make no junk!

The Nodal Axis is the purest symbol of the workings of that spiral of consciousness described earlier. It is a spectrum, stretching between two points which are opposite and yet exactly the same. The goal, or aspiration of a lifetime (masculine expression of the ideal), is to strive to achieve success and manifest accomplishments through the North Node point in the spectrum. It is true that a deep sense of fulfillment does accompany the expression of energy via the North Node. It is also true that the nature of the actual deed or energy expressed through the North Node can usually be described by a mastery at the South. Rarely does anyone talk about the inherent gifts symbolic of the South Node, or the fact that *what often manifests at the North Node is the result of the natal abilities and innate talents described by the South Node.*

I have discovered that mastery of this axis is enhanced and facilitated when the South Node is described to the individual as a point of equal value and worth to the North Node. Rather than a point to be avoided at all cost, the Lunar South Node represents a skill which can be used in service and directed through its North Node counterpart. The South Node is one's inheritance, *a natural gift and a point of automatic mastery with which one is blessed at birth.* The North Node is one's legacy, *the aspiration to serve with that gift and the ability* (or lack of it) *to create a vehicle through which that service can be manifest.*

More often than can be attributed to chance, the South Node is in the same sign as the Sun or Moon of one of the parents. That parent, as guardian of the energy of the individual, becomes the dominant influence in the early training of the child. The South Node represents an innate ability which is as natural to the individual as breathing. The parent whose planets contact the South Node is the model/teacher for that natural expression. This does not always occur in a positive or pleasant way. We learn from all experience and sometimes the teachings take the form of suffering the abuses of one's own negative potential. It is of great benefit to a client to frame the lunar South Node in terms of its more positive qualities and as a point of tremendous worth/value, a natural proclivity which, when directed toward service, can be the source of a great sense of success and accomplishment in the world.

Humans tend not to place a value on what comes naturally. If things come too easily, they must not be worth anything, or they must be something everyone can do. This attitude is born of cultural bias. In an earlier, more primitive time, when each member of the tribal community was a very valuable commodity, necessary to the survival of the group, I believe a different attitude prevailed. New life, if it survived, was precious. Rather than trying to create a pathway for that new life and mold it into a particular role, children were observed and watched in order to discern the natural proclivities they possessed. It was assumed that the little boy who always seemed to gravitate to the toolmaker, watching, listening and practicing his art, had a natural talent for toolmaking and should be encouraged to develop that inherent skill for the sake of the future of the tribe. If a little girl followed the medicine person around and always seemed to be there when healing was being administered, it was honored that she was choosing her own training. A human being was too valuable to waste time and energy trying to shape what was not there. Lifespans were short. Time was at a premium. Survival depended on honoring the gifts and preferences of each individual, the South Node in each chart.

To work the spectrum demands the ability to creatively blend the polarities represented by the nodal axis in sign and by house placement. Simply put, the North Node is the direction and describes the activity through which energy must flow in order to capitalize on the gifts of the South Node. For example:

If the South Node is in:	The innate gift is:	To be directed in such a way:
Aries 1st House	To be so firmly anchored in a sense of Self and your ability to survive . .	that you can relate equally and fairly with others and resist the temptation to project onto them.
Taurus 2nd House	To understand the worth and value of a thing so well . . .	that you only invest time and energy into that which has evolutionary potential.
Gemini 3rd House	To be so in tune with the here and now experience of life . . .	that you can apply acute and immediate awareness to future goals and aspirations.
Cancer 4th House	To nurture and maintain yourself, take responsibility for emotional needs and honor your personal boundaries . .	that you possess the strength, stamina and desire to take on responsibility for outer world structures necessary to the support of the larger whole.
Leo 5th House	To understand and believe in your own	that you can be a powerfully creative force,

If the South Node is in:	The innate gift is:	To be directed in such a way:
Leo, (cont.)	and be so strongly centered in your own divinity . . .	to reflect higher will in whatever group you choose to align with.
Virgo 6th House	To innately understand natural logic and law which underlies all earthly systems . . .	that you can function with ease in situations which demand that order be created out of confusion.
Libra 7th House	To understand the power of relationship to be that of reflection and a tool for self-awareness . .	that you can grow and model greater self-awareness through relationship.
Scorpio 8th House	To innately understand the power/ value of a thing in terms of its latent potential, and ability to wait for its unfoldment . .	that you can manifest the most solid foundations of unquestionable worth in the physical world (both material and spiritual).
Sagittarius 9th House	To possess vision and an innate understanding of whole systems and how they operate; awareness which transcends personal experience . . .	that you can apply the best parts of all systems (those most suited) to whatever system you choose to align with.

If the South Node is in:	The innate gift is:	To be directed in such a way:
Aquarius *11th House*	An innate understanding that the power of the group depends upon the freedom to create by each individual, and the ability to insist on that right . . .	that you develop and model a confidence in your own personal creative potential which serves both the self and others.
Pisces *12th House*	An innate understanding of the universality and connectedness of all things and the ability to access in emotional understanding all possibilities within the flux of changing universal rhythms . . .	that you can naturally assess any situation in terms of the larger picture and successfully plot the best course of action relative to all considerations of the

CONCLUSION

It will take many years and many writers to thoroughly treat the subject of the feminine in astrology, to reframe those concepts imbued with egg consciousness in a way which reflects an equal value and understanding of the feminine end of the spiral of consciousness. This is just the beginning—a suggestion—some food for thought. The time is very ripe right now for such activity. As the outer planets align themselves in the powerfully feminine signs of Scorpio and Capricorn, that end of the spectrum so long ignored and denied will emerge. It is emerging. And the painful ramifications of the prolonged imbalance are already in evidence. All collective systems and structures which are based on this imbalance are subject to dramatic change, if not destruction, over the next few years. We must revive in memory those tools and proper ceremonies once used to deal with such reality as exists at this end of the spectrum.

The Goddess of Necessity is alive and well and walking on the planet. She is touching each inhabitant in both personal and collective ways. Some know Her well, have missed Her in Her dormancy, and welcome Her return. Some fear Her because they do not understand Her principles. They only know the stuff of fairy tales and the distorted perversions of Her myths. Initially, as Her walk begins, Chaos accompanies Her. This isn't good. This isn't bad. This just is. With Chaos comes confusion and fear—necessary prerequisites to facilitate the kind of dramatic changes required of us over the next 15 to 20 years. There are those who will resist, desperately struggling to maintain the chasm which has kept Her at a distance for so many years. But there really is no choice but to honor Her process. This will become increasingly evident as Pluto and Neptune move deeper into Her end of the spectrum. The end result, hopefully—a world of balance and a consciousness described by the automatic assumption of equality—the Aquarian Ideal. We, as astrologers, can play a vital role in the creation of that new world view. We can begin by reframing those concepts and principles within our own field which have for too long been allowed to support the imbalance and reflect the ignorance and lack of understanding of the feminine side of consciousness. As translators of Universal Truth, we owe it to ourselves and to all whom we serve with this art-science.

The Goddess of Necessity is knocking. She does not wield a lightning bolt. She does not strike down those who fail to recognize and honor Her. She simply knocks. If not soon heeded and welcomed in, the knocking will become a pounding, the reverberations of which will shake our world and change the face of this planet in ways we have yet to imagine. This isn't good. This isn't bad. This just is.

Kathleen Burt

An astrologer for 17 years, Kathleen's orientation is toward the spiritual and esoteric. She and her husband reside in Solana Beach, California, and she teaches astrology as well as Indian history at Mira Costa College, Community Services Branch at Del Mar.

She is a Fullbright scholar to India and formerly taught at Roosevelt University in Chicago, Illinois.

Kathleen is currently presenting workshops on the theme of her latest book, *Archetypes of the Zodiac*, published by Llewellyn Publications.

Besides doing everyday astrology for her clients, Kathleen also offers esoteric chart readings, which she recommends for those who are interested in understanding the spiritual side of their nature and who have a basic knowledge of astrology. These readings include an interpretation of the esoteric rulers of the signs according to Alice Bailey and Isabel Hickey. Sanskrit vocabulary of karma and dharma is used in these delineations.

THE SPIRITUAL RULERS:
THEIR PRACTICAL ROLE
IN THE TRANSFORMATION

As the Age of Aquarius draws nearer, an article on the practical application of the spiritual (esoteric) rulers seems timely. Even five years ago would have been too soon. I remember attending a conference in 1983, at which I mentioned to several colleagues my use of the esoteric rulers, as well as the Moon's Nodes and planetary exaltations, falls and detriments in client work. They raised their eyebrows and exchanged disparaging glances with each other. One woman asked, "Don't you really think that the Alice Bailey/Isabel Hickey approach is old-fashioned and impractical? After all the average client merely wants to know when the ideal partner is to appear on the scene, or when the big break is coming professionally, or when they'll win the state lottery. They want to know about the mundane issues—love and money, emotional and financial security." I remember thinking, "The time is not yet ripe to talk about this."

Of course, many people still come with purely mundane questions and are content to live life instinctually, unconsciously, at the personality level. The exoteric (mundane) planetary rulers will, of course, not become extinct in the New Age; they will still be needed to answer questions about the *outer* world, wherein many desires and ambitions can be fulfilled. There are, however, an increasing number of spiritual seekers appearing in the astrologer's office— people whose background and interests are connected with the inner work of meditation, introspection, dream

77

interpretation and active imagination, the growth techniques of the New Age. These people do not ask, "How can I persuade or convert those around me to my will, or *my* philosophy?" But rather, "How can I change myself? How can I get in touch with my soul, instead of just living in the mundane horoscope? Is there a way to transcend from the personality to the soul? Is there a bridge, or at least a middle ground where I can stand and watch myself think, feel and intuit? Where I can respond consciously rather than instinctively in a manner appropriate to the situation of the moment?"

Yes, there is! In *Esoteric Astrology (Treatise on the Seven Rays, III*, pp 514 and following) Alice Bailey outlines the approach. The traditional natal chart describes the work of the personality in the outer world, while the esoteric chart describes the inner work, the work of the Soul. Delineation of the soul chart is discussed elsewhere in this anthology, so I will focus upon the importance of the spiritual ruler of the Ascendant. Alice Bailey emphasizes the role of the Ascendant, or rising sign, and of its esoteric ruler in spiritual growth. This approach is important in India as well, because the Ascendant—the attitude—is considered to be of primary importance on the spiritual path. The individual's work in a given incarnation concerns this attitudinal change. That is the *real* meaning of the transformation.

BECOMING CONSCIOUS OF THE ASCENDANT

I have found that by mid-to-late-forties my average clients are becoming conscious of the importance of their Ascendant, the pattern of their reaction to people, events and circumstances in the outer world. Prior to that, their reactions were pretty instinctual. The Fire signs tended to react impulsively, or to overreact; the Water signs tended to react sensitively or hypersensitively, often seeing slights where none were meant; the Air signs tended to react by talking and analyzing the outer world mentally, often rationalizing away their own responses instead of altering their behavior patterns; the Earth signs tended to react in an earnest, heavy manner, feeling burdened by the outer world like the god Atlas with the weight of the globe on his shoulders—taking themselves too seriously. The mutable signs tended to react through the flight instinct. "This is too much for my central nervous system. I'm going to leave the project unfinished and move on to a new environment— learn new things from new people and situations." The Cardinal signs tended to respond authoritatively. "If I cannot lead, I'll go elsewhere and hang out my shingle. I'll take my marbles and go home." The Fixed signs tended to respond stubbornly: "Why should I back down and change my stand—he's the one who is wrong!"

By midlife, people seem to have dealt with the primary goals of their Sun signs, through accomplishing them, compromising them, or relinquishing them. The more conscious clients have also caught the Moon at its emotional games. The questions asked by those between the ages of 40 and 50 frequently indicate a readiness to understand the Ascendant and to consciously work on their attitudes. Becoming conscious of instinctual action/reaction patterns improves their ability to use their free will. With transiting Uranus and Jupiter opposing their natal positions at midlife, freedom becomes an important issue. This search for freedom and conscious understanding may be connected to the motion of these expansive planets of freedom and learning. In the second half of life we may feel limited by time and an aging body, but we have lived long enough to gain experience. We know that though not always free to act as we choose, we have more insight, are better able to consciously determine our reactions and to try new approaches.

ESOTERIC RULERSHIPS

The esoteric ruler, considered a more subtle influence, can come into play for the conscious client at midlife.

Attunement to its positive qualities (and of course, avoid-ance of its negative traits) will help them shift gears in their forties and fifties.

The esoteric rulers are:
Aries: Mercury
Taurus: Vulcan-Haephestus
Gemini: Venus
Cancer: Neptune
Leo: The Sun of Illumination
Virgo: The Moon (Mother of Form)
Libra: Uranus
Scorpio: Mars (the Spiritual Warrior)
Sagittarius: The Earth (Groundedness)
Capricorn: Saturn (Duty beyond personal ambition)
Aquarius: Jupiter
Pisces: Pluto

Many clients with such stubborn, willful Ascendants as Leo and Scorpio may spend the first half of life trying to control the world around them, to change others. Prior to age 45 they may ask, "What practical purpose would I achieve by changing my attitude? Why should *I* have to compromise? *Others* should change, not me." But close to age 45, many seem to meet with a stalemate, or even a checkmate situation in their outer world. Their spouse may pack and move out, or the corporation may close its plant in their city and sell the office building. All the alternatives seem to be unacceptable; they could lose what they worked most of their adult lives to accomplish by remaining intran-sigent, submitting their resignations, or compromising and taking a look at the company's out-of-state office in Texas, New York or Chicago. "But I don't want to budge," is an attitude that may no longer work.

If the astrologer can help "Fixed" clients attune to the

esoteric ruler of their Ascendant, the change in the outer world can be viewed as an opportunity rather than an obstacle. If the esoteric ruler is well-aspected in the natal chart, clients may have viewed the planet as a hobby subject rather than a career or something important in their lives. Trines to the esoteric ruler may indicate past life success in that field; these persons enjoy the talent recreationally this lifetime, but are not challenged to work with it as they would have been were it a natal square. In the second half of life they may return to the trine of the esoteric ruler, go deeper into that area of life and find some peace, some joy, or some meaningful creative release through it.

LEO ASCENDANT

Many Leo rising clients have been thrown by midlife changes imposed by the outer world only to discover that their esoteric Ascendant ruler, the Illumined Sun, shone magnificently for them as they allowed it to shine. By letting go of hurt pride or lost face (wounded mundane Ego, with the lower Sun as ruler), they enjoyed a new freedom—the freedom of living where they liked. The Sun of Illumination, the esoteric ruler of Leo, took them to a spiritual environment, such as a temple that offered courses in yoga, tai chi, meditation, or brought them into contact with a Friends of Jung group in the area of relocation. The Jungian path of Individuation appeals quite naturally to many Leo rising and Leo Sun people who seek wholeness and the ability to express themselves creatively in cooperation with the Unconscious. Thus, it helps if the astrologer can focus on the Sun of Enlightenment—Leos shift at midlife from extroverting activity toward a sense of inner fulfillment, of growth in "becoming" themselves. (See *Archetypes of the Zodiac* by Kathleen Burt, Chapter 5.) Concentration at the Sun Center (Ajna Chakra) in meditation will accelerate the attunement to the esoteric ruler and help Leo mentally, spiritually, emotionally and even physically, since meditation promotes relaxation and relieves stress.

SCORPIO ASCENDANT:

Like Leo rising, Scorpio Ascendants may suffer at midlife from loss of control, power or emotional security. With Pluto as mundane ruler, Scorpio rising is more likely to respond bitterly or vindictively to change, ready to strike back at the outer world. For example, transiting Pluto square natal Pluto can become severely depressed by frustrated desires. Such negative response patterns impede progress in both the inner and outer world. A change of attitude can be effected by positive attunement to Mars, the esoteric ruler of Scorpio. This will help Scorpio to fight the inner battle. Pluto often prefers to live in the past, but Mars lives in the present and courageously fights his own battles. (Depression does not immobilize a Mars ruled Aries, for instance.) Rather than use the Scorpion's tail to sting those who challenge them in the outer world, many Scorpio rising individuals have attuned to Mars and been energized at midlife. Facing the Shadow, the inner darkness, moving beyond depression into the purifying emotional fire Mars generates, is like performing an alchemical process.

The Phoenix/Scorpios experience their next combust within, at the nadir of the pesonality, and emerge purified, resourceful and strong, with greater magnetism and creative power than before. Several Scorpio rising clients have become therapists as a result of their inner death and rebirth journey—shamans who help others in crisis. Some have gotten in touch with Mars in a more literal manner; they have studied karate, kung fu, run in marathons or taught aerobic dance. Motion, exercise and activity are all Mars ruled approaches which have proved helpful. Mars activities function as a release valve for the emotions as well as the body. Mars also rules the sex life, the lower chakras. Becoming too absorbed in sex as exercise (energy release) is a Pluto square Pluto tendency. It is important, esoterically speaking, to lead a balanced life, one that circulates energy through the upper, as well as the lower chakras. The martial arts systems of the Orient, as well as all forms of yoga, are recommended to balance the energy in the chakras.

AQUARIUS ASCENDANT:

The Ego usually identifies with the attitude of the planet that rules the Ascendant at the mundane level. In the case of a Fixed rising sign, the planet may fight for stability and control, versus change and growth. This is particularly true of Taurus where Venus/Aphrodite as mundane ruler clings to emotional and financial security, and it is true even of broad-minded Aquarius which is attached to its community or its group of friends and can be surprisingly resistant to change. (Mental stimulation comes from the feedback that Uranus, the mundane ruler, receives from the group.) Jupiter, the esoteric ruler of Aquarius, complements Uranus and raises its mental curiosity and humanitarianism to a higher, more spiritual level. Jupiter often impels the conscious Aquarius rising toward a mid-life relocation—a totally new community or 11th house environment. (If transits of Jupiter are checked in the charts of those Aquarius rising clients who are seekers, this pattern can be observed. Jupiter's compassion goes beyond scientific or clinical logic; it opens the Aquarian heart to non-scientific or New Age areas of life which require Jupiterian faith. Aquarius rising men often remark at midlife, "My wife has bugged me to have an astrology reading for years. I guess I wasn't ready. I had no faith in anything my fellow scientists (*the group*) disdain." The move to California or New York changed the group around him, and therefore, his attitude. Jupiter also enhances generosity after midlife when it can bring affluence to Aquarius rising; in many cases after 45, these people have enough money to pursue their altruistic work. There- fore I speak in the Jupiter vocabulary to Aquarius rising clients who, at midlife, are faced with pulling up roots or are losing their funding at their scientific/educational institu- tion and are forced to move on. The aspects to natal Jupiter as well as Jupiter's role in the soul chart can provide clues for the astrologer's approach. Aquarius rising is often an indicator of the New Age scientist, teacher or healer. Jupiter's midlife transits may offer the advanced souls an oppor- tunity to draw close to a Guru, its Hindu meaning, by introducing them to a new group of spiritually-minded people.

TAURUS ASCENDANT:
Taurus is an interesting Ascendant for the esoteric stu- dent because in Greek mythology the mundane ruler, Aphrodite (Venus) was married to the esoteric ruler Haephestus (Latin name: Vulcan). Zeus (all wise Jupiter) arranged the wedding himself, so it was meant to be. "Beauty" in the form of Aphrodite married to "the Beast," Haephes- tus the ugly dwarf. Many people are familiar with Aphrodite's mythology, but few with that of Haephestus. We know that she was vain, somewhat snobbish (she ruled aesthetics) and very seductive. She hated to work and she hated coarse environments like the battlefield of life. Haephestus was ugly, but had the wisdom of the Earth itself. (See Jung's essay on dwarfs and smiths in Vision Seminars, I.) Esoteric Taureans have that common sense wisdom of which Jung speaks; we find it in the Buddha's sermons and the stories about Swami Sri Yukteswar in Yogananda's *Autobiography of a Yogi*. Both are astrologically connected with Taurus. Marie Louise von Franz adds a choice morsel of informa- tion in her study of *Apuleius and the Golden Ass*. (See Notes.) Haephestus was the only one of the gods who worked. He worked constantly and earnestly at his forge, transforming

base metals into beautiful art forms through alchemy. According to von Franz, the other gods disliked him for his workaholic termperament. Perhaps he put them to shame.

How does this relate to the life of the Taurus rising people? At the mundane level, Aphrodite can be especially lazy. At midlife, Taurean Ascendant individuals will often remark wistfully, "I have an artistic creative side, but (sigh) I don't want to give up my comfortable standard of living to develop it. Will my prince come and save me? I loathe having to support myself, I should be able to quit and stay home and fix up the house, or take courses that stimulate my inner, creative nature." I have thought a lot about this over the years. Aphrodite had to remain married to Haephestus. She had to work in order to create. "But I want free time to smell the roses," says Ferdinand the Bull. Haephestus was capable of making beautiful objects like the shield of Achilles, which Homer raved about in the *Iliad*. But he kept the forge fire burning constantly, patiently, every day. For the Taurus attitude (Ascendant), midlife often brings a Vulcan earthquake, an upheaval in the outer world (often some transit of Saturn or Uranus to Venus/Aphrodite, mundane ruler). Due to the upheaval, they are forced to work on their attitude, whether they want to or not. Haephestus worked not only in making spears and shields, but on his relationship with the feminine, his mother. This is part of the journey to creativity releasing the inner feminine. (The Moon is exalted, symbolically, in Taurus.) At midlife I check out the Moon for Taureans. I ask about their mother. Is she still living? Was she supportive of their personality/spiritual growth? Is there work remaining to be done with mother or mother figures?

At midlife, tending the inner fire or the alchemical forge of transformation refers to relating, for both Venus and Haephestus. They worked hard at it and had to achieve a compromise to develop a soul beauty that is more than skin deep. Vulcan's earthquake opens up the land, but it also destroys old structures, old lunar attachements. Receptivity will help a spiritual client deal with midlife changes creatively and will attract happiness in relationships if the attitude is positive and open. Understanding Haephestus' role can help.

The Uranus Opposition

In my discussion of the Attitude (Ascendant) and its esoteric ruler, I chose to present the Fixed signs first for a reason. In the esoteric tradition Fixity is a type of inertia. It is harder to work with than Mutability or Cardinality. A horoscope with several Fixed squares indicates habits entrenched for many lifetimes. Though there may be more Ego in the leadership signs (Cardinal), they are less rigid in their instinctual behavior. Once Cardinal signs have consciously understood their habit patterns, they are usually able to alter them more quickly than the Fixed sign Ascendants. Mutable signs rising are the most adaptable to change. If they err, it's on the side of inconstancy and impressionability.

Though the Fixed rising signs seem to draw opposition, stalemate or checkmate from the outer world at midlife, perhaps *because* of their resistance to change, this is not true of everyone. We all have encountered persons whose charts are composed mainly of trines and sextiles, who have led placid, uneventful lives until Uranus opposed Uranus (close to age 42). They may remark, "How dull life is, how boring. Something's missing, but I don't know what. I know it's something important and I'm ready for a change, but what sort of change? Mostly, I guess I'm just restless." On the mundane level, the astrologer will look at the houses affected by Uranus and identify the outer changes by house position, aspects and so on. But what about the "something missing?" How to put the client in touch with that? If the

Ascendant is in a Cardinal or Mutable sign, they have an adaptable or open attitude ot change and may even welcome it (unless, of course, they also have a Fixed Grand Cross or T-Square).

To put the client in touch with what's missing at midlife, the astrologer must not only be acquainted with the esoteric ruler of their rising sign, but with the esoteric and mundane rulers of their Sun sign, as well. The spiritually aware clients (those who vaguely mention that something's missing) will usually link their Ego's (Sun sign) unhappiness with some area of life they used to enjoy or be stimulated by. They then list their symptoms—co-worker problems, allergies, traffic, smog and so forth. We have to be familiar with: 1) what the Ego has been doing with itself in the outer world and 2) (esoterically) what the Ego would like to do on the soul level. This often describes the cause behind the symptoms. "I need to get out of the smog and feel alive." The esoteric ruler may be a wide open spaces environment planet, Jupiter, or a planet that requires a New Age environment, such as Uranus, the esoteric ruler of Libra relationships with real seekers who can be found in a New Age community in the wide open spaces. I cannot be much more specific here, as horoscopes, like snowflakes, are each different. The aspects to the esoteric ruler of the Ascendant and to the esoteric ruler of the Sun will be important for the soul journey, as well as for personality integration, for happiness in the inner and outer worlds.

I list the esoteric rulers of the Sun and Ascendant to each other and find them in the soul chart, as well as the natal chart. The attitude (Ascendant) fosters our new goals and draws the right people, events and circumstances into our lives. These planets need to work in harmony with each other. Sometimes I draw the esoteric ruler on the Ascendant large, in order to visualize it. Then I draw, also large, the esoteric ruler of the Sun sign into the house where the natal Sun is posited. I just look at those two planets, unencumbered by asteroids or other planets, nodes, etc. on an otherwise blank sheet of paper. What do they have in common? Are both Feminine? Masculine? Mental? Spiritual? What approach will they take? Are they already well-aspected to each other in the natal chart or not? Will it be easy to integrate their energy or will it take work and time? Is the client used to working in a profession that has developed one or both of them? That is, if Mercury and Jupiter, two mental planets, or Mercury and Uranus, are the esoteric rulers, and they are in trine in the natal chart, and the person is a teacher, a salesperson or counselor—in any communicating career—then they have already been developing them. Such, unfortunately is not often the case. In the first half of life most of us are more attracted toward natal squares than natal trines. If the esoteric rulers are in trine in the natal chart, the person may have organized others' communication projects as an administrative assistant. In the second half of life, they will be more likely to go forward and do their own communicating—having observed others do it well over the years. Is the person doing *inner* work? In therapy? Meditating? These are important things to find out early in the session. Inner work helps promote the transcendance; the blending of energies from natal to esoteric chart happens more quickly and easily.

I then ponder the mythology of the esoteric and mundane rulers. As C. G. Jung has said, the gods and goddesses are all within us. These planets represent our contact with the sacred, so it's good to get to know them. Are both esoteric rulers feeling planets? or religious planets? or intuitive planets, like Neptune and the Moon? Suppose the esoteric rulers of the Ascendant and the Sun are spiritual planets, but for 45 years, the person has been so driven to succeed materially that he or she has paid no attention at all to them? Then a crisis of values may occur at midlife for the

Soul is not satisfied and the client is becoming conscious: "There should be a purpose to life, shouldn't there? Though I'm financially comfortable, I am somehow dissatisfied."

Often the new outer direction or solar goal does not matter as much as the new approach that the Ascendant takes for the second half of life's journey. Perhaps the Ego has so often identified with thinking or feeling or sensing or intuiting that the personality has become lopsided, and the journey to wholeness involves a shift toward a different function. People may become bored with the superior function through which they have automatically been reacting to life. The "something's missing" may be soul functions, a part of themselves they enjoyed in youth but set aside as they grew older. The second strongest (auxiliary) function which the person also feels good at may be indicated. If the client has worked consciously to develop two functions, then it is likely that the esoteric rulers will yield a third function, a greater challenge because it has never been developed. The fourth or inferior function—the troublesome function they are most out of touch with or avoid like the plague— usually does not surface from the unconscious in the esoteric reading, but may appear as soon as the individual begins consciously to work with the second and third functions. It emerges in the environment around them. They try it and people say, "My, you're a mess at that."

Our journey to wholeness involves integration of the archetypal functions in order to reach our inner center, the middle ground which lies beyond them, and which Marie Louise von Franz discusses in her essay, "The Inferior Function." Counselors who reach this middle ground within can observe themselves thinking, feeling, sensing, intuiting. They are of greater service to their clients, for they can consciously select the appropriate response for a particular client on a particular day under particular circumstances.

THE ASCENDANT'S ROLE IN COUNSELING

The first step toward this middle ground would seem to be, astrologically speaking, conscious attunement to the esoteric ruler of the Ascendant and the blending of its energies with the talents of the mundane ruler, already instinctively operating. For example, many *Cancer rising* counselors automatically, instinctively "mother" the client, whatever the circumstances. The feeling function unconsciously nurtures. The client becomes dependent upon Mother to hold his or her hand. A *Gemini rising* counselor will automatically provide lots of facts, alternative suggestions, objective remarks and cool logic through the thinking function. This counselor is instinctively working through Mercury—communicating, as the Cancer rising counselor was instinctively reacting through the Moon, supporting. The *Aquarius rising* counselors are similar to Gemini rising, "but I was so shocked when one day she met me in the grocery store and failed to recognize me. I spent every Tuesday afternoon with her for three years. I felt as if I was a case to her—a footnote in her next article, not a human being. We had no personal relationship at all."

Aries rising counselors may tell their clients the first thing that occurs to them, frankly and directly, or urge the client to take action and do something about their problems soon. They are instinctively tuned in to Mars. *Leo rising* may automatically take control of the client's session to the point that the client is overwhelmed. They may leave with the feeling that Leo is overdirecting their process or dominating them. It takes a strong will to interrupt and/or contradict Leo rising. Like Leo, *Scorpio rising* tends to control. As a deep water sign, Scorpio is not flamboyant but operates from beneath the surface and has a sexual magnetism which can get the counselor into trouble by unconsciously sending mixed signals to the client. At the mundane level Pluto tends toward unconscious manipulation.

Capricorn rising counselors, tuned in to mundane Saturn, and grounded in reality, may provide the common sense answer 90% of the time. But is the common sense response always the best one? We might ask this same question of *Taurus rising*. Taureans may project their own personal concerns with financial/emotional security onto the client and attempt to help them structure their life. But if the clients have a stellium in Aquarius and are free-spirited, this may not appeal to them at all; they may find the session irrelevant.

Pisces rising counselors, idealistic and impressionable, with perhaps a bit of the Messiah complex operating, may try to *save* their clients, or they may tune in to their client's hopes without any sense of the practical possibilities or lack thereof. This is especially true if Pisces rising is low in Earth, the concrete, specific, practical energy. Pisces and Cancer rising may become drained psychically. Their clients feel loved and nurtured, but sometimes become overly dependent.

Libra rising counselors like to please or to balance their client's point of view with their own perspective, to play the devil's advocate. "Yes, X is a good possibility, but let's talk about Y, which is also workable." The client is charmed, admires Libra, but many times leaves confused. *Sagittarius rising* is another charming, positive thinking Ascendant like Libra. Like Pisces rising, Sagittarius sees the whole cloth but may miss the specifics, such as the transits of Saturn as a delay factor. Sagittarians are inspirational counselors but may be too direct; they can strike their target with an arrow (piece of information) the client is not emotionally ready to handle.

Virgo Ascendants see the specifics but not the whole cloth and may pick at their clients. Where the Fire sign Ascendants inspire and motivate, Virgo may deflate or spread uncertainty. "Well," the client may think on the way out, "I guess this is a good time to change jobs, but then again, there are these minor adverse aspects. I'll have to remember to make my appearance in the new office at exactly 2:43 pm to avoid them." A client with many planets in the feeling element, Water, who discontinued working with her Virgo rising counselor told me, "I feel as if she just wants to apply a bandage to my psyche and get me back into the marketplace as soon as possible. I want to see where the Unconscious is taking me. My husband says he makes a good living and there's no need to return so quickly to a job I hate."

At the esoteric level, individuals can direct the instincts and the talents of their mundane rulers more consciously, more spiritually. As counselors, they could contribute a good deal more to their clients, for they have by now learned from their own inner esoteric world. I have just listed some of the positive and negative traits of the mundane level Ascendants for counselors. If we could find twelve counselors at the esoteric level (one from each of the signs) how might they work with people?

Cancer Rising:
Cancer rising comes to mind first, probably because I have so many counselors with this Ascendant as clients. At the esoteric level, Cancers do not automatically nurture because their esoteric ruler, Neptune, leads them to trust their intuition. Moon ruled Cancers still feel for their clients, but Neptune intuition curbs the instinctual mothering and dissolves the dependency cord that binds the client and drains Cancer. As esoteric ruler of the thrifty and cautious Cancer Ascendant, Neptune also dissolves its inner fears. "If I don't mother them, they may not need me. They may not come back and I need the money." Eventually, through attunement to Neptune in meditation, psychic study, trust in the Self and God, Cancers transcend their unconscious

inhibitions, the instinctual limits their personality places upon the soul, and emerge from their crab shell as intuitives. In the personal life, Neptune dissolves the tie to a negative mother, if they have one, and enables them to develop their own inner femininity, their creative capacity.

Gemini Rising:

The Gemini rising counselor is ruled esoterically by Venus. In Plato's philosophy, Venus is the higher mind—the good, the true and beautiful in the world of ideas. Venus also represents the ability to adhere to a personal value system, rather than simply to look at everyone else's and say, "Yes, I can see the truth in that." Participating in the idea of the good, the true and the beautiful, the harmony of the cosmos and the planetary order, Geminis see not only the dual alternatives but the synthesis of all energies; they see a unity beyond individual or concrete facts. They are like the abstract scientist who sees integrated fields in beauty and harmony. Moving in their own minds from analysis to synthesis, Gemini Ascendants now appear warm and human; they seem to be going to the heart of the problem rather than meeting it head-on. They abandon their sarcastic wit and glibness for a kinder, Venusian approach. I have observed clients' reactions to a Gemini rising who is on the spiritual path, who has begun to do the esoteric inner work. Clients will remark to each other, "She isn't as aloof anymore. She seems to have more depth." Plato's Heavenly Aphrodite, Aphrodite/Urania, had a good deal of depth. She was the principle of harmony that united the opposites in a dualistic world.

Aquarius Rising:

Aquarius rising at the esoteric level is ruled by Jupiter. Jupiter represents kindness and compassion; it is the classical ruler of Pisces. It is also a social planet with warmth and concern as well as vision. Aquarius rising at the Jupiterian, esoteric level projects these qualities to the client, so they do not feel like a case study or a footnote.

Aries Rising:

The Aries rising counselor under the mundane influence of Mars infuses others with infectious optimism, but may also leave them thinking that problems are easier to resolve than is, in fact, the case. The battering rams knock over the obstacles in their own path, but this is not always possible, or comfortable, as an approach for other people. Thrice Great Hermes, the Greek Mercury, is Aries' esoteric ruler. Mercury enables all Aries to stand back from their own energetic, instinctual approach of: "Let's get ourselves in gear and go and *do* and *act*," in order to look at the chart and the predicament from the client's point of view, which with an Earth sign client is often that of the tortoise, not the hare. Mercury signifies patient study—the natal chart, the esoteric chart, progressions, transits, etc. Thrice Great Hermes was a magical healer. The esoteric Aries knowledge and enthusiasm leave the client feeling better off both mentally and emotionally. With Mercury also at work, Mars comes through as a wise counsel as well as courageous, confident, inspirational and motivating.

Leo Rising:

Leos, although more patient than Mars ruled Aries, also tend to project their own decisive approach into the client's session. At the esoteric level (the Illumined Sun) Leo's flamboyant style no longer overwhelms the client. No longer under Leo's domination, clients find it easier to develop confidence in their own creative talent and use their own will.

Scorpio Rising:

Like Leo, Scorpio has a powerful will. At the esoteric level, Scorpio is ruled by Mars which brings a conscious directness to Pluto's unconscious depths. Esoteric Scorpio Ascendants can cut to the crux of the problem with laser-like intensity. They are psychic surgeons, healers or shamans with the ability to stimulate the client's will to fight back at life to transform themselves.

Capricorn Rising:

I have many Capricorn rising clients who are nurses, masseuses and counselors of various types. It's been a joy to watch them move beyond the self-imposed limitations of Saturn as mundane ruler to Saturn at its esoteric level. Capricorn rising seen from the vantage point of esoteric Saturn knows that seemingly conflicting duties to Self, to children, to parents, to the community, to God can be reconciled and integrated if they flow with the day and quit attempting to fix everything through concrete or common sense methods. If they recall the presence of God as Father who carries the burden for them, who is the real Doer, they need not take themselves so seriously, or be quite so demanding on the self and others, quite so saturnine. They can be part of the cosmic plan and realize that others are too, that nobody is inexpendable. There's time to find joy, to play, to meditate. The clients will say, "My Capricorn rising counselor no longer seems so judgmental. I used to think of her as a parent figure who would dislike me if she found out I didn't measure up to her standards. Now I am not quite so concerned about that—she's my age, not my mother's and she's human as well as wise."

Taurus Rising:

Taurus rising individuals are often found in the same service related professions as Capricorn Ascendants. As

Earth signs they work through the body as well as through the mind. They are usually found in structured professions and generally hesitate to make changes (take risks) in life and career. Those who have developed themselves by investing in therapy, education and inner work, express the depth and creativity of Haephestus in counseling or healing. They do not attempt to structure clients so much as to encourage their growth process, along with the financial/emotional risks that process may entail. Those in physical healing professions will be unafraid to employ their own techniques and experiences, rather than only following the traditional approach.

Pisces Rising:

The Pisces rising person often says, "I went into counseling to help others with such high ideals. Maybe I was gullible about people, but my clients exhaust me. I give so much. There's so much sadness out there I could never do enough, no matter how hard I tried." I often think of the Pisces rising elementary school teacher who was told by the principal, "Just teach 'em, don't save 'em. You'll never last if you try to save 'em." Many a Pisces rising burns out in counseling when discrimination and common sense (Earth qualities) are low in the chart, or there is little Fire and the body becomes easily fatigued. Pisces feet hurt at night as they stood on their intuition all day long without employing any other function.

Pisceans need to develop their will, set limits, stand back and let others learn from their mistakes. Pluto, the esoteric ruler, represents will and determination, inner resources, tough-mindedness. It helps set boundaries for Pisces' hypersensitivity. It dissolves the attachment to "not having done enough;" it helps Pisceans to take a stand or stand alone. Sometimes it plunges Pisces into the depths, like Jonah who was swallowed by the whale. Pisces can only trust that things will come out all right in the end. Pluto is an analytical planet and tends to lift Pisceans out of their idealistic absolutism; their do it, skip it philosophy. Alice Bailey says that Pluto dissolves the silver cord of attachment between the two fishes (the Pisces glyph) so that the spiritual fish is freed. Pisceans learn many deep Pluto lessons in the counseling field, but tend to move on to an emotionally less stressful occupation.

Libra Rising:

My clientele includes several Libra rising marriage counselors, for marriage is the Libran issue. We have seen that at the mundane level, Libra tries to balance others, which leaves them feeling equivocal and often confused. Libra tries to please just as Venus tried to win her beauty contest; Libra Ascendants may try to win their own popularity contest. "I have so many referrals from satisfied clients." Ruled by an emotional planet on the mundane level, subjective Aphrodite, Libra is the least objective of the Air signs. Uranus, the esoteric ruler, raises Aphrodite beyond her petty nature. Uranus is unafraid to tell the cold, objective truth when it is necessary. Sometimes people have been living at one end of the scales for years—in the thinking function exclusively, or in the feeling or sensate function. They need to swing back and integrate a different function for a few years. They may need to be without a relationship—to study, to travel or go off to a monastery in Japan. Uranus understands that a radical change might restore the client's balance. Natal Aphrodite in the counselor's unconscious would likely say, "I notice progressed Sun conjunct natal Venus. True, it's in the 9th, the house of travel and religion, but I think you'll be getting married. So give up the cave in India idea." Aphrodite rose from the ocean foam (Unconscious/feeling element) to live in the air. She was the daughter of Uranus, scientific objectivity.

Blending thinking and feeling is an inner function marriage that occurs in many esoteric Libra rising counselors and clients alike.

Sagittarius Rising:

Sagittarius on the mundane level is a positive if restless Ascendant. In dealing with others, Sagittarians are blunt, direct and straightforward. Impressionable and idealistic, Sagittarians try to tell others the truth, whether or not they want to hear it. The esoteric ruler is Earth—groundedness. It brings balance to Sagittarians through its solidity and helps them move from procrastination to the ability to finish what they start. The glyph for Earth is like an image of the Soul, the mandala circle divided into four quadrants. It refers to a need to retreat inward from the adventuresome extroverted search in the outer world. At midlife many Sagittarius rising people do just that. Patience, and the ability to focus on the step-by-step approach—these techniques come at midlife if Sagittarius Ascendants attune to the esoteric ruler. Their clients remark, "She interrupts me less now and seems to answer my specific questions much more satisfactorily. She isn't as argumentative either." Sagittarius is a visionary Ascendant. The esoteric ruler helps them keep their feet on the ground while their heads are in the clouds.

Virgo Rising:

I have fewer Virgo rising counselors who stay with the profession than I do counselors in the other rising signs. At first this seemed strange to me as Virgo is a service oriented Ascendant and so many of them have degrees in psychology, sociology and counseling. Several have returned to school in business related areas and now seem content to work behind the scenes as accountants, secretaries, medical technicians, or in service environments such as schools, hospitals and government welfare agencies. Like the other Mutable rising signs, Virgoan's nervous systems suffer cumulatively from burdensome responsibility, deadlines, and the stress of decision making. They prefer to leave the pressures to others, unless calm Libran planets or other cardinality prevails in the chart, or physical stamina is enhanced by Fire planets and/or a strongly placed Mars.

Virgo is an anxiety prone Ascendant and these people often look for a secure niche, a narrow area of specialization and work where they feel knowledgeable. When Virgos feel on top of things, they can demonstrate a superior attitude and a critical approach to others' work that alienates those around them who take the job less seriously. This compensates Virgos for the many areas of life, such as social participation, where they may feel shy, inadequate or even inferior.

The Moon is the esoteric ruler of Virgo rising. In medical astrology it is connected with the stomach—the digestion process. Joan McEvers puts it quite well in her book *12 Times 12*, when she says that this sign "singlehandedly keeps the Tums company in business." (p. 115) Esoterically this means that Virgo Ascendants need to assimilate, to digest life experiences in the course of their own spiritual journey, rather than simply focusing on what they do well, or feel good about. Otherwise Virgos tend to internalize pressures and develop stomach or duodenal ulcers. The Moon suggests going with the creative flow, but Virgos would rather fix or tidy up the situation. In a series of dreams, for instance, one must remain open and observe the lunar unconscious as it proceeds to inform the thinking mind (Mercury, the mundane ruler) about its growth direction. The Moon ruled feeling function is often the inferior function for Virgo rising. They naturally tend toward serving or helping others with their creative projects, but unless the creative planets are strong in the chart, it is difficult for

Virgos to give birth to their own creativity. Tuning in to the Mother of Form (Moon) will help.

CONCLUSION

I have ended with Virgo rising because it is the most literal, concrete Ascendant and the mind/body link between the mundane and esoteric rulers is easy to discern when the mind makes the body ill. But all of us need to digest our life experience.

I hope that these concrete examples in the outer world have demonstrated the practical application of the esoteric rulers. Useful work is important to many New Age seekers and the quality of this work will improve as counselors transform themselves. Who we are makes at least as great an impression upon our clients as what we know—the skills and techniques we possess.

I do not mean to imply that it is easy to integrate or blend the instinctual talents of the mundane Ascendant ruler with the esoteric one. It takes time and patient effort once the person has consciously analyzed the matter. It is not always fun either, especially if two different functions are involved, one governed by the mundane and one by the esoteric ruler. Then too, the midlife shift in goals, the raising of the Sun sign to its esoteric level usually requires still further effort.

References

Alice Bailey, "Esoteric Astrology," Vol. III in *Treatise on the Seven Rays*, Lucis Press, New York, NY, 1976.

Kathleen Burt, *Archetypes of the Zodiac*, Llewellyn Publications, St. Paul, MN, 1988.

Marsilio Ficino, *Commentary on Plato's Symposium on Love*, Jayne Sears transl., Spring Publications, Dallas, ND, 1985.

Marie Louise von Franz, *Lectures on Jung's Typology*, "The Inferior Function," Spring Publications, Dallas, ND, 1971.

Marie Louise von Franz, *A Psychological Interpretation of the Golden Ass of Apuleius*, Spring Publications, Dallas, ND, 1985.

Isabel Hickey, *Astrology: A Cosmic Science*, Altieri Press, Bridgeport, CT, 1975.

James Hillman, *Lectures on Jung's Typology*, "The Feeling Function," Spring Publications, Dallas, ND, 1971.

Robert A. Johnson, *Inner Work*, Harper & Row, San Francisco, CA, 1986.

C. G. Jung, *Visions Seminar*, Vol. I "Dwarfs," Spring Publications, Dallas, ND.

Joan McEvers, *12 Times 12*, ACS Publications, San Diego, CA, 1983.

Joseph Campbell ed., *The Portable Jung*, Chapter 8, "Psychological Types," Penguin Books, New York, NY, 1986.

Parmahansa Yogananda, *Autobiography of a Yogi*, S.R.F. Press, Los Angeles, CA, 1973.

Swami Sri Yukteswar Giri, *The Holy Science*. S.R.F. Press, Los Angeles, CA, 1974.

Shirley Lyons Meier

Shirley's astrological initiation did not arrive until shortly before her 40th birthday. After reading all the astrology books she could find, she eventually connected with Carl Payne Tobey.

In September, 1977, she founded SLM Astro-Counseling Service, which eventually grew into a successful practice. Her traditionally accepted credentials (Registered Nurse; B.S., summa cum laude; M.Ed. with a focus on counseling) attracted the professional community.

In January, 1980, she became associated with Llewellyn's Personal Services as a writer and contributed to their annual Calendars, Moon and Sun Sign Books.

In December, 1981, the largest paper in Vermont ran a full page human interest story on her business. She received acknowledgments from publishers of *Who's Who in the East, The World Who's Who of Women* and other type biographicals— recognition she had never attained while living a traditionally accepted life style.

Her first book: *Elemental Voids: More Than Meets the Eye*, was published May, 1984. Currently she works full time as a Health Care Specialist in a local Community Correctional Center, sees astrological clients, and is working on a novel.

THE SECRETS BEHIND
CARL PAYNE TOBEY'S
SECONDARY CHART

It started out as a clear, beautiful, sunny fall day . . . November 12, 1984, to be precise. Excitement was in the air as I awaited the visit of a young friend who had spent the past several weeks traveling through Europe. At the sound of her Honda pulling into the driveway, I bounded down the stairs, threw open the door and welcomed her into the foyer with a warm bear hug. Her vivid quilted parka, tasseled knit cap and chubby rosy cheeks were clear indications of the nip in the air—perhaps meant to be an omen of the chills I would be experiencing within the next few hours.

It was hard to believe that this innocent looking cherub with dark round eyes and baby smooth complexion was approaching her thirty-first birthday, and was about to overwhelm me with her newly found (yet actually maturing and innate) talent for making contact with the spirit world. But such were the facts. Her January birthday was rapidly approaching and since she was returning to Italy before the year ended, I had promised to gift her with an updated reading on her chart. Once that was accomplished, she decided she wanted to do something nice for me, so she asked for my watch, made herself comfortable in my favorite chair and then proceeded to stare off into space.

A few years back, I had told her that once she began ridding herself of all the ungrounded fears which had been detrimental to her health, she would discover her psychic abilities coming to the surface—fast and furiously. I saw according to her chart, a release coming during the fall of '84, and by late '85 good health would be hers. Hence, my expectations as to her psychic talents on this day were hovering around the moderate range. Suffice it to say, I was definitely proven wrong.

Slowly she began telling me what she was feeling from my watch. And then, without changing her facial expression one iota, she suddenly remarked, "Oh my goodness! There is an elderly gentleman coming in and he wants me to give you some messages." She described, in great detail, his physical appearance, and that's when my nape hairs took note of what was happening and I quickly paid attention.

She then began interpreting his actions as he seemed inclined toward guessing games rather than outright answers. She came to the conclusion that when he was alive (spirits of living persons stay off in the distance and remain hazy, whereas souls who have already crossed over into the spirit world are more brave and will stand directly in front of her), he was a researcher; he wrote books and other materials; and there was a third thing he was noted for—but she could not figure out what he was showing her. I asked her what she was seeing and she responded, "Well, I see all sorts of numbers and geometric designs surrounding him, but I don't know what they mean." In a tremulous voice I quizzed, "How about a mathematician?" She perked up and exclaimed, "You know him—don't you!" You bet I did. It had to be none other than my mentor—*Carl Payne Tobey*.

Yet I had to be sure so I rooted around in my office for pictures of men in CPT's age range. I showed her two. Neither of them was Carl but one was close enough in appearance to pass as his twin. She paused over the latter, remarked that he might be the one but she was actually seeing a younger looking man. I then brought forth pictures of men in their 50's. One happened to be the picture of Carl found on the back cover of *Astrology of Inner Space*, and that was the picture she immediately pounced upon. I was satisfied, and somewhat envious, knowing she could see him while I could not.

Once the charades were out of the way, Carl decided to get down to business by advising me on a number of family/personal matters. I was stunned by the information he was channeling through my friend; it was so accurate. And then he began to act out a scene for her to observe. She saw him sitting at his desk. He slowly opened each drawer. The first one had brightness about it and he was pleased with its contents. The second one was empty so he quickly closed it. The third one was full of light and he was acting very pleased about that one. He then explained to Barb that the first one is my book now out on the market (Elemental Voids: More Than Meets The Eye - May 1984) My second book holds nothing of interest for him (hence the emptiness and quick closing), but it will be all right for others. The third book is the one he is going to assist me with—not for another few years yet, but Carl insisted I would know when the time was right. I was told the book will be a large one, perhaps consisting of two volumes or made up of a number of books within the greater book.

On that unforgettable fall day in 1984, I was completely in the dark as to books number two and three. Today the fog has lifted and he is absolutely correct about number two, begun earlier this year, holding no interest for him—it was to be a fictional novel. Forty-six days after the start of number two, I was invited to participate in this anthology; a number of books within the greater book. As to my choice of topics, all I can say is, "Carl made me do it." And all I can hope is that he is presently here to assist me with the writing.

Yet, I can't help but wonder "why me?" when there are so many other fine students to his credit. Why not Andy, who sat with him until the very end? Why not Judi, who ws his assistant until ill health forced him into selling his business? Why not Betty, who has relentlessly spent the past several years in search of all his written works so that others may learn of and utilize his ideas?

However, I cannot overlook the fact that Carl and I share a mutual birthday—April 27th. During the two years I studied under his guidance, I was constantly and acutely attuned to his health fluctuations—much to his amazement and mine as he was residing in Arizona while I was here in Vermont. Eleven years ago today, I received a letter from Carl (via Judy) telling me to do as much testing as possible regarding my discovery of a new way of working with his Secondary chart. It was then that he remarked he wanted me to write up my discoveries with the goal of one day having them published.

This then, must be the right time, so I'll wonder no more as I begin applying myself to sharing and expanding Carl's great ideas. If, in fact, Carl is watching over my shoulder, there will be short pauses as we hotly debate areas where I seem to have gone astray from his original teachings—the first obvious difference being that I choose to call his Secondary Chart the Shadow chart. Carl and I share many similarities. We were born on the same date in practically the same locale, both with 5th House Suns. Our natal charts sport Sagittarius Ascendants; Venus and the Sun rulers are the point focus in Mutable T-Squares; he has Uranus on his Ascendant and, my Uranus conjoins Sun/ Mercury; his Moon is in Capricorn while my mine conjuncts Saturn in Pisces. However, there are also striking differences between us (other than age and gender factors). A major one is his Saturn square Mars/Mercury/Sun whereas my Saturn sextiles Uranus/Sun/Mercury. Thus his word is *law*, but I am more flexible in changing rules if they do not work for me. I once commented to Carl that after studying all the people I know with Saturn/Mercury squares in their charts, I had come to the conclusion that the majority of them were driven by causes and a sense of duty to teach and/or spread the word to others. On the other hand, they frequently came across to others as being quite opinionated. Carl laughingly responded, "I may be opinionated but only because I'm always right." See what I'm up against?

CARL'S SECONDARY CHART

Carl would be the first one to tell you that the basis of his Secondary chart is not an original concept on his part. Many of you have never heard of a Secondary chart and yet you are well acquainted with the Part of Fortune or Fortuna, which is routinely included in each natal chart. Formula: Longitude of Ascendant plus Longitude of Moon minus Longitude of Sun equals Part of Fortune ⊗. The house position of this symbol tells us where people feel most comfortable in expressing their personality, hence the areas of life in which they will (or could) receive their greatest financial rewards. Although it is absolutely essential to have a correct birthtime in order to determine the true Ascendant degree, Fortuna's house position (but not its sign or degree) can be found by setting up a solar chart, placing the Sun's longitude on the 1st House cusp and then dividing the 12 houses into 30 degree segments with the Sun's longitudinal degree on each cusp. By so doing, the Moon will fall into the same house or segment of the chart as Fortuna does in a timed chart.

Each planetary figure has its own personal Part or Point and is found in the same way as Fortuna—ASC + Planet - Sun = Point of Planet. This system of finding an additional set of points for each planet dates back to the ancient Arabics. Hence they are called Arabian Points or Parts.

Carl went one step further with this arabic concept.

He theorized that since each planet has its own special point, why not the Ascendant as well? The mathematician went to work. Carl frequently took long walks in order to mull over the problems he was working on. Through a visionary process, he would eventually discover the answers he was seeking. The answer to the missing Ascendant was a simple one. The same longitudinal distance between Ascendant and Sun measured in the opposite direction from the Ascendant will point out a new Ascendant degree and sign. Thus, if the Sun is below the horizon and 60 degrees from the present Ascendant, measure 60 degrees from the Ascendant above the horizon to find the new Ascendant. *Formula:* ASC + ASC - Sun = Arabic ASC.

Thus, the Arabic chart becomes a mirror image of the natal chart, but only in the sense that all planets are found in the exact same house locations and distances from house cusps and from one another—providing, of course, that an Equal House system is used. Although Carl suggested that his students experiment with unequal houses, he himself was a firm believer in the Equal House system. He constantly stressed the value of simplicity—if an easy solution works, why complicate matters by finding a more difficult solution? This notion is also evidenced in his renaming the Arabic chart, "Secondary chart." Rather than call the two charts natal and Arabic, he simply called them Primary and Secondary.

Both charts can be interpreted independently for a more total picture of an individual. However, the important cross-ties between charts are the most informative and revealing connections to consider. Another important aspect is the fact that the Secondary chart is just as sensitive to transiting and progressed activations as the Primary chart— albeit the Secondary will indicate different responses (according to planetary signs) as well as different areas of life being affected (houses Secondary planets rule). Often a Primary chart will indicate routine or normal activities for an individual but said person claims such is not the case at all. The mystery is solved when a number of simultaneous activations are noted in the Secondary chart. When one has the proper tools, few answers are elusive.

Now for a quick lesson in setting up the Secondary chart. See Carl's Primary chart (Figure #1 on page 115). Using the formula:

	Sign	°	Min.
ASC 23°Sag 05′	= 9	23	05
	+ 9	23	05
	18	46	10
Sun 6°Taurus 54′	- 2	6	54
	16	39	16
12 zodiac signs	-12		
	4	39	16
30 degrees	= 5	9	16 = Sec. ASC 9 Leo 16′

Not only do we now know the Secondary Ascendant, but with a quick glance at the Primary chart, we also know the secondary placements of the two lights. Secondary Moon is 21° Leo 40′ as the Part of Fortune was extracted from formula ASC + Moon - Sun = Fortuna. And Secondary Sun will *always* be the same longitudinal reading as the Primary Ascendant. Why? Simply because the source of the Arabic chart is based upon the natal chart and the rotation of the Sun's position to the exact longitudinal position of the natal Ascendant. This implies all the other planets are rotating as well—hence, the new zodiacal positions or Points. However, since Carl's Secondary chart has its very own Ascendant, all Secondary planets will remain in their natal house positions. Therefore, cusps and luminaries will be positioned as seen in Figure #2 on page 116.

In order to position the other planets, it is a simple matter involving addition and subtraction—from planet to planet or planet to house cusp. In the Primary chart, the North Node at 4° Scorpio 21′ is 1° 09′ less than the Moon at 5° Capricorn 30′ . . . and we are dealing with a sextile aspect. Secondary Moon is 21° Leo 40′. Therefore, Secondary Node is 20° 31′ and sextile aspect places it in Gemini. Primary Uranus is 2° 13′ shy of the ASC at 23° Sagittarius 05′ so in the Secondary chart, Uranus is at 7° Leo 03′. Primary Saturn is 34° 38′ beyond the ASC. Adding 34° 38′ to 9° Leo 16′ = 13° Virgo 54′. The difference between Primary Saturn and Jupiter is 17° 13′, which when added to Secondary Saturn at 13° Virgo 54′ = 1° Libra 07′ for Secondary Jupiter. Primary Venus is 2° 20′ away from the 4th House cusp. This amount subtracted from the Secondary 4th cusp at 9° Scorpio 16′ = Secondary Venus at 7° Scorpio 07′.

The above should give you a good idea of different ways for calculating the Secondary positions. Now try your hand at coming up with the four remaining Secondary placements. The completed Secondary chart should look like Figure #3 on page 117.

You will notice a number of smaller planetary symbols straddling the perimeter of these charts. The "s" and "p" indicate the cross connections between charts such as "s" (Secondary) Venus conjoining "p" (Primary) Node in the 11th House. The circled symbols indicate the planetary Nodes and their connections to personal points in Primary and Secondary charts. In all cases, I use no more than a 3° orb.

Let's pause a second to discuss the planetary nodes. Carl placed great value on nodal connections to personal points in a natus. Therefore he used the *heliocentric* planetary

Nodes in all his work—with no discrimination as to whether the South or North Node was involved. Results were the same. He described the activated personal points as being modified by or forced to accept the coloration and energy associated with the Node involved. Upon testing his theory I found such to be the case. Hence I can affirm that he turned me into a true believer and faithful user of planetary Nodes.

A few examples should prove his point. Joe Louis, a gentleman with an extraordinary talent for boxing, has a Taurus Sun conjunct the Node of Mars. Senator Edward Kennedy, wealthy politician, has the Node of Jupiter directly on his Capricorn Ascendant. Sex symbol/actress Marilyn Monroe was born with her Ascendant degree hovering over the Node of Neptune. And Carl himself, whom I mentioned earlier as having a talent or gift for visualizing answers to problems, has the Node of Neptune conjunct his Secondary chart Ascendant.

For those of you who would like to test this theory on your own charts, there follows the only information you will need to locate nodal positions. Please note they are listed in ten year spans.

Mercury   annual increment 42.6″
1900	17° 10′ 48″ Taurus	1950	17° 45′ 18″ Taurus
1910	17° 16′ 54″	1960	17° 52′ 24″
1920	17° 24′ 00″	1970	17° 59′ 30″
1930	17° 31′ 06″	1980	18° 06′ 36″
1940	17° 38′ 12	1990	18° 13′ 42″

Venus   annual increment 32.4″
1900	15° 45′ 36″ Gemini	1950	16° 13′ 56″ Gemini
1910	15° 45′ 36″	1960	16° 19′ 36″
1920	15° 56′ 56″	1970	16° 25′ 16″
1930	16° 02′ 36″	1980	16° 30′ 40″
1940	16° 08′ 16″	1990	16° 36′ 04″

Mars   annual increment 27.7″
1900	18° 57′ 22″ Taurus	1950	19° 20′ 17″ Taurus
1910	19° 01′ 59″	1960	19° 24′ 54″
1920	19° 06′ 36″	1970	19° 29′ 31″
1930	19° 11′ 03″	1980	19° 34′ 08″
1940	19° 15′ 03″	1990	19° 38′ 55″

Jupiter   annual increment 36.7″
1900	9° 28′ 12″ Cancer	1950	9° 58′ 47″ Cancer
1910	9° 34′ 19″	1960	10° 02′ 56″
1920	9° 40′ 26″	1970	10° 09′ 03″
1930	9° 46′ 33″	1980	10° 15′ 10″
1940	9° 52′ 40″	1990	10° 21′ 17″

Saturn   annual increment 31.4″
1900	22° 47′ 05″ Cancer	1950	23° 12′ 15″ Cancer
1910	22° 52′ 19″	1960	23° 17′ 29″
1920	22° 57′ 33″	1970	23° 22′ 43″
1930	23° 02′ 47″	1980	23° 27′ 57″
1940	23° 07′ 01″	1990	23° 33′ 11″

Uranus   annual increment 18.0"

1900	13° 29' 24 Gemini	1950	13° 44' 24" Gemini
1910	13° 32' 24"	1960	13° 47' 24"
1920	13° 35' 24"	1970	13° 50' 24"
1930	13° 38' 24"	1980	13° 53' 24"
1940	13° 41' 24"	1990	13° 56' 24"

Neptune   annual increment 39.4"

1900	10° 40' 51" Leo	1950	11° 13' 41" Leo
1910	10° 47' 25"	1960	11° 20' 15"
1920	10° 53' 59"	1970	11° 26' 49"
1930	11° 00' 33"	1980	11° 33' 23"
1940	11° 07' 07"	1990	11° 39' 57"

Pluto   annual increment 48.8"

1900	18° 57' 21" Cancer	1950	19° 38' 01" Cancer
1910	19° 05' 29"	1960	19° 46' 09"
1920	19° 13' 37"	1970	19° 54' 17"
1930	19° 21' 45"	1980	20° 02' 25"
1940	19° 29' 53"	1990	20° 10' 33"

Shadow: to follow closely, especially in secret

Carl Gustav Jung, psychologist and psychiatrist, introduced the world to such terms as *extrovert, introvert, persona, archetype, anima, animus, shadow,* terms which today are part of our ordinary vocabulary. Jung's life-time quest was to find the answer to the secret governing the human personality. No one was more driven to such a task than Jung, a man who made frequent references to his Number 1 and Number 2 personalities, to the shadow within, to the struggle between his unconscious and conscious selves. Jung eventually came to the realization that the secret of the personality was enclosed within each individual. When one was ready to acknowledge and pay heed to all his/her inner voices, the personality would emerge as one—a more powerful and confident human being. It is no wonder that having come to terms with the reality of the shadow within himself, he felt freer to be, rather than to do, all that he had discovered and wanted life to become.

As James Michener succinctly wrote: "For this is the journey men make: to find themselves. If they fail in this, it doesn't matter what else they find."

We, as astrologers, know these words to be true and self-evident. We have at our fingertips the perfect tool, the natal horoscope, which can unlock secrets to be found within all of us. Carl's Secondary chart provides us with another aspect of ourselves which we may well be experiencing but are not really seeing in the natal lifeprint plan (horoscope) itself.

In Carl's Primary chart (see figure #1) we see a Capricorn Moon opposing Neptune in the last degree of Gemini. This man was a people gatherer, a man surrounded by creative, artistic and theatrical people (also note the Ascendant ruler, Jupiter, conjunct Secondary chart Neptune and the Sun ruler, Venus in Pisces) and yet he was fearful or held back from sharing his own psychic gifts with them. That would not be the intellectual (Sagittarius Ascendant) thing to do as it would devalue his reputation (Ascendant ruler in the 2nd House) in their eyes, hearts and minds (Jupiter square 5th House Mercury, ruler of the 7th and 10th Houses and the Sun, ruler of the 9th).

However, the Secondary chart (see Figure #3) is more open along those lines as the Moon is now in Leo while opposing the Aquarian Neptune; hence he is more willing to take chances. The Moon in the 1st rules the 12th House, so he finds it much easier to bring his hidden talents to the surface in order to share them with loved ones, students, and others who appear to admire, adore and look up to him for inspiration. The latter was a necessity in order for him to

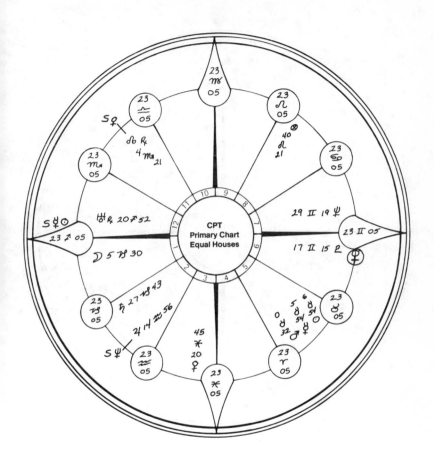

Figure 1
Carl Payne Tobey   April 27, 1902
10:32 pm EST, New York, NY
Data from Tobey

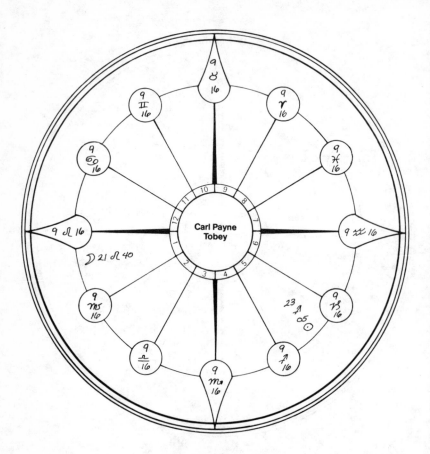

Figure 2
Step 1 — Secondary Chart

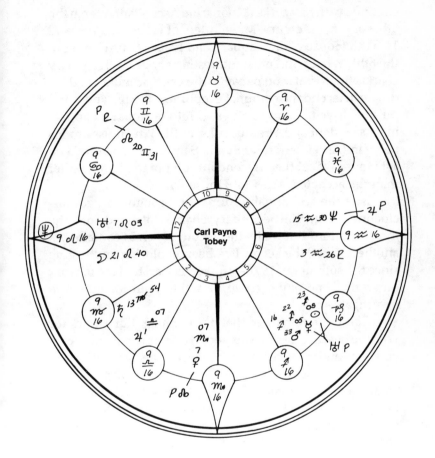

Figure 3
Completed Secondary Chart

continue with his works (Moon trine Ascendant ruler in the 5th, conjunct Mercury/Mars, rulers of Houses 2, 4, 9, and 11. Fifth House planets square 2nd House Saturn, ruler of the 6th). What I find most interesting about his Secondary chart is the correlation between the Leo Ascendant and his dream (Ascendant conjunct Neptune's Node) and compulsive drive to convert others (Pluto in Aquarius opposing Ascendant and Uranus, ruler of the 7th House) to his belief in (Ascendant ruler Sun in Sagittarius) a natural Leo 1st House wheel (Leo Ascendant ruler in the 5th)—rather than the accepted Aries 1st House wheel.

Isn't the additional information brought to light fascinating when the Secondary chart is blended into the interpretation? But wait—the Secondary chart contains yet another secret, the secret I've been exploring and testing since the summer of 1976—the secret Carl told me to work on so that one day it could be written out for others to investigate.

Carl often remarked that if something didn't work for you, the best thing to do was get rid of it, as it will only get in your way and prevent you from learning and growing. And so I must confess that by the late 70's, I found myself favoring an unequal house system. It wasn't because the Equal House no longer worked for me, but simply because I frequently felt uncomfortable using it—as though I was missing out on something I shouldn't have overlooked. Fortunately I have a wonderful little astrological computer, so I was able to test out my charts using all known house systems. In the end, I chose a house system almost as old as the Equal House— Porphyry, which trisects the four quadrants. However, I must also admit that I mentally superimpose the equal houses over the Porphyry chart in order to check for planets occupying two houses. I also view the house cusps as the most intense sectors in a chart. Therefore, any planet positioned within six degrees of a cusp, on either side, is inter-

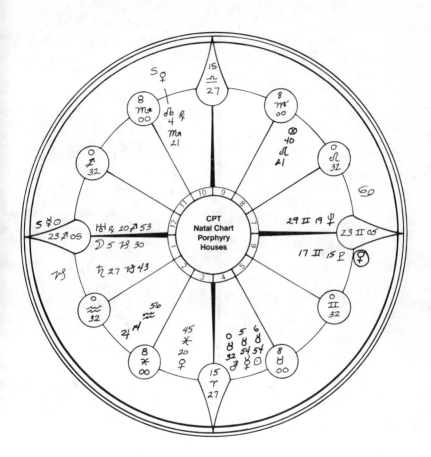

Figure 4

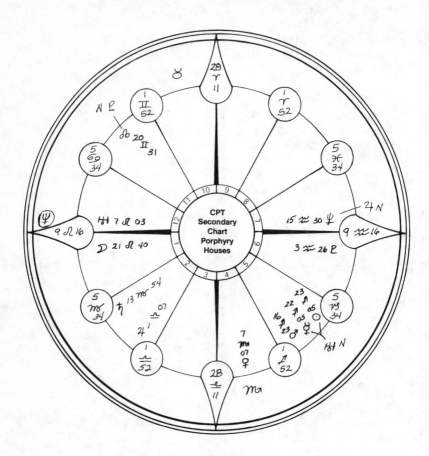

Figure 5

preted as being in that house.

By using the Porphyry system, I found that my Secondary chart discovery worked more often than not. Generally, the 'nots' included those persons born at sunrise—with them what you see is who they are. But, if they have an early or very late degree on their natal Ascendant, causing it to shift into the next sign, or if a 3-4 degree shift will cause the Secondary Ascendant to fall on a planetary Node, then there will be more to them than meets the eye.

Out of fairness to Carl, I will be the first to admit his Equal House method is far easier to set up. So if that is your preference, go with it. If you favor Koch, Placidus or any other method, please continue using it. If it works for you, use it.

Figure #4 on page 119 is Carl's natal chart using the Porphyry house cusps. The most obvious difference between the two systems is the change in house cusps, which for me, is the important factor regarding interpretation of the Secondary chart's secret. I also believe this chart makes a stronger statement regarding Carl's life than the Equal House chart does. For instance, Sagittarius on the 12th and 1st Houses with Capricorn sharing rulership of the 1st (Capricorn intercepted) and both rulers in the 2nd House (Saturn is within less than 3 degrees of the 2nd cusp) certainly indicates a person capable of earning a livelihood through his own initiative, as well as through writing and his associations with producers, directors and other powerful behind-the-scenes type persons (12th House).

Gemini on the 6th cusp and Capricorn in the 1st, along with the rulers in square aspect to each other, surely describes the health condition he suffered from—crippling arthritis, especially in his hands. Toward the end, his negative thought patterns simply wore him out; or perhaps he chose to give up. I really don't know. However, Andy's last letter to me prior to Carl's passing mentioned the fact that

Carl had come down with pneumonia. He also remarked " . . . at this stage of life, Carl isn't capable of writing too well. He is also partially deaf so it makes it difficult to communicate with him. The last time I called him, he couldn't hear me at all." Sorry Carl, but I do find it easier to read these facts in the unequal rather than the equal house system.

The problem in using an unequal method is the additional math required in order to erect charts. More time (and perhaps frustration) is involved. The normal procedure is to find sidereal time which gives the MC/10th House cusp. Then, based upon birth latitude, the Ascendant and intermediate house cusps are found. This procedure is slightly reversed when setting up Carl's Secondary chart. With this chart, we already know the Ascendant which has been derived from the natal chart. Now we must find 9° Leo 16′ in the 1st cusp (Ascendant) column and at the birth latitude in the Table of Houses. Once located, we can then calculate MC and intermediate house cusps. When figuring out the Secondary positions of the planets, the 1st and 7th cusps are the only ones that can be used to measure distances to and from. If you prefer an unequal system, this last point is important to remember if you want correct longitudinal readings for the planetary positions.

In Carl's Secondary chart using the Porphyry house system, we find 28° Aries 11′ on the MC/ 10th with Taurus sharing house space (intercepted). (See Figure #5) In his Porphyry natal chart, Libra is on the 10th cusp with the ruler, Venus in the 3rd House, implying career success can be attained through sharing his ideas (Libra), either verbally or through written words (3rd House), with business contacts (Libra) and/or students (Taurus on the 5th). The Secondary chart expands on this theme by telling us his career growth will come about as a result of his own initiative (Aries MC conjunct natal Mars) and his ability to follow through (Taurus) on daring or pioneering ideas (Aries). Mars in the 5th House suggests he can attain success based upon a hobby or sometime activity he enjoys very much. This activity will lead to travel, contacts with professionals, publishing, ideas which might well encounter resistance due to their foreign or unusual qualities, and other 9th House matters (Mars also rules the 9th). Venus in the 4th implies a strong likelihood of one day owning his own business as well as operating out of his home. With Libra on the 3rd House cusp we find another indication of great success (Jupiter conjunct that cusp) involving communications and consultant, mediator and/or counseling type roles (Libra).

I feel certain the above information can be found in the Equal House chart, but for me, not as readily as when using the unequal system. I suppose my own Libra/Mars retrograde in the 10th House as the point focus of a Yod to my 3rd House Moon/Saturn and 5th House Uranus/Sun/Mercury has something to do with my resistance to exclusive use of the Equal House system. The additional information gleaned from using the Porphyry house system is one of the secrets behind Carl's Secondary chart.

Only after the above discovery did I find more validity in the original concept I shared with Carl eleven years ago. He told me to test and test the idea until I really felt comfortable with my findings. I now feel comfortable enough to share it with you; hopefully it will excite you into wanting to test it out on your own collection of charts.

Simply look at the zodiacal sign on the Ascendant of the Secondary chart and then find the natal cusp it occupies, or if intercepted, the house where it's located. In Carl's Porphyry natal chart, 0 degrees Leo falls on his 8th House cusp. This immediately tells me that 8th House matters, good and bad, had a tremendous impact upon his life. In fact, those astrologers who knew him well, likely experienced him as an 8th House, rather than 5th House, Sun person. He constantly stressed the need for research and statistical proof in order to advance astrological findings. More telling examples are the titles he gave to some of his correspondence course lessons—"The Unconscious Interpretive Apparatus and Three Survival Dynamics," "The Survival Dynamic Reactors," "The Non-Survival Dynamics," "**The Art of Interpretation**," "Analytical Interpretation," "Survival or Non-Survival," "**The Mysterious Social Survival Problems**" and "**Seeds of Mental Illness**."

Granted, the natal Equal House chart has the ruler of the 8th in the 1st House providing us with like information. However, the intensity of the 8th House impact is not shown in the Equal House system due to the fact that the Moon only opposes Neptune and trines the 5th House planets. These connections suggest that those areas of life he found enjoyable and interesting stimulated a naturally creative and productive flow of energies from him. Other areas in which he encountered or had opposing viewpoints were a different matter. I'm inclined to think that if he didn't get his own way, he'd turn his back on a situation and/or person and then do it on his own.

Back to the unequal Secondary chart (Figure #5). The sign on the 8th cusp describes how Carl dealt with the impact of those areas in his life (see bold print course titles as an example). Neptune in the 7th House making valid connections to *every* planet (Mercury/Sun's association with Mars and Pluto's tie to the 7th House cusp are valid connections) in this chart surely expresses the intensity he experienced in dealing with 8th House situations.

One final secret to share is to assure you that the Secondary chart can be progressed and is just as valid as the progressed natal chart. Secondary progressions making 1 degree orb connections to personal points in Secondary, Natal and Progressed natal charts are quite revealing and

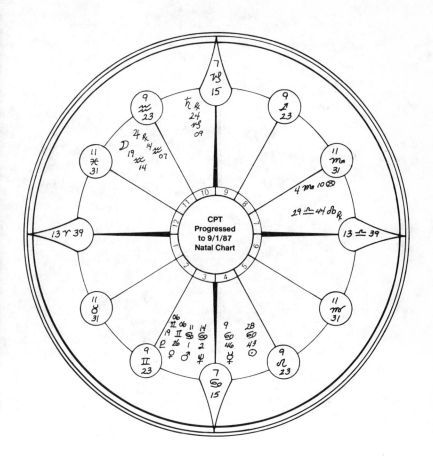

Figure 6

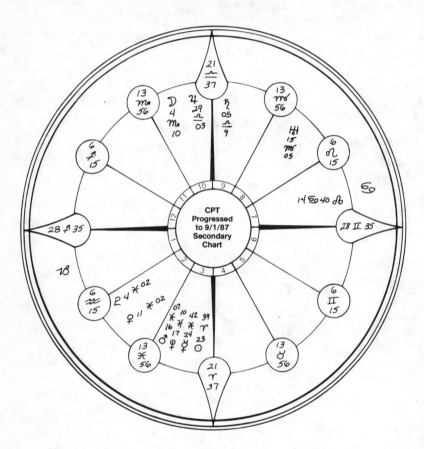

Figure 7

helpful in the interpretive and predictive processes, as are the transits activating Secondary and Progressed Secondary charts.

Note transiting Pluto activating Figure #5, Venus/Uranus square (12/85—9/87), indicating a compulsive need to bring old ideas/values to light (Pluto/Scorpio—rebirth process) so that others may evaluate, judge, and use in order to increase awareness and further their own goals. And the house cusps on Figure #7 are practically the same cusps as the natal Figure #4, pointing out the significance of this period of time for Carl. Finally, my progressed secondary Moon is at 0 degrees Virgo 45' as I write this material . . . sitting in Carl's unequal natal 8th House and trining his 4th House Mars, ruler of the 4th and 11th Houses. While in my own natal chart, progressed secondary Moon makes a trine from the 9th to the 5th House Uranus, ruler of my 3rd.

Truly, as I started this material I had every intention of sharing with you a variety of well-known personality charts. But with Carl's progressed secondary Saturn conjunct my natal Mars, such was not possible. This was meant to be his article and since he has the upper hand right now, I seem to have had little choice as to who would receive top billing. No matter—if perchance any of you are interested in receiving some of the charts I had already prepared, please let me know and they will be yours. And, if you're lucky, Carl just may tag along to surprise *you* with one of his visits.

Jeff Jawer

Jeff Jawer has been a professional astrologer since 1973 and holds a special B.A. in "The History and Science of Astrology" from the University of Massachusetts at Amherst. Jeff was a founder of AFAN and served on its Steering Committeee for four years. He was one of the organizers of the United Astrology Congress (UAC) and has participated in several other organizations as both a member and an administrator.

One of the pioneers in Astrodrama, Jeff wrote a major article about it in 1978 for *Astrology Now* magazine. In addition, he has written dozens of articles for astrology publications in the U.S. and abroad. Jeff has been a faculty member at more than 30 astrology conferences and has lectured extensively throughout the United States, Canada, Europe and Brazil.

In addition to his private practice, Jeff has been a corporate astrologer, helped develop the first handheld astrological calculator and participated in several astrologically based plays as an actor, writer and director. He has had his own radio programs in Massachusetts and Georgia and has made numerous appearances on radio and television in several countries.

ASTRODRAMA

"As above, so below" is the ancient axiom upon which astrology is based. It tells us that what exists in the sky also exists for us here on Earth. One could say, however, that modern astrologers have developed a view which says, "As above, forget below." By this I mean that we astrologers have become fixated on the mind, "the above," in our work and have lost sight of "the below," our bodies and our emotions. We have lost sight of our roots and the roots of astrology. Astrodrama, the dramatization of astrological principles, means to reconnect these two dimensions.

Dane Rudhyar has written that every astrology reflects the culture in which it exists. Today we are living in a world where we have separated mind and body. This, of course, is the result of many things. But, as astrologers, we can see this most easily in the proliferation of techniques for our heads—new methods, new systems, all geared to fill us with more facts and all, in some way, pushing us further away from the truth of who we are.

The conventional history of astrology is that it was developed in Babylonia by wise men, who carefully observed and plotted the movements of the heavens from their ziggaurats or step-pyramids. We are led to believe that after centuries of observation, correlations were made between these movements and life on Earth. But, I would like to suggest that the roots of astrology are much deeper and that its development originated from a much older source.

Before the rationalism of Aristotle and the monotheism of the ancient Hebrews the world was very different. God was not the one Father in heaven who spoke through the male priests. God, or rather the gods, were multiple in form, appearing everywhere in nature, and when represented in human form usually were *female*. A great deal of literature has been written recently supporting this and it has important implications for astrology.

The matriarch of the pre-Arian era had a consciousness of the universe vastly different from ours today. The pantheistic view of God-in-everything did not allow for the separation of "the above" and "the below." The distinction between human beings and nature did not exist so clearly. In the age of the gods and goddesses all things were alive and one did not discover the meaning of the universe through calculations and objective analyses. It was not necessary to observe the movements of Jupiter to understand its influence. Jupiter was not out there to be studied as a foreign object. It was here in our world, in our bodies where it could be felt directly. Even as late as Ptolemy, in the 2nd century A.D., the planets were not seen as symbols or even as the homes of gods. They were seen as the living gods themselves.

The rise of the male-dominated religions and the rationalism of the later Greeks separated us from nature and from the planets. They contributed to our sense of separation from one another. Astrology became more focussed on the individual and less on the collective.

The original astrology was not based on the individual. Its focus was for the utilization of the group and its techniques included ritual, prayer, dance, meditation and art. It was those times which taught us to know the planets in our bodies and in our hearts. It was thousands of years before we separated our minds and our identities and developed the astrology that we know today.

The contributions of the male-dominated cultures that

gave birth to modern astrology and the modern world were considerable, but in the process we have lost touch with the whole. This has brought us to the brink of self-destruction. In our striving for individual identity we have forgotten who we are collectively and have placed ourselves in great peril.

THE REBIRTH OF ASTRODRAMA

The purpose of astrodrama is to help us reconnect to one another, to the planets, and to the life force within ourselves. It does not presuppose the elimination of any of the other astrological methods currently employed. It seeks, rather, to compliment the explosion of intellectual energies with a holistic relationship with our universe.

Astrodrama is the original astrology returned to us when we need it most. An astrology that does not serve the health and well-being of the culture is doomed to fail. Unlike our scientific technology which has brought both wonder and terror, we must connect astrology with life and with the spirit of the human species. Accurate analyses of personality traits and life cycles are not enough. Astrology can and must reconnect us with the roots of feelings which lie buried deeply in our bodies.

The modern rebirth of astrodrama, or experiential astrology, grew out of the social changes and ferment of the 1960s. The spiritual community of Findhorn (Scotland) began to use astrological rituals and celebrations while individuals in the United States and Europe were developing other forms of astrodrama. The desire of the hippies to return to nature, to feel life beyond the intellect, influenced many of us. And today, in spite of the "Me Generation" and the yuppification of the Western world, its spirit remains.

A look at the calendar of astrological classes and workshops shows more astrodrama activities. The astrological vision quests of Dan Giamario, the theatrical productions of Michael Lutin of New York, the workshops and rituals of Angel Thompson in Los Angeles and Barbara Schermer in Chicago, the astrodrama retreats in Europe with Friedel Roggenbuck and the astrodramatic creations in Arizona are all part of this growing current in our field. We find the rebirth of experiential astrology everywhere. Astrologers are reconnecting to a sense of sacredness in their work, the public is being entertained and informed, and we are all learning a great deal more about astrology and ourselves.

The many techniques of astrodrama serve to enrich astrological education as well as to inspire. The only requirement is a willingness to play, a little imagination and a letting go of limited concepts of a "right" kind of astrology. When we open our hearts and our emotions we can discover the essential powers of the planets and signs, and most importantly ourselves.

Astrodrama techniques include role-playing, meditation, visualization, rituals, walks, skits, games and more. It draws inspiration from psychodrama, gestalt therapy, psychosynthesis, storytelling, children's games, goddess worship, nature religions and Sufism. Let's take a look at some of the ways it can be used.

In learning astrology one of the most important factors is the development of a rich vocabulary for describing astrological principles. The more ideas you have for any principle, the wider choice you have in chart interpretation and forecasting. A limited vocabulary of keywords will inhibit the potentials you can see for yourself and your clients. A useful technique, called the "keyboard circle," involves the use of a group to supply a variety of keywords for any astrological concept. In teaching the elements, for example, you seat the group in a circle. Ask each person to say one word for the given element. For Fire the words may be hot, warm, burn, heat, passion, red, yellow, bright, anger, love, lightning, fast, etc. Additionally, astrological terms such as Mars, Aries, Leo and so forth can be used.

To prepare the group for this exercise some simple suggestions are recommended. First, ask each person to speak in turn quickly to keep the energy of the group moving. When forced to move quickly we access the unconscious mind and intuition flows more easily. This also promotes surprises which can enrich the exercise. It is also important to remind the group that there are no wrong statements. If someone says "cool" for Fire they may discover something about themselves, about their feelings about the Fire energy that could expand the group's understanding of the element. (I know several Fire sign people who discharge all of their heat and often feel physically cold.) It is also important to tell the group that they can repeat what others have already said as keeping the steady rhythm of responses helps the exercise immensely.

After the group has made several rounds of statements you can stop and discuss what came up. Was anyone surprised by any of the words they heard? These can be the basis for investigation, both as to the meaning for the individual who said it and for the group. There are other techniques you can use to enliven this exercise. For example, you can light a candle and place it in the center of the circle so that the physical element of fire is present. (A bowl of water for Water, a block of wood for Earth, a bird's feather for Air, may work for these elements.) You can have objects or pictures related to the Fire principle in the room to further stimulate the group. You can even ask people to wear fiery colors to the class and plan it on a night when the Moon is in a Fire sign or some other astrological correspondence occurs. Music is another way to enrich the environment according to what you are working with.

Another additional variation is to request sounds or gestures as well as words in this exercise. Sometimes it's even best to start with a round or two of gestures or sounds to warm up the group before using words. Physical activities, such as rubbing the hands together very quickly to generate heat, or jumping up and down, will add to the fiery atmosphere prior to using the keywords. Stamping the feet or self-massage is a way to contact Earth energy. Air would utilize breath and feelings of lightness. Water might involve using memory pictures of home and family. Use your imagination and you'll find endless variations.

The keyword circle can be used for any astrological concept, elements, planets, signs, etc. There are no wrong statements, as the purpose is to open possibilities. When we don't allow "mistakes" we inhibit creativity, free expression and the possibility of discovering new ideas.

OTHER EXPLORATIVE TECHNIQUES

A rich field of exploration for the experiential astrologer is the human body. The body has an intelligence of its own. We learn many things in our heads which never touch us deeply. The body is a door to the emotions and the capacity to learn and remember is keyed to this emotional memory. The use of gestures in the keyword circle is one way to integrate the body in the astrodrama process. The use of walks is another.

The concept of planetary walks has been used in some branches of Sufism. The idea is to connect the planets with the body as we walk. One way to do this is to ask someone to walk and inquire of the group as to what planet the walk most represents. Another way is to request the group (or individual) to walk as a specific planet. For example, the walk of the Sun is centered in the heart, in the chest, and is characterized by the qualities of openness and confidence. Learning to walk like the Sun is much more than an astrology lesson. It is a lesson in courage and self-expressiveness.

The Moon walk focusses on the stomach and emphasizes receptivity. A very slight concave shape can contribute to lunar consciousness. The purpose here is to receive, to feel the impressions of the environment and your sensitivity to them. After practicing both walks you can divide the group in two and have them walk toward one another mirroring (copying) the person opposite. You can have half the group do the Sun walk and the other half the Moon walk. After they walk toward one another, have them return to the starting point, reverse roles and do it again. You can ask which of the walks is more comfortable for each person. If someone prefers the Moon walk, is it because they find it easier to be receptive or because they are uncomfortable with the expressiveness of the Sun? Perhaps there are other reasons. An atmosphere of non-judgmental inquiry allows the greatest openness of response to your questions.

The Mars walk focusses on the head, the arms, and the muscles in general. The Venus walk emphasizes balance and grace with attention to the hips. The Jupiter walk is wide open and expansive, motivated by the thighs. The Saturn walk is centered in the skeletal system (bones) and is characterized by its upright posture.(Can you walk like Saturn without being rigid? This is a good exercise in developing structure without losing flexibility.)

When a group is paired off in combinations of planets such as Venus/Mars or Jupiter/Saturn it can be fun to watch their reactions to one another. Will the Mars people attack the Venus people? Will the Venus group seduce the Mars group? You can have the Saturn group link arms in a horizontal line and ask the Jupiter walkers to try to get around them or over them. You can even ask a line of Mars walkers to try to break through a Saturn line. The traditional astrological correlations between the planets and body parts and types will provide plenty of material for this exercise.

I want to add that these walks are very useful for individuals as well as for groups. In your everyday life you can practice, not simply to learn more about astrology, but to teach yourself how to contact the essences of the planets. You do not have to be exaggerated when using these walks in public. If, for example, you lack the drive and motivation associated with Mars, a slightly more strident walk, head forward, arms swinging more than normally, can be a profound stimulant for change. The patterns of the body are so ingrained that a slight, but regular, shift can be significant. Underlying this idea is a very important concept. Astrology is not something we learn only to help others or to cope with the limits of our natal charts. It is, essentially, a tool for personal transformation. When we connect with the planetary archetypes, we train ourselves to use their qualities. We discover the essence of the planetary gods within. The natal chart offers a precise picture of individual perspective, but it is also quite limiting in principle. As human beings we have access to all the information of collective human experience. As spirits in this universe we are part of everything in it. Experiential astrology helps us discover the pure essences of the signs and planets so that we can use them as we desire. The limits of the natal chart are not limits in fact, but limits in perception. Collective consciousness in astrology allows us to have both the personal and universal perspective at our disposal for dealing with life's problems and discovering its multitudes of joys.

DIRECTIONAL EXERCISES

Another physical aspect of astrology is the spatial relationships we experience in everyday life. This is often ignored as we turn our attention heavenward and forget the Earth. Most native peoples have a deep feeling for the meanings of the four directions. Their use in rituals and daily life are guiding principles in many cultures. The Hopi Indians, for example, associate the direction South with social activity. To go South is to go to the social area in the community. This may also be seen in the meaning of the Midheaven (the southernmost point in the horoscope) as indicating one's place in society. But, more important is the basic concept that we live on the Earth and that the four directions have a profound influence upon us.

A simple compass can be quite helpful in this work. When you work at your desk which way are you facing? Which way do you sleep? These are fundamental questions that are not generally considered to be part of astrology. But, we use the four directions in our charts, each with its own meaning—why not in our lives? What is on the West wall of your bedroom? Does it reflect the qualities in the western portion of your horoscope? Alignment with the four directions is a way to observe heaven's force on the Earth. Chinese astrologers, sometimes called "Wind and Water Masters," are very concerned with the location of physical objects on the Earth. The relationship of your house with the lay of the land, water, mountains, roads and so forth, is vital information to the Wind and Water Master.

If you were born with Venus in the 7th House, it was West of your birthplace. Perhaps this is the direction in which you are most able to contact the qualities of Venus. Of course, this may vary for each person, but beginning to notice the relationships of the planets and our physical place can do much to broaden our consciousness. Additionally, this sense of direction can be very useful in personal astrological work. If you have a question or problem regarding Venus, you might align yourself with Venus in your birth chart and then meditate on its meaning. (Venus in the 2nd House, for example, is in the Northeast portion of the horoscope. You can either sit in or face this direction.) You can also align yourself with the planets of the moment to have a clearer and more direct experience of their present influences. This is an important factor in astrological ritual work which we will explore a bit later on.

PSYCHODRAMA ADAPTED TO ASTROLOGY

Psychodrama, developed by Jacob Moreno, offers some specific techniques which are easily adapted for astrology. One of the most useful is called "doubling." The purpose of this exercise is to explore the range of possibilities in any given situation. In astrodrama work this can be used for natal chart issues, but is also very valuable for working with current transits or progressions. An individual may have a major transit coming up which is of concern. A transit of Pluto to the Moon, for example, is rich with possible meanings. In doubling, the astrodrama group can discover a variety of emotions and experiences which this can trigger.

One of the interesting aspects of the doubling technique is its use of walking. Moreno felt that when we move, our emotions are opened and we are less able to block them. This principle of the use of movement is fundamental to some of the ideas mentioned earlier, specifically that the body has an intelligence of its own. When we integrate the body with the therapeutic process of dialogue, the possibilities for learning and changing are enhanced.

In the doubling exercise two people are needed to assist the protagonist, the person on whom the exercise is focussed. One of the assistants ("doublers") represents all the negative aspects of the situation. The other represents all the positives. They stand on each side of the protagonist and act as parts of his or her mind, offering thoughts and ideas about the situation. The three walk slowly together and begin to speak of the issue at hand. The two assistants are not to argue directly with one another, but to play two parts of the protagonist's mind. As the three walk, one assistant discusses all of the negatives and the other all of the positives. The protagonist is free to respond to either and to share his or her own inner thoughts. The goal here is not to reach specific conclusions about the outcome of the transit, but to open the protagonist to a wide variety of ideas about its possible implications.

In the example of the transit of Pluto to the Moon, we designate one assistant as the negative Pluto and the other as the positive Pluto. The negative Pluto may describe all of the fearful and terrible things this planet can bring when contacting the Moon. "You will lose your job, your home. Your mother may die and you'll have intense family problems. You will be in physical danger and have horrible nightmares. Your deepest, most private secrets will be exposed," and so on. At the same time, in a sort of overlapping dialogue, the positive Pluto assistant might say, "This is going to be a wonderful time of transformation. You will get rid of those bad habits and awful fears you no longer need. You'll finally clean up your family problems, maybe even remodel the house," etc.

The protagonist can respond or not to any of these remarks. Ideally, the three people develop a rhythm in their talking and walking that allows them to exchange information easily. It is all right for some of the conversation to overlap, but it is not necessary for any of the participants to talk all the time. Sometimes they may walk in silence, feeling and gathering their thoughts. A space of at least 15-20 feet in length is needed so that the three can develop some rhythm to the walk. When they reach the end of the space they should turn together and walk in the opposite direction continuing the conversation.

Psychodrama work requires that one person play the role of the director, the leader. This is also necessary in most astrodrama exercises. It is the job of the director to supply additional information to the players and to guide the exercises. She or he can, for example, whisper cues or ideas to the assistants in the doubling exercise if needed. It is also the job of the director to stop the exercise when she or he feels it is most appropriate. With the doubling exercise, as with all astrodrama work, there needs to be discussion afterwards. She or he can ask the assistants if they had any difficulties with their roles. (Perhaps they would like to change roles and do the exercise again.) The protagonist is asked his or her feeling about the exercise. This can give rise to further conversation within the group to explore possibilities or strategies in the given situation.

I understand that one of the objections to this exercise is the possibility of presenting negative ideas which will precondition the protagonist to bring these into being (self-fulfilling prophesies). This concern, in fact, is one that is raised generally with respect to astrological counseling. If the astrologer says negative things, the client will be more likely to accept (and even unconsciously seek) these in life. If the astrologer says only positive things to the client the session is unlikely to be realistic in serving the needs for growth and self-awareness. So with the doubling exercise we confront one of the basic questions of astrological work. If we believe that all is predestined by the planets we deny free will and individual choice. If we believe that the client is free to choose attitudes and actions exclusive of the planets, we deny astrology.

The philosophy behind the doubling exercise, and behind most effective astrological counseling, is that individuals with knowledge of themselves and their cycles will be best equipped to deal with their lives. Awareness of the choices and the materials with which one chooses, gives choice. In fact, major patterns in the natal chart, as well as by transit and progression, generally express in a variety of ways, both positively and negatively. It is unlikely that a single behavior pattern or response will exist for any of us. As we change and grow, variety teaches and enriches us. It is also true that many of the most difficult transits or progressions correspond to times of difficulty in life. But, it is often these very crises that lead us to our fullest potentials. When ideas are offered in an atmosphere of love and acceptance, growth is stimulated. Of course, compassion and sensitivity are essential for any counselor and must be a part of any astrodrama work.

ROLE-PLAYING

Role-playing is a psychodrama technique that has found its way into other therapies as well. For the astrodramatist this is one of the most useful methods for gaining insight into the potentials of the natal chart or current patterns. A useful way to apply this technique with astrology is to ask for someone with a hard aspect (conjunction, square or opposition) to volunteer. (In actual practice you can use any aspect, planet or group of planets in the chart. Hard aspects, though, are more dynamic and active in the life and in the roleplay.) Let's take the example of a person with the Moon in Aries in the 10th House square Saturn in Capricorn in the 7th. The issue may be one of personal freedom, related to career (Moon in Aries in the 10th) versus responsibilities in relationships (Saturn in Capricorn in the 7th). The director then must create a scene which dramatizes the conflict. (The group can also help create the scene.)

One approach might be to tell a story of someone who has a restrictive partner, one who is very concerned with time limits, etc. The partner might be portrayed as someone older who plays an authority role in the person's life. (It is not vitally important that the situation reflect the precise life situation. We are making living metaphors of the symbols to bring them into high relief. The subject can be invited to say whether the characters have any meaning for him/her.) The Moon in Aries, though, is very involved with career and frequently loses track of time, spending long hours at work. The director asks for a volunteer to help the protagonist play the scene. The volunteer may play the restrictive spouse while the protagonist plays the work-oriented role.

The partner (Saturn) has invited some guests home for dinner. The protagonist, though, has forgotten this and arrives home late from work, several hours after the guests have arrived. In fact, they've already left, to the embarrassment of Saturn. Saturn feels betrayed, the protagonist feels restricted by Saturn's rigidity. Each player is asked to enrich their role with appropriate body postures and voice tones. The director can also add information during the role-play. For example, he or she might suggest that Saturn is being too soft or that the Moon should show a bit more anger. The idea is to develop the essential qualities of the planets to heighten awareness of the underlying energies present.

Of course, there are many different stories we could tell to describe this aspect. The limitations are only those of the imaginations of the director, the players and the group. After playing the scene once, the players are asked to reverse roles and play the scene again. Following this the participants are asked to describe their experiences in playing the roles. The group can add its observations and questions. The protagonist, though, is the focus of most of the time and attention after the role-play. Questions about the words used or omitted, body language, voice tone, etc., can be asked. Sometimes these scenes can be very explosive, sometimes sluggish. There may be no comfortable resolution to the issues raised. At other times the players find a way to hear each other and solve the problem. Suggestions from the group and the director may be helpful. The players may be invited to redo the scene with the suggestions offered. Another person may replace the original assistant and the scene replayed. When there is no comfortable resolution, the protagonist is directed to consider the feelings raised after the session. In an ongoing group these may provide the basis for discussion at the next meeting.

In role-playing the idea is to allow the archetypes of the planets to express themselves openly and directly. Each of the planets may represent what are called "sub-personalities" in psychosynthesis. The issue with sub-personalities is that they may be dominant or repressed in our lives. Direct confrontation with them, though, offers the possibility of something more balanced. Both the Moon in Aries and Saturn in Capricorn have their needs and their gifts. Through the dialogue of the role-play, greater clarity of these needs and gifts may be seen.

Additionally, other planets (players) may be added to the scene to ameliorate the differences between the first two. (This is most clear when two planets in opposition have a third planet sextile and trine.) By utilizing all of the elements of the personality (all of the planets), integration may be enhanced. Ultimately, these role-plays can be extended to exercises in which the entire chart is played, a person representing each planet. Such performances can include make-up and costumes, which has been done both in the United States and Europe. These lengthier works can be a powerful stimulus for the protagonist. She or he can question the planets, argue with them, play the role of one of them, etc. The transits and progressions can also be added in a more elaborate piece.

The role-playing of full charts also works best when the four directions are used to properly set the positions of the planets. The actual physical alignment helps to recreate the birth moment and adds authenticity. This type of work, though, is not limited to natal charts. In fact, it is such work at the time of New and Full Moons, Solstices, Equinoxes and the cross-quarters (when the Sun is at 15 degrees of the Fixed signs) which comes closest to the original rituals of astrology.

These special moments in the sky provide us with opportunities to align our will with that of the heavens, to bring the below to the above and vice versa. The powerful moments of the lunation cycle and major shifts of the solar cycle are times for celebration. Each of these moments has its own purpose. For example, the Full Moon in Cancer is the time when the consciousness of social responsibility (the Sun in Capricorn opposed the Moon) versus family and personal needs (Moon in Cancer) is clearest. By aligning ourselves with the planets at this time we connect with their intention. Our intention meets those of the planets and the ancient bonds that connect us are remembered. These are useful times for meditation, prayer and celebration.

USING SPECIFIC CHARTS WITH ASTRODRAMA

You can also experience these individually if you like. Calculate the chart for the event (New Moon, Full Moon, etc.) for your location. Find a quiet, private space in which to work. You might want to mark the positions of the planets with crystals, stones or other objects. (Ideally, these will have some connection with the meanings of the planets, at least to you.) Walk through this magic circle. Say the name and sign on the angles and of each of the planets as you pass their place. You can begin at any point and walk in any direction (although entering at the East may be most appropriate for beginnings). You walk the circle several times, feeling the influence of each planet as you pass its place. You can stop at any point and contemplate the feelings you have about that point or planet. If the Moon is highlighted you could then sit or stand at the place of the Moon and meditate. If it is the Full Moon in Cancer, the issues of security, family, feelings, etc. would be appropriate subjects for your meditation. If that Moon falls in the 6th House locally, you should consider it in light of 6th House matters such as work, health and so forth. You can offer prayers for yourself or others or use this time in any way personally appropriate. (While it is best to make these rituals at the precise time of the event, it is possible to do them up to 24 hours before or after with good results. Just calculate the chart for the time when you actually perform the ritual.)

This ritual, then, is yours to be enhanced by candles, incense, pictures, music or anything you like. There are quite a number of books available on the subject of rituals to assist you if you don't have a tradition or method of your own. What is most important is the spirit of openness and the awareness of the bridge you are building between heaven and earth.

When the heart is open, magic happens. When we align ourselves with the cosmos we open and become magical. This is the astrology of our ancestors. It is not limited to the natal chart, but is the remembrance of the unity of our universe. This is the astrology that teaches us that we are each all of the planets, all of the signs. Our individuality is meaningless without these connections. When my concept of Saturn is only that of "my Saturn" I suffer, astrology suffers, and our world slips further into the darkness. The richness of astrology is its universality. Each of the planets has at least two faces for each of us. There is the face we meet at birth which colors our perceptions of reality. But, there is also the essential face, the pure energy of each planet, each perfect, each a divine teacher and friend. Through the connection of ourselves with the essences of the planets we remember this. We help to heal the earth and ourselves. "As above, so below" becomes not the measure of a distant relationship then, but the embodiment of an intimacy with all of life and its beauty.

Donna Van Toen

Donna is a popular Canadian lecturer/writer/teacher based in Toronto, Ontario. Her work has appeared in numerous magazines; additionally, she is the author of *The Astrologer's Node Book* and *The Mars Book* (forthcoming), both published by Samuel Weiser.

Currently President of Astrology Toronto, Donna is chair of the FCA Speaker's Bureau, a member of the AFAN Steering Committee and the 1989 UAC Planning Committee. She has been a faculty member at NORWAC, UAC, AFA and at FCA regional and national conferences in addition to lecturing for many Canadian and U.S. astrology groups.

ALICE BAILEY REVISITED

For decades astrologers have been debating the value of the Alice Bailey books—particularly the material in *Esoteric Astrology, Esoteric Psychology* and *The Destiny of the Nations*. A large number of astrologers gave up on the notion of esoteric astrology before they really got started, becoming perplexed by the non-traditional sign rulerships, bored by the rather ponderous writing style and irritated by the somewhat arrogant assurance that those who may understand shall. Some astrologers who actually finish the books freely admit the material made no sense whatsoever to them and let it go at that. A few people purport to understand, but decline to explain. And a few people actually *do* understand and try to share their understanding.

Alice Bailey's teachings were channeled. Her "guide" was a Tibetan sage named Dwajl Khul. The books were written in different times for people with a somewhat different concept of spiritual enlightenment than they have today. The metaphysical tone of those times smacked of "occult" (in the sense of hidden), stressed that knowledge was available only to the spiritually elite and must of necessity be obscured as a safeguard against misuse by the unevolved. Remember, these books reflect the Piscean Age. Spiritually, service to others and the realms beyond were idealized, as they are today. However, at that time in history they were idealized in a 12th House way—as a powerful source of strength, but a source that if misused could lead to self-

147

undoing. Hence the vagueness and guardedness.

This manner of presentation may have been fine thirty or forty years ago. Now, however, we have entered the Aquarian Age—or at least are on the cusp of it, depending on which theory you believe. Times have changed. With these changes there must be a re-examination of the products of the old age, so that we let neither impatience or frustration cause us to overreact and cut down perfectly good concepts that have as yet not blossomed. Nor should we enter the new age with excess jargon that merely clutters, impedes and trips us up. With this in mind, what do we do with the Alice Bailey material? Do we dump it as just a bunch of vague fantasizing? Or do we bring it with us, clarifying and refurbishing where necessary to make it more useful?

We know that each Age tends to bring something of a reaction against the previous one. The Piscean Age was an age of mysticism, solitary contemplation and a not totally unjustified fear of martyrdom or persecution for beliefs espoused openly. The Aquarian Age, on the other hand, is more an Age of, "Let it all hang out and tough luck if you can't take the consequences." The Piscean Age way was to have mystery schools, initiations and a variety of idealized servers, such as saints, gurus, and Masters, who could be approached for guidance and direction by those seeking or traveling the Path. The Aquarian Age way is not to wait for the approach, but rather to advertise, promote, and/or disseminate the teachings in a way that makes them easily grasped by anyone interested. Initiations and mystical degrees? Far too elitist for the Aquarian Age. Throw 'em out! Make it clear that each person can be their own channel, master, or guru. In fact, not only *can* they be, they have an obligation to be! If the Piscean Age symbol was the guru on the mountain top, the Aquarian age symbol is more apt to be a boy scout dragging protesting people across a street they aren't sure they want to cross!

So much for the differences between the Piscean and Aquarian Ages. Again we must ask: How do these differences affect the relevance of the Alice Bailey teachings? It's clear that if these *do* have a place in the New Age, they must move beyond the boundaries of the theosophist, be freely disseminated, and above all else be "translated" into plain English. No longer can the astrologer presumptuously determine whether or not the client is "on the Path." No longer can they arbitrarily divide people into "evolved" and "unevolved" categories. No longer can they smile rather smugly and say, "If you are to understand, you will." Rather, the Aquarian Age astrologer will operate from the premise that everyone is on the path, everyone is evolving and that those who *do* want to understand are entitled to some explanations.

The teachings of the Tibetan, as recorded in Alice Bailey's books, revolve around a system of esoteric rulerships that varies considerably from those used in traditional exoteric astrology. At first glance these rulerships are somewhat disconcerting, to say the least, and a couple of them appear to make no sense whatsoever, at least according to traditional astrology's tenets. If we are to take these teachings into the Aquarian Age, the first thing we must do is make some sort of sense out of this system. Unlike the Piscean Age, where feeling is believing, the Aquarian Age stresses knowing how any system of correspondences works and understanding its construction. In other words, before this system is accepted, astrologers must clarify how the system is best utilized and why.

The Tibetan stated that these esoteric rulerships were only valid for a certain segment of astrologers—"evolved people." The second thing we must do is look at that statement. The Aquarian Age philosophy is that we are all evolving. What works for only a select few under select conditions is at best undemocratic (and for that reason suspect);

at worst, it is wishful thinking and just plain wrong. So, if these teachings are to serve a purpose in the Aquarian Age, they have to be demystified and made more accessible to whatever segment of the public expresses interest in them.

With this in mind, the remainder of this essay is an attempt to restate the basic principles of "Esoteric Astrology" in plain English. The rulership system is meant to complement rather than replace that of traditional exoteric astrology; as long as we live in the material world and are involved with parents, spouses, jobs and the many other externals that make up day-to-day life, exoteric astrology will remain a useful and valid tool. However, we exist simultaneously on many levels. One of these levels involves the relationship between our inner voice and our outer actions and realities. Just as synastry techniques help clarify what is going on in relationships, just as locational techniques shed light on our reactions to and experiences in various parts of the world, so esoteric astrology can shed light on our inner dialogue, explaining why we sometimes feel compelled to enter into situations or relationships others advise against, why we can have "everything" yet still be discontented, why some skills come to us naturally while others elude us, no matter how hard we try to acquire them. It goes without saying then, that one purpose of esoteric astrology might be to follow the thread between past lives and present. From that perspective, let's look once again at those esoteric rulerships:

Aries - Mercury: In exoteric astrology, Aries is described as a pioneering, courageous, and above all else, physical sign. Mercury, while not a non-physical planet, is usually connected more with mental activity than with physical. So how do we justify this rulership? For starters, remember that Mercury was the mythological messenger of the gods. As such, he was both physically and mentally active—not just an ivory-tower intellectual, but rather a god who was right out there in action.

Remember too, the occult maxim, "Thoughts are things." Before any circumstance can manifest in the material world, it first must manifest in someone's mind. This is the crucial link to understanding Mercury's esoteric rulership of Aries. In order to actually take action, you must use your mind to select the action you are going to take. Esoterically, the selection process may entail reviewing past-life actions and learning to draw conclusions from these before selecting the lifestyle options you want to pursue this time, as well as the actions you will need to take to bring about your chosen lifestyle. Esoterically then, Mercury may tell us a bit about past-life learning or skills we've brought into the present to utilize in career, hobby, or private life areas.

If Aries is emphasized in a natal chart, the soul may be here not so much to take concrete action through doing or creating, but rather to plant ideas in others and inflame them with the desire to bring those ideas into manifestation. So the influence of Aries on an exoteric level is to take action, while from an esoteric standpoint it might be to inspire and/or incite action, rather than to personally accomplish a task single-handedly. Note how this tallies with the exoteric stereotype of Aries as a sign that doesn't finish what it starts. On the soul level, Aries may feel a task is "finished" once someone else has started on the manifestation; therefore they may sense that no further action needs to be taken, since they have assigned the work to someone motivated and capable of seeing it through.

Taurus - Vulcan: The first problem we encounter in understanding this rulership is that Vulcan is as yet undiscovered. Being a hypothetical planet, it is not a part of exoteric astrology. What we know about this planet is that, according to existing literature, it is supposed to be intra-

Mercurial. A number of planets and other bodies have been hypothesized as "the" Vulcan. Not all of these, however, are intra-Mercurial in orbit, and as yet, none have been accepted by all esoteric astrologers. Among present contenders for the Vulcan crown we have a hypothetical Vulcan as described by L. H. Weston in *Vulcan, Its History, Nature and Tables*, Carl Stahl in *Vulcan, The Intra-Mercurial Planet*, the asteroid Icarus (note that the asteroid Vulcan is *not* a serious contender), Chiron, the Moon's True apogee point (the so-called European Lilith), and Transpluto. I leave it to you to explore or reject any or all of these at your leisure; if this appears to be a mind-boggling task, you might start by considering Vulcan's influence on the house of your natal chart where Taurus is found.

Esoterically, Taurus has to do with justifying your existence by accomplishing something or getting tangible results. The rationale behind this is easily understood by looking at the mythological Vulcan. Unlike the other gods, Vulcan was not physically perfect. He was, in fact, crippled and was often ridiculed or humiliated by the other deities (particularly Mars). In order to survive, Vulcan became servant to the other gods, making their armor and functioning as their blacksmith.

If Vulcan is the Avis of the mythological kingdom, then by analogy Taurus may be thought of as the process of starting from self-acceptance or acceptance of what you cannot change. Taurus in a natal chart can often indicate an area of life where physical, psychological or other types of damage have left scars on the soul. Yet we must remember that each sign, and each experience, serves a purpose. In fact, the Buddha was said to have achieved enlightenment during a Taurus Full Moon. Growing awareness can involve painful realizations as well as joyous ones, so we might say that Taurus symbolizes how and where we strive for enlightenment. Had the Buddha not initially tried other paths and found them (or himself) wanting, enlightenment might not have come at all.

Esoterically, Taurus is the work done to justify existence in the Light. If we prefer to fritter away our time on earth eating, drinking and consuming other sensual goodies, then our path is lit by neon, which for some people may not only be enough, but just what they need. However, to turn the inner light on, we must give as well as take. We must pay the price for what we want. In connection with this, Taurus may have esoterically to do with clarifying desires, accepting what cannot be changed, and seeking security within, rather than through objects or experiences without.

Gemini - Venus: Exoterically, Gemini is associated with duality and variety, while Venus is more connected with maintaining the status quo, being nice, and preventing disruptions. How on earth then can these two be esoterically linked? Well, let's think about it. One of the prime exoteric correspondences of Venus is relationships. Don't relationships involve two people (at least), a variety of experiences, and a lot of learning? Now let's take it one step further. Jungian psychology states that even though we are born in a physical body displaying either male or female characteristics, the mind, soul and psyche are androgynous, consisting of both "male" (active, impulsive, physical) and "female" (passive, receptive, emotional) characteristics. Should we attempt to repress either the animus (male) or anima (female) because one of these is awkward or uncomfortable to incorporate into our physical behavior? If we do, we are apt to feel a lack and then we might meet someone of the appropriate sex who can serve as a mirror of the repressed traits. This is what is known as projection. Note that while the person may indeed share these repressed traits, the fact that you are expecting them to act out not only their own but yours, as well, invariably leads to problems. (After all, if the Cosmic Steering Committee had decreed that it was only appropriate for men to have a Mars, they would have undoubtedly structured the Universe so that women were born only when Mars was void-of-course, transiting some other galaxy, or at least intercepted in the 12th House) Venus, as esoteric ruler of Gemini, simply amplifies the concept of other people as mirrors. It stresses the need to unite not only exoterically, but also esoterically. In other words, Gemini is the process of uniting the male and the female within us.

Another process symbolized by Gemini is that of acquiring what the Buddhists call right knowledge. Right knowledge is more than seeing that our facts are straight; we can memorize all the books in the world and still not have right knowledge. Right knowledge is the process that allows us to use factual information to create. Our creation may be a book, a home, or a healthy, competent, productive self. In each case, the ingredient needed to create this thing of value is more than mere book learning. The necessary ingredient is love. Only when we love and value the raw materials of facts and experiences can we create something that will be loved and valued by others. All we need to do to bear this out is to look at the difficulties in the lives of unwanted children. Gemini says that knowing how to do it (or get it done) is not enough. Rather, we must understand that we cannot attract from outside ourselves. Only when we have learned to accept and love ourselves can we teach or love another person, subject or thing.

Planets in Gemini can simultaneously detach from the ego (our "theory" about ourselves) and become consciously owned or acknowledged (right knowledge of ourselves). This involves learning that to be at peace with ourselves, we must speak from our hearts and not from our heads. This has to do with making sustained efforts toward wholeness, with realizing that a mirror is no earthly good unless we stand still long enough to see our reflected image, and with learning that what we value is more important than what anyone else values. If we are untrue to our values, we won't be able to live with ourselves. If we are unable to live with ourselves, it is unlikely that anyone else will be able to live with us either. Think of Gemini then as a process of going from external to internal consensus.

Cancer - Neptune: Cancer and Neptune are both emotional energies, but whereas Cancer involves security and centering, Neptune is traditionally described as confusing and hard to pin down. Aside from the fact that both are indicators of emotional sensitivity, how can we relate these two?

Where Cancer represents the material womb, Neptune represents the spiritual womb. Where exoterically Cancer has a lot to do with responses conditioned by our upbringing, our concepts of security, and our genetic family roots, Neptune has to do with responses and roots laid down in past lives. Instead of describing our security within our immediate environment, it describes our internal security in relation to the universal environment, one which extends beyond domestic, national or even earthy planes. Esoterically, Cancer represents the process of relying on externals to provide an outer environment that is conducive to finding security within. In this sense, it has a lot to do with living in our own bodies and trusting our own "light source" rather than trying to live in the reflected light of other people's concepts of "good" and "not good." In this way, we go from being dependent on others for nurturing and sustenance to believing in the universe and invoking our own higher self to provide necessary support. So in many respects, Cancer is about growing up on a soul level.

Leo - Sun: Exoterically and esoterically, the Sun rules

Leo. The principle here is one of recognizing what we are and being all that we can be.

Where Leo and the Sun are placed in our natal chart is where we want to let our light shine. And we can, once we decide where the power switch for our light will be. If it is situated in our ego, then our light will shine brightly so long as other people do what we want; should they refuse to do our bidding, our power source will be diminished, possibly to the point where a fuse is blown and our light is put out temporarily. If, on the other hand, we realize that the more in touch we are with our own center or essence, the stronger our light will be; we have a potentially endless light source that may dim on occasion but can never really burn out or short circuit.

When Leo energies in a natal chart are powered by the ego, they often generate popularity or recognition. In contrast, when these same energies are powered by the soul, there may or may not be the same level of popularity, but there will be greater self-esteem as well as recognition of and respect for our originality. For this to happen, power must be decentralized and the ego needs not given priority over the need to express the soul. To go from "I am the center of the Universe" to "I am a spoke in the Universal wheel" requires discipline and self-awareness; adulation and attention can be just as addictive and reality-distorting as alcohol and drugs. Leo, then, symbolizes the task of moving from dependence on personality to dependence on impersonality. In plain English, this means that Leo experiences have to do with having faith in the Universe to put you where you can shine, rather than putting yourself where *you* think the center of the Universe is and refusing to budge.

Virgo - Moon: Virgo and its esoteric ruler, the Moon, show the concrete manifestations of karma in this lifetime in terms of events and other external phenomena.

Exoterically, Virgo is ruled by Mercury. Virgo has a lot to do with reasoning skills, with analyzing the results of our actions and with modifying our behavior accordingly. Esoterically, Virgo symbolizes this same process, only not so much in the here and now as in terms of analysis and subsequent conclusions drawn from past-life experiences in between the last lifetime and this one.

When there is heavy emphasis on Virgo in a natal chart, there is often what I call a cosmic fertility problem. There is an abundance of potential, but because the person is still hung up on—and identifying with—past-life details or experiences, the potential is blocked and the crop of possibilities does not bear fruit. To fertilize this potential, knowledge garnered from past and present life experiences must be digested and converted into wisdom. Tradition has it that this is why we are given a quiet time, or rest period, between lifetimes. These may however, be instances where in order to finish required tasks the rest period was cut short—either voluntarily, at the soul's insistence, or involuntarily, by the Cosmic Steering Committee because of past due Karma. In such cases, the dividing line between "then" and "now" may be hard to distinguish and the digestion process from a last lifetime is still incomplete.

Libra - Uranus: At first glance, this rulership seems to make no sense whatsoever. The planet of divorce, rebellion and individuality ruling the sign of marriage, harmony and cooperation? Preposterous, at least until you look at Saturn, which is a common bond they share. Saturn is traditionally exalted in Libra; before the discovery of Uranus, it was also given rulership of Aquarius. Both Libra and Aquarius are Air signs, which means they have a lot to do with social order. Saturn is a so-called karmic planet; hence we can safely suspect that any sign connected with Saturn has some tie-in with karmic laws. In the case of Libra, there are a number of laws or maxims that come to mind. Among them is "Judge not, lest ye shall be judged." Since we know Uranus is, to say the least, paradoxical, a couple of other laws just might fit this Libra/Uranus combination. One is, "Be careful what you wish for, you just might get it." Another is, "What you hate, you ultimately become."

Libra is the stage upon which we perform the age-old ritual of opposites attracting, interacting and reacting. This process of confronting just what we have always wanted gives us spiritual nausea; or conversely, confronting just what we've never wanted may feel like dying and going to heaven. Both are spiritual catalysts for the soul; they can open the third eye, spark spiritual awakenings and pave the way to break free from merely existing so we can truly live—not only in this life and on this plane but in other lives and beyond the material world.

Scorpio - Mars: Mars had rulership of Scorpio until Pluto's discovery so this rulership is easier to understand than some of the others. Mars represents motivation, including perhaps what motivated us to come back here. Scorpio represents where or what we have to fight, or how to accomplish a difficult task before we can have what we want. Some astrologers say that where Scorpio is in the chart is where we confront our own shadow. My own feeling is that this is where we have been told, "Go ahead and try it, but we'll be watching you. And if you abuse your privileges, it'll be a cold day on Earth before we let you try this one again." Sort of like the first time we got to take the family car on a Saturday night, remember? Only what we are being given is a lot more powerful, a lot more valuable, and potentially a lot more dangerous to us and others if not handled with maturity as well as understanding of its powers and drawbacks.

We might get the feeling from this that where Scorpio predominates in our chart, we are more or less on trial or probation. This may well be the case. Scorpio could be seen as the sign which denotes a place where there's a final exam or at best, a test of competence. This is the place where we have been practicing or auditioning, perhaps for lifetimes. Now we have a chance to *be* or *get* the real thing.

Any diploma, of course, takes hard work and occasional sacrifice. Scorpio rules annihilation, while Mars traditionally has a warlike, aggressive nature. Where Scorpio and Mars are placed, we face a need to confront certain realities. These may be painful to look at and deal with. However, refusing to face them can be equally painful, because what we refuse to confront and deal with is invariably what destroys us. Only by confrontation can we put out the destructive fire and walk beyond it. Therefore, we must learn to differentiate between harmful silence and harmless speech, positive action and meddling, positive apathy and negative buck-passing. We must confront egotistical desires and transmute them to self-aware desires based on universal love. Above all else, we must go from a stance of fearful combativeness to one of emotional calm based on the knowledge that the only thing to be feared in life is fear itself. Fear cripples and kills; confrontation leads to understanding, which ultimately leads to healing.

Sagittarius - The Earth: The Earth in your chart is always directly opposite the Sun. Traditionally, and for reasons I've been unable to determine, esoterically, the rulership of the human race is given to Sagittarius.

The Earth is where we live physically. Sagittarius tells us about the goals we set for ourselves before coming back here, goals that could best be filled—or perhaps only be filled—by yet another life on this earthly merry-go-round. There may be one goal; there may be several. We may have chosen one goal before coming down, only to discover as we get here that this goal leads to still others that we didn't know we had, because we were unaware any options existed until we returned.

Traditionally, the sign Sagittarius is connected with the gifts of prophecy and foreknowledge. Esoterically, people with prominent placements in Sagittarius pave the way for things to come. They may do this through teaching others, through acting as channels or through serving as examples for others in some respect. At first glance, this sounds ever so special and evolved. It can be, but it might be worth mentioning that people have been known to teach or pave the way by setting bad as well as good examples. As astrologers, we all know the hazards of self-fulfilling prophecies. Before we can be masters, we must first be students, and teachers. Placements in Sagittarius show where we are doing our fieldwork to get our B.A. in life. As part of the curriculum, we learn to think before speaking and speak from our hearts rather than just from our heads. We must learn the difference between wise discrimination and unwise choices based on hearsay or prejudice. We must be very clear on what we are seeking, because until we truly know we will not find it.

Capricorn - Saturn: Here's another case of identical esoteric and exoteric rulerships. The principle is that what oppresses, restricts, or limits the immature soul, frees the mature one.

Capricorn is the path of duty; Saturn is the planet of Karma. Where we have Capricorn and Saturn, we are well-advised to think about the duties we might have undertaken before reincarnating. Where we find Capricorn is where we signed a binding contract with the Cosmic Steering Committee. To ignore it or pretend we don't remember could be quite risky. They will remember and they'll catch up with us. They have our astral signature on that contract. They will have no qualms about reminding us that failure to deliver is likely to result in unattained goals, thwarted plans and loss of respect from other souls.

Where we have Carpricorn is a place where we can literally have it all, so long as we honor the terms of our contract. The problem is that we can also be blinded by the light and glamor, drawn to an either/or situation much as a moth is drawn to a flame. The temptation is great to either put all our eggs in the basket of material achievement or conversely to turn our backs and focus on something non-material. What can be forgotten in the pressure of life is that we can actually fill both baskets simultaneously, so long as we honor the terms of our contract. To do this requires a heart that's warm and open to people, but not a head that equates love with patronizing, or catering to greedy egos. It requires us to look for failures even though those around us may only see or comment on our successes. It requires flexibility since each egg of accomplishment will need careful attention so that it does not break, crack other eggs with its weight, or unbalance the basket. However, so long as we honor our responsibilities to ourselves (for that is what the contract is all about), we will continue to acquire the eggs and choose where to put them.

Aquarius - Jupiter: Jupiter is connected with expansion, philosophy and teaching. Aquarius has been called the water of life. So this combination could be said to symbolize knowledge as truth or knowledge as freedom. Certainly there's a clear inference that knowledge is a necessity of life.

The esoteric relationship between Jupiter and Aquarius may explain to some extent why Aquarians are often motivated to focus their energies on human rights and scientific causes, or when they promulgate astrology and other consciousness expanding studies.

As an Air sign, Aquarius is connected with distribution and circulation. With Jupiter as its esoteric ruler, it might be safe to assume that placements in Aquarius have to do with sharing the wealth or sharing knowledge. This means that where Aquarius is in the natal chart, we can acquire so long as we are giving; what we hoard will ultimately dry up and evaporate, doing no one any good. We must operate here on the basis of democracy and universality rather than on the basis of "the rules don't apply to me 'cause I'm special." When Aquarius is emphasized in the natal chart there is often an unusual intuitive, psychic or intellectual gift. If this is shared freely and honestly without thought of ego gratification, it will blossom. If it is made a fetish of, pouring it unsolicited upon those who don't want it in order to quench our own egos, it will dry up leaving us dependent on others to refill us spiritually, until such time as we are capable of operating our own shut-off valve and regulating our own psychic/intellectual flow.

Pisces - Pluto: Both Pisces and Pluto are in a sense "the end of the line." We have been here before and done it all. It's time to move on, burn the bridge, cut the umbilical cord. But before we venture off into the unknown, it might be wise to take a look around and see if there is anything worth saving before we call in the wreckers.

Pisces and its esoteric ruler, Pluto, represent the promise that we will be resurrected, that though the body may be ready for the zodiacal garbage heap (as Pisces was once called), our soul essence will continue to live and experience new cycles of unfoldment—on Earth or perhaps elsewhere.

Pisces can be likened to the time in psychotherapy when a choice must be made as to whether we really want to change or merely want to perfect our neuroses. If we earnestly desire change, then we must find some practical means of fusing our ideals with some of the annoying but unavoidable realities of living in the material world. We need to focus on where we are going and what is in our path, rather than pretending that nothing is in our way, and then falling flat on our faces because we missed the danger signals. We need to bring body and soul, logic and emotions together for an executive meeting, delegate duties to each and set a time to reconvene for a progress report.

Change—real change—may mean letting go of familiar relationships, past history, possessions, or any one of a multitude of other things. Perfecting our neuroses, on the other hand, simply means making our addictions more socially acceptable. For example, we can switch from compulsive eating to anorexia, from talking about our grudges to merely thinking about them and overtly denying their existence, from dependent relationships to co-dependent relationships. Where we have Pisces placements we must ask ourselves "Do I really want to be here or am I simply too tired to pack up and leave? Is the party over? Am I just trying to postpone cleaning up the debris, washing the rosy-colored glasses and vacuuming the karmic crumbs from the carpet? Is this all there is?"

It's always sad to close the door and bring things to an end, but until we do, we are not free to rest, to go on to new things or to be anywhere else but where we are. Until we get up and say good-bye, what we have is all there is and it is apt to get less and less jolly as others move on. Finally, Pisces is the end of the chapter, just as Aries is the beginning of the new chapter. It is up to us to decide when the time is ripe to start that new chapter. And that is what Pisces is about.

Philip Sedgwick

Philip Sedgwick began his study of astrology in 1969. He started astrological counseling in 1975, becoming a full time professional in 1980. He has lectured internationally and has conducted classes and seminars in many major conferences and conventions. His areas of expertise include metaphysics and parapsychology.

Co-founder and President of Delta Dynamics—an Astrological Consulting and Research Company, Philip has used astrology with business clients ranging from sole proprietors to Fortune 500 corporations. He is currently working with the entertainment industry as well as programs to assist in increasing commercial aviation safety.

Together with some astrological giants, he pioneered the realm of Galactic Astrology which includes Galactic effects such as black holes, quasars, the Galactic center and Halley's Comet. He is exploring research correlating planetary patterns with solar disturbances.

He has a series of works in print including: *The Astrology of Transcendence* (1980). Seek-It Publishers; *The Astrology of Deep Space* (1984), Seek-It Publishers; Contributing writer, *Llewellyn's Sun Sign Books*, 1986, 1988.

GALACTIC STUDIES

In June of 1983, a U.S. space probe reached a milestone in space. Early in that month, the probe, launched several years earlier, crossed over the outermost perimeter of the solar system. This perimeter, at that moment in Universal Time, derived its reference from the distance which the planet Neptune held from the Sun. Due to a January, 1979 trading of places between Pluto and Neptune, Neptune was just over 35 million miles further from the Sun than Pluto. Thus, as the space probe left the Neptunian demarcation, a new dimension of Galactic Consciousness began.

Symbolically, this event defined the origins of a new realm of conscious awareness. From that moment forward the technological advancement of humanity, symbolized by the space probe, began a curious investigation into the deep, dark, mysterious realms of distant space. Humankind had broken through the definition of the solar system once and for all. The consciousness shift based upon this leap states that from an astrological point of view one cannot be limited solely by the perceptions of the solar system. Extending from the deliberate penetration into space by Earth's developing technology, all forces outside of the solar system achieve relevance to the development of astrological consciousness back on Earth.

Perhaps this achievement in technology opens a 'cosmic can of worms'—perhaps not. The most significant statement notes the need for astrology and astrologers to maintain a sense of galactic current affairs. The 1986 passage of

Comet Halley, the supernova explosion of February, 1987, and the July, 1987 announcement of two suspected black holes (galaxies M-31 and M-32) all must fall under the watchful study of contemporary astrologers. The realm of Galactic Astrology undisputedly knocks upon the windows of the mind and the doors of our hearts and souls.

The world of humanistic astrology as spearheaded by the late Dane Rudhyar and his contemporaries noted difficulties with the hard-line, deterministic astrological patterns entrenched in consciousness over the ages. Changing conditions in life, rather than responding to external circumstances, gained momentum as the astrological state of the art. Astrologers sought to provide clients with choices in life, rather than predicting events over which no control existed. Astrology evolved to meet the needs of a more responsible society. Still, retention of the ideas of the astrologer telling the client how life will be, thereby reducing motivation, perceptions of free will, and most damagingly, creating negative dependency upon the astrologer, remains. The inbred philosophies within Galactic Studies strive to induce a paradigm shift in astrology. All invalid astrological concepts must fall. Clients shifting responsibility for life onto astrologers must be redirected. Astrology must follow developments generated by science and Galactic Studies to maintain its position as a contemporary science. This is not just desirable; it is inevitable.

Galactic dimensions offer a more wholistic and spiritualized approach to astrology. However, this wholism must be differentiated from the spiritualism often seen before. The "airy-fairy," spaced-out format containing abundances of rationalizations and excuses for not progressing, based upon the cosmic scapegoat—Karma—evaporates with this approach. Spirituality reaches down to the level of the mundane. Perhaps the most spiritual thing a human can do is meet the conditions of the mundane, daily requirements with responsibility, integrity, lovingness and an attitude of healing adversities. Compared to the levels of realization in Galactic magnitude, many problems perceived lose significance.

Developing the fundamentals of Galactic Studies is not difficult. First of all, a symbolic approach presents a basic foundation. As will be seen with black holes, the actual astrophysical dynamics of the object portray a symbolic behavior pattern for humanity to individualize. Secondly, the emanations of the object in its radiation spectrum suggest the levels of consciousness affected. Finally, the periodicities of the galactic entity also create a timeliness exhibited by the recipient of the galactic source. For instance, a black hole with an eclipsing pattern of 5.6 days yields an awareness cycle in the individual connected to that interval. A black hole with an x-ray burst of 285 seconds suggests a look at an idea with devoted attention for four minutes forty-four seconds to obtain the entire picture.

Closer to home, a new mythology for planetary pictures emerges in the forefront of our conscious attention. This can be correlated to the breakthroughs taking place in the galactic realm. The image of the space shuttle Challenger crew as gods and goddesses rising above the planet to ascend into the heavens contains the seeds of future mythology. One reference to the peace proponent, Gandhi, noted that in future years it may be difficult to perceive that such a courageous and enlightened person ever existed. Perhaps if one looks far enough, the images created by the PTL religious scandal and the Iran-Contragate extravaganza will create similar images of demigods—for better or for worse.

Upgraded images of transcendence also extend from the models of Galactic Studies. The idea of Karma, as it is known, must change to fit with the new perspectives created. Cause and effect, the confines of Karma, come from Newtonian models of physics and have been exceeded for nearly a century with the innovations of individuals such as Albert Einstein. Cause and effect fits the mode of linear thinking, a grossly limited pattern. At best, linear thinking can be bent creating somewhat circular thoughts, generally repetitive. This mental agenda permits the adage of historical repetition to refresh itself. Historical regeneration of activity tends to suggest that the mechanism behind humanity has not been understood—condemning humanity to evolutionary redundancy, much like marrying the same soul in a multitude of lifetimes. Are we evolving or just revolving?

The images involved in Galactic Studies evoke the possibilities of distorting reality as it is known. The deceptiveness of appearance long pointed out by mystical masters comes into focus. Time dilation and space warping may actually cause events at different times to occur simultaneously. Places separated by great distances may be neighboring stages for consciousness evolution. Astrophysics has problems with many of the ideas seen in this realm. Astrophysicists say that such metaphors violate causality. Hallelujah! Finally, the condemnation of the cause and effect universe is exceeded. Future lives can now co-exist in harmony with past lives. Perhaps the Karma one experiences in a relationship pattern is actually a lifetime from three thousand years ahead of our current time perceptions, back for resolution now. So, according to this model, when the future life does occur, it will be better. This goes on to note that the end result is that the life now is better because of it being better in the future. Certainly a more optimistic model of karmic obligation develops releasing justification for many negative interactions between growing souls. Clearly, cause and effect no longer exist. The time of instant Karma pervades the pursuit of galactic phenomena.

Before discussing the astrological dynamics of Galactic Studies, several points must be definitively stated so that the context of Galactic Astrology will not bear negative tones of cause and effect. First, Galactic Astrology is in its infancy; billions of points need yet to be studied. So far only a few hundred have been examined. It must be realized that references should be weighed against fact. Should one emerge from this treatise realizing that eight natal planets connect with black holes, it tends to create an astrological elitism of chart superiority. Yet, an individual with such strong connections must actualize the power within those connections. This process takes great perseverance, consciousness and will.

Secondly, working with galactic points definitely enhances the quality of life. Still, there exist many individuals with galactic potential which remains unfocused, and complications then appear in even the most basic elements of daily living. This realization contains a good bit of the overall insight of galactic alignments; use and cooperation creates understanding and contentment.

Third, with applied research, especially through the turn of the century, catalogues of galactic energy with an astrological basis can be established. The ultimate realization would be an awareness of the energy emanating from each discrete sign of the zodiac so each degree emerges as being special, unique unto itself, full of understanding and penetrating enlightenment brought forth by the radiation of that degree.

GENERAL PERSONALITY TRAITS

From the initial view of galactic studies astrologically applied, a series of consistent personality traits emerge. These unique characteristics include:

- An increased sense of personal magnetism, sometimes seen as enigmatic qualities. This effect is immeasurably present with black hole connections.

- A sense of timelessness. Time dilation (warping) provides the native with both regression and progression capabilities without the need to alter consciousness (as in trancing). These natives shift between alternate realities in the blink of an eye and can pursue visions of other dimensions.

- An increased sense of destiny or purpose prevails when the contact is realized.

- The personality bears qualities noted as controversial, radical, or bizarre.

- The individual has an innate ability to teach regardless of formal or informal teaching environments.

- The person has a perception of understanding energy of an etheric nature. This brings a strong sense of sexual presence whether actively applied or not.

- Often a bizarre sense of humor prevails. Nothing is considered sacred, nor should it be.

- A sense of alienation exists in the communication of inner awareness and urges. A need for more time alone—something which must be understood in all personal one to one relationships.

- Communication often comes from other realms. As such, the message is unfamiliar, exciting, risk-oriented, often highly confrontive.

To grasp a sense of relative intensities, the milder of the galactic points seem to resonate at the quantitative amounts of five Jupiters or two Plutos. In dealing with black holes, the most powerful of the galactic sources, the intensity level rivals ten times the powerful magnitude of Pluto—even if Pluto *is* potentially being downgraded from planetary status.

Changes in reality yield changes in manifestation. Expanding realities expand the spectrum of manifestations. Imagining realities beyond your current visions produces a way of life which exceeds your wildest dreams.

THE NATURE OF ENERGY, GALACTICALLY

The galactic nature of energy can be established in a somewhat generic method. The following types of energy/ forces fall into these basic families:

Gravity - Strongly weighted with influence, perceived as heavy or immovable. Saturn-like in feeling. Conscious mind.

Infrared (IFR) - Relates to the subconscious mind, memory provoking, releasing mental/emotional blockage. Activates the Root Chakra.

Ultraviolet (UV) - Refers to the preconsciouos (uncorrupted and innocent) mind. Known as superconscious, this vibration lights up the top chakra, the Crown Center.

Radio Energy - Generates consistent and repeating messages to ensure reception and acknowledgement. Skilled at communicating key points.

X-rays (XR) - Zone of the two most potent energies, this emanation seeks to penetrate the core for objective understanding. This internal viewing is the knowing of the soul and recognizes others at the soul level. Relates to the Sanskrit term *namaste* which implies mutual recognition at the most inner and divine level of existence.

Neutrons - The second of the strongest energies. Neutrons are all pervading, containing the essence of inner healing—that which is healed at the cause level. Neutrons are regenerative and transformative.

Gamma Rays - Gamma radiation strives for transmutation which is similar to transformation except that it occurs through external catalyzation while transformation is an internal occurence.

From the galactic points the above types of energy accompany the light perceived and the degree of heat received from those points. These vibrations are subtle, yet influential. It is much like realizing that the light of the Sun, per se, does not burn your skin or heal germs. These conditions come from the ultraviolet nature of the Sun which coexists with the warmth felt and daylight seen.

The frequency and duration of intrinsic radiation vary with each of the observed galactic points. Emanation is the overall interval in which the energy cycle of the point repeats. Periods range from just under 5 hours to 35 days in black holes and up to 164 days in other objects. The pulse width is the time interval in which the energy is "on" or active. These bursts run from thousandths of a second up to 284 seconds. The period and pulse correlate to creative, inspirational cycles and the time elements in which the insights flash through the consciousness. It is interesting to note that such insights burst into the brain faster than the conscious mind can grasp. Thus galactic factors come experientially; they contain the essence of underlying knowledge and philosophy without the linear details of data and information transmission. This image shows the learning and comprehension necessary to free humanity from the limited view of education based upon memorization without understanding. Such a model is encouraging for the newcomer to astrology. It is not necessary to memorize Venus in the signs or houses. It is only necessary to *understand* the nature of Venus, signs and houses. Then unlimited synthesis occurs naturally and resonately. This frees the learning astrologer from the dogma of only knowing what has been stated or written. Undisputedly, it is impossible to teach another everything there is to know about any astrological component. Galactic Astrology frees the astrologer from the confines of linear thought and opens the way for understanding and fully experiencing astrology at its most subtle and powerful level!

GALACTIC COORDINATES

Astrophysicists do not generally give the zodiacal longitude with which astrologers are familiar when they encounter a significant point. Even if they were accomodating, the point may be listed sidereally and would require conversion to the tropical zodiac. The astronomical coordinates given are right ascension and declination. Through trigonometric tricks the zodiacal longitude can be calculated. Right ascension and declination are usually related in epoch 1950.0 which means January 1, 1950, at 0000 hours GMT. Since points far removed in space (fixed points) advance or precess at a rate of roughly one degree per 72 years, providing a position for mid-century usually serves the entire century with minimal accuracy. Unlike planets, the galactic points are not contained within the realm of declination or latitude that planets in our solar system are. Some points explored may range well above or below the usual planes of vertical reference. To assume that only those points within range of "natural planetary declinations" contain significant effects borders on tunnel vision. Granted, the nature of these points traversing so far north or south may require re-orienting the head to see such things. Maybe a new point of view will be good. (Remember your Mother telling you to look up and down the street when she really meant look left and right?) Some extra effort may be needed to tune into the bandwidths of some of the extreme points of orientation. Perhaps this consideration suggests an alternate point of view, one workable beyond the contained view of options naturally perceived in solar system vision. An energy grid develops which is the networking of the Cosmos.

GALACTIC PLAYERS

With all the preliminaries out of the way, a microcosmic view of the macrocosm can begin. Volumes can be written about the very few points now known astrologically of the galactic domain. These points are merely intended to introduce, to excite, and to induce further exploration of what lies beyond. Astrologically, it is virgin territory.

The first point which exposed the intradimensionality of galactic astrology originated within the core of our galaxy. The galactic center is now relatively known in astrological circles. Located at 26 Sagittarius 09 (Latitude 5S36, Declination 28S59, Right Ascension 265 37 30) the Galactic Center (symbolized by Z or GC) bears the same relationship with our Sun that the Sun maintains with the Earth. The Earth revolves around the Sun every 365.4 days. The Sun similarly revolves around the Galactic Center in a cool 250 million year period. Given 5 billion years of solar existence, this cycle has repeated some 20 times.

Our Sun is 30,000 light years from the Galactic Center. The galaxy at large maintains a radius of 50,000 light years. The Sun actually sits between two arms of the galaxy's spirals. These arms are the Sagittarius Arm (the Milky Way) and the Perseus Arm.

Because of our involvement with the Sun, this galactic point is highly relevant in our scheme of things. Any object which is in itself a nucleus has a certain sense of centrality. This suggests that the point automatically finds itself containing other influences (or people) within its grasp, presumably in the interest of leading toward a common, highly

purposeful goal. Recognition and advancement of an uncomfortable nature go hand in hand with this point. In any
situation where an individual gains prominence there exists
a reason for the visibility. With the Galactic Center as a
guide the reason is enlightenment.

Individuals with connections to the Galactic Center
automatically acquire information of an enlightened nature.
The information, however, can be blocked and such block-
ing creates additional complications in life, the least of
which is an inability to think logically about life situations.
In essence, the Galactic Center refers to ignorance. This
semantical ignorance does not connote lack of knowledge,
rather it refers to the access of information, higher and
enlightened information which the individual chooses to
ignore.

The information exuding from the Galactic Center is
ahead of its time by six to fifteen months. The person using
this data is likely to encounter resistance. The typical reaction to such new input is that the connectee to the Galactic
Center is accusing others of being wrong through the dis-
semination of insight. Alternate realities of right answers
universally exist without a conflict of information. This
realization fits neatly into the awareness of the Galactic
Center. To ensure that this infrared information, which may
be somewhat ahead of its time, is received subconsciously,
it needs to be imparted objectively. The third party technique works effectively. Starting sentences with phrases like,
"I knew someone who . . ." or "I read where . . . ," and other
similar non-confrontive phrases, works well. The Galactic
Center presents an urgency of expression and although it
may seem premature, it is not. In reality, the subconscious is
seeded with the next steps. The Root Chakra, the releaser of
blockage and creator of receptivity, activates and opens the
psychic door for use of the seeds planted. It will take time.

An interesting phenomena results when the individual

imparts the channelled information of the Galactic Center. This person receives a bonus for imparting such wisdom, an insight which can be applied collectively and usually bears a strong personal statement for the individual tuning in. The formation of this second bit of information does not build consciously without the data becoming focused either by speaking or writing.

Information from the Galactic Center falls into the category of channelled input. However, this type of channelling does not require losing consciousness, trancing or altering one's state of mind; it just happens. The beauty of this method is that it remains completely inconspicuous. Only those beings connected with the pipeline from the Galactic Center recognize the symptoms of that mode of channelling.

The Galactic Center challenges those connecting with it to be radical, courageous in spreading information, speculative without attachment to rightness (or righteous-nous) and open to free and abstract association in the mind. These people, in reality, just make it up. These are the innovators of new ideas, those willing to use new, untested and untried ideas, and in true Sagittarian fashion, they are the ones relied upon to get from here to there in less time and in a more directed manner. Progress is a strange entity—odd, eccentric and very upsetting to those enjoying their habituations and homeostasis.

THE BLACK HOLE, MEMBRANE AND METAPHOR

Undoubtedly the most intriguing and perplexing enigma in modern astro-physics is the black hole. Full of paradox and mind stretching concepts, just to allow the black hole to exist, this galactic oddity may be responsible for more evolution in the next fifty years than any other previously established concept in the history of humanity. To perceive the black hole you must give up most of what you know about reality. You cannot enter here holding on to logical precepts and mental dogma. You must free your mind of what you know to be true and what can be possible. What is possible on the next pages are ideas probably not conceivable in your mind now.

To begin, a black hole is a dead star which started out having at least three times the mass of our own Sun. As a part of the star's decaying evolution it reaches a condition of critical mass within its nuclear furnace and explodes into a supernova. As the supernova cools, a long time after the explosion, the gasses can no longer be supported by the once active stellar core. The gasses begin to contract, gaining density; gravity begins to accumulate; the gasses combine, collect, collapse and dive head first toward the former stellar core. Soon the process of contraction and collapse becomes so strong that no force known to nature can halt the collapse. The massive accumulation continues until suddenly the star punches a hole in the "stuff" of the Universe! The remains of the star are now invisible while it continues to plunge into the inescapable unknown—past the point of disappearance and continuing into infinite smallness.

Soon the achievements of the black hole will be a cosmic orafice possessing attributes of infinite gravitational density, infinite curvature of space and maximum warping of time. This invisible point now becomes the most powerful entity known in nature.

The point which gives birth to the black hole results when it disappears from view. A radius, based upon stellar mass, creates the perimeter of the black hole. This perimeter is known as the event horizon. If Jupiter became a black hole, the event horizon would be 9 feet. Should a star with an initial mass ten times that of our Sun collapse into a black hole, it would black out of view when the compression had reduced the matter to a diameter of 37 miles! The point at which the black hole contraction maximizes is known as the singularity. The singularity and event horizon provide the main components of a black hole.

Since the black hole, as the name implies, is invisible, it can only be detected indirectly. This detection usually occurs when the hole begins eating another star in space. The enormous devouring act transfers a phenomenal amount of energy corresponding to the laws of physics. As the star plunges into the depths of the black hole, the surrounding atmosphere heats up to millions of degrees in temperature. The by-product of the thermal transmission generates gamma rays and intense X-ray emanations. An orbital eclipsing pattern of the star and the black hole often results, creating what is known as an X-ray eclipsing binary. Such interactions provide astrophysics with the best existing evidence for black hole phenomena.

The purpose for discussing the nature of black holes is to present a set of contradictions designed to wipe out reality as it is known. This serves as a metaphor for the vast amounts of knowledge contained within the strong teaching disciplines of the black hole. Does it exist or does it not exist? Is it real or not real? Does it matter or not matter? Black holes point out that if you think it is real, it is. If you believe it matters, it does, even if it does not. Understanding this series of statements which could be construed by linear thinking conservatives as mumbo-jumbo, is actually the state of awareness sought in many Eastern disciplines. Transcendence occurs when nothing matters, yet everything does. Enlightenment results when no questions remain. Black holes suck the synapses of the brain, struggling and screaming, into the orafice of enlightenment. The energy used in the transfer of entering the black hole purges the mind, emptying it so that space is vacated in the conscious perception for new information.

Releasing, healing and letting go result. Now the person exists within the alternate dimension. Once this state is achieved, the individual frequently, and at first uncontrollably, shifts back and forth between virtual realities. The image conjured up suggests that information of another dimension must be imparted to a more structured and fearful dimension.

Since those things drawn into the black hole are not readily evident, it takes significant insight to reveal the images of this new found multi-dimensionality. The maximum approach comes from living a Divine example of the understandings encountered. It will be only a matter of time before others sense the difference in the knowing one's life. At that point, the black hole teacher leads the seeker to the event horizon and points out the singularity. The seeker plunges into the depths of true consciousness which cannot be taught. The seeker may, at first, resist the plunge, but resisting does no good.

The realization that *Karma is now* becomes emblazoned on the heart of the seeker. No longer are past lives, cause and effect used as rationalizations to avoid life. What was *is* and what will be also *is*. It is like a look at the evolution of the individual soul by glancing "somewhen" and "elsewhen." Consciousness ceases to be regulated by time and space and falls into the Cosmic jurisdiction of light-like parameters. A lightness toward life co-exists with the magnitude of events. Perspective begins.

The black hole natives have great magnitude and power. They draw in others almost as if against their will. The truth here is that on the most fundamental level of quantum physics, things which are attracted to one another will be attracted to each other, no matter what. From the quantum physics point of view things interact through either attractive or repulsive energies, with no judgement on the nature of the description of the energies. One merely polarizes opposite the other.

Black holes inspire an elegant simplicity of understanding and seek to find the absolute bottom line in any situation. Individuals must be seen at the soul level. The eyes X-ray, seeking to see the inner structure of being, the core of the soul. No judgment exists here. It is just as it is.

At first the flirtation with the black hole is obsessive, then consuming, and finally, ever so enlightening. One may feel somewhat devoured by a black hole native. Strangely, this intrigues, captivates and generates electric healing.

A miniature view into each of the theorized black holes follows. Realize that black holes are still speculative. The black hole model provides scientists and soul seekers with one of the most astute models of understanding ever rationally devised. The information referring to these points is initial, speculative data. It provides a peek into the massive swirl of totality and nothingness. The leap is up to you. Realize that once you look in, you have chosen to take the consciousness plunge.

THE BLACK HOLES

M-31 (3U0021+42) *24 Aries 06*, Latitude 35N51, Decl. 42N00, RA 005 27 00

The first black hole is in galaxy M-3 (which is actually a bit later in Aries, but the X-rays emanate from this degree), a part of the Andromeda Galaxy. This point was classified a black hole in July, 1987, just following Jupiter's conjunction to its longitude. Devotion and peacefulness are indicated here once one learns acceptance. Conflict comes from fighting one's own nature. Achievement is all within the grasp of one's potential. Models of mediocrity and anything which does not allow full development of the soul should be abolished.

CASSIOPEIA A (3C 461, 3U2321+58) *26 Aries 42,* Latitude 58N33, Decl. 54N15 RA 350 18 15.

This black hole is relatively young, resulting from a supernova of just over 300 years ago. This powerful Aries point suggests the ability to conduct past life regressions almost at will. It seeks to locate the uncorrupted, child-like innocence (not naivete). Self-acceptance, self-forgiveness and self-love comprise its primary disciplines. It implies that one should "get into one's self," and plunge into the discovery of the inner being by locating the trusting, loving soul which once existed.

M-32 *26 Aries 56,* Latitude 33N00, Decl. 40n36 RA 010 00 00.

M-32 coexists with M-31 as part of the local group in Andromeda. Primal perseverance constitutes its theme. The question is—when should relentless effort be considered perseverance and when does it constitute banging one's head against the wall, Aries style? The key is timeliness and timelessness. All things come at the right time. Being consistent creates the mainstay of perseverance. Waiting and patience for what is already done are virtues.

M-82 (Ngc 3034) *28 Cancer 17,* Latitude 69N56 Decl. 52N07 RA 147 58 30.

M-82 addresses the consideration of support as it relates to something outside of the self. A black hole forces the plunge within, therefore the implication of this late Cancer point seeks to locate internal support—support of and for the self. Self-contained support can never cease to exist. Its symbol could be the giving of a hug to oneself. When this function is realized, Cancer lets go of all need for external security. An emotional wholism develops and a completely non-interfering policy regarding others becomes the mode of life.

VELA XR-1 (Vela X, 3U0838-45, PULSAR 0833-45) *2 Leo 43*, Latitude 45S03 Decl. 60S25, RA 128 24 00.

This strong X-ray source is estimated to be between 10,000 and 100,000 years old. It represents the shift between ego and soul knowledge and enhances true knowledge. Negatively, there may be feeble attempts at faking it, hyping the self and other self-seeking proclamations. The irony is the fact that no one can provide emotional confidence for another. It must ultimately come from within. Guilt for being the self must be released. Strength becomes the attribute and suggestion becomes the vehicle of influence.

3U0900-40 *6 Virgo 22*, Latitude 40S22, Decl. 53S56, RA 135 03 45.

This black hole comprises part of an X-ray eclipsing binary star system. The star HD77581 falls slowly into its grasp. It has an eclipse period of 8.95 days with a long X-ray pulse of 284 seconds, the longest pulse width recorded in suspected black holes. Purity, simplicity, and grace show strongly here. Order becomes a Divine state of affairs and is probably where the phrase, "cleanliness is next to Godliness" got its start. Order does suggest freedom from clutter. This black hole demands focus; focusing on an initial thought for its full duration. That duration is 284 seconds (almost 5 minutes) and this seems like a long time to ponder a complete thought. Thoughts held should be seen at the structural level, not within the clutter of informational content. Distraction should not occur and perception of places, individuals, souls and relationships must receive the same graces as ideas and abstractions. A wonderful blend of the logical and the abstract can coexist peacefully here.

VIRGO A (M-87, NGC 4486, 3U1228+12 Super-Galactic Center) *1 Libra 05*, Latitude 12N42, Decl. 14N26, RA 187 01 15.

Undoubtedly this black hole is the most powerful. It was once a star 100 million times the size of our Sun! Thus its magnitude is monumental, phenomenal, overpowering, irresistible, compelling, magnetic and devouring. This black hole contains our galaxy and a series of other galaxies in its grasp. But it contains perhaps the simplest message of all. Create the ultimate relationship. The ultimate relationship results when the ego and spirit align in love to allow unconditional acceptance of the self. Should this realization not occur, the individual tends to go through relationship with one of the partners complaining about feeling consumed, used, depleted, ejected. Those words illustrate the worst side of this huge hole in the heavens. Negatively, people with a planet aspecting this point can be relieved of relationship responsibilities to regenerate love of self. Know, accept, and love the beauty within.

CENTAURUS X-3 (sU1118-60, V799 Centauri) *28 Libra 31*, Latitude 60S19, Decl. 56S19 RA 169 43 45.

The last of the Libra black holes completes an intense Cardinal T-Square of black hole entities. This X-ray eclipsing binary maintains a period of 2.1 days with a corresponding X-ray pulse of 4.8 seconds, both on the short term side. Like its counterpart in Libra, the message of this black hole is simple. It points out the difference between being alone and being lonely. Being alone develops by choice and being lonely results from dependency on emotional sustenance. Being alone is being all one. Libra is an Air sign and subject to Air's occasional coolness and indifference. Unless the person emotionally recharges periodically, the Universe intervenes, removing relationships to ensure this action. Having much to share emotionally, being in a relationship is needed to remain functional, but the understanding of these relationships, both personal and impersonal, must be added.

CENTAURUS A (3U1322-42) *6 Scorpio 56*, Latitude 42S45, Decl. 31S20, RA 200 36 00.

Run silent, deep, and true. This soul seeks to achieve a state of incorruptibility. Nothing can induce falling from grace. What is done is done by conscious choice; the intention is to upgrade and evolve. All answers are found in the stillness within. Serenity is there for the taking; it comprises a part of your innermost being. This black hole realizes, more than the others, that many teachings are not done with words. Choices and actions present the clearest vehicle of enlightenment.

CIRCINUS X-1 (Cir X-1, 3U1516-56) *3 Sagittarius 25*, Latitude 56S59, Decl. 37S15, RA 229 11 00.

Circinus X-1 starts a stellium of Sagittarian black holes. This early degree directs the native to understand information, acquiring complete knowledge in the process. In-depth study leads to the comprehension that knowledge helps to develop a life force of its own. This creates a condition known as consciousness. The individual finds it easier to live life based upon consistency between thought and action. Initially some resistance to new knowledge may occur. Of course, as with all black holes, resistance is futile.

HERCULES X-1 (HZ Her, 3U1653-35) *4 Sagittarius 11*, Latitude 35N36, Decl. 57N33, RA 253 18 00.

This black hole holds some of the more unusual cyclic rhythms. HZ here falls into the category of an X-ray eclipsing binary with an eclipse period of 1.7 days. The duration of the pulse is 1.24 seconds, a short term exposure. An overall 35 day cycle contains a clearly defined "on" and "off" time. The "on" runs 10 to 11 days. Then, mysteriously, the emissions shut down for 25 days before again initiating X-ray transmissions. This point seems to direct the native toward truth based on the use of knowledge; correctness in action, *sans* judgment, as black holes insist, emerges to guide the person. Insights of truth are passed on only when asked, and the person does not fanatically dump beliefs onto others. For 10 days or so the individual receives an influx of information and insight which must be applied to life in the following three plus weeks, before the cycle turns off. A period of great inspiration precedes the interval of cognitive reduction of information. It is a natural *tao*. Forcing insight outside the natural periods only generates mental blocks and lapses in consciousness.

SCO X-1 (3U1617-15) *5 Sagittarius 09*, Latitude 14S32, Decl. 5N43, RA 244 16 45.

Scorpio X-1 seems to be sucking in the tasty stellar morsels of the star V818 Scorpii. The reference to Scorpio and Sagittarius comes from the disparity of degrees between the sidereal and tropical zodiac system. This black hole depicts an awakening to an initial sense of destiny. There seems to be a direction, a plan, a guiding light. There *is* a light at the end of this black hole. Allow yourself to be naturally guided in the way of the Higher Directive without knowing what it means. The experience contains the insight and the knowing. A large scale perspective begins to develop. This perspective makes allowances for multiple points of view, the choice to know one's place and create peace in one's experience.

3U1700-37 *17 Sagittarius 52*, Latitude 37S46, Decl. 14S57, RA 255 06 30.

If your actions and beliefs do not line up, which do you modify? A large question which requires a larger answer looms in the center of this singularity. Consistency of consciousness stands out as the primary consideration. Practicing what you preach is essential. If you experience consciousness—theological, education or philosophical superiority over others—the doctrines prescribed are violated. What value is placed upon belief systems and dogmatic principles? What can be said for open-mindedness and flexibility? This black hole requires that the native be open, objective and perceptive, that all thoughts and dimensions of consciousness be included. Just as soon as a model of belief firms up, this black hole will ensure that it is uprooted. Ongoing growth yields enlightenment. The enlightenment of today soon becomes the kindergarten of consciousness of tomorrow.

GX339-4 *18 Sagittarius 53*, Latitude 48S44, Decl. 25S52, RA 275 06 30.

This Sagittarian point concludes the parade of black holes in the Archer's range. GX339-4 parallels the input of its predecessor 3U1700-37.

Inconsistencies may emerge in the person's doctrine. The value of being wrong presents the ego and consciousness with remarkable growth potential. A tendency to perceive the self as a demigod will not be accepted. Rationalization and justification as a mode of excuse will be obliterated. Cosmic Justice prevails, but interestingly, no real judgment is felt. Most outsiders in a position to judge will recognize similar shortcomings in their own souls and will not cast stones of ridicule. All souls grow through experiences of error. No judgment, no blame results. It just is as it is, and that is truth.

SGR X-4 (SGR 4, NGC 6624, 3U1820-30) *4 Capricorn 26*, Latitude 30S32, Decl. 7S23, RA 275 06 30.

Of all the black hole contenders, Capricorn commands the greatest promise as a comedian. To this point everything is funny or should be funny. What is going on that can be taken seriously? The use of laughter as a healing tool involves the native with connections to this point. Humor becomes the antidote for cynicism and creates freedom from the vices of the material plane, particularly money abuse, drug addiction and sexual decadence. These are conditions of phases certain souls go through, but don't deny. SGR X-4 points out a healthful approach to food, finance and frolic. Responsibility for emotional attachments comes with such pursuits. A concern for natural resources formulates in the heart. In order to prevent an atrophication of spirit, the native must commit to the absolute use of all the inner qualities.

SMC X-1 (SK 160, 3U0115-73) *11 Aquarius 39*. Latitude 73S42, Decl. 66S26, RA 018 49 45.

This hole falls in the Small Megellenic Cloud (SMC). The object is an X-ray elipsing binary with a period of 3.9 days and a pulse duration of 0.7 seconds. Quick processing of information and heightened ability to receive input are the attributes of this black hole. Multitudes of experiences, at maximum intensity and depth, pervade your being. Realization of self comes from objective observation of the self, and this breeds a complete sense of personal wholism known as individuality. Avant garde style and non-responsiveness to social pressure are other components of this degree of Aquarius.

CYGNUS X-1 (3U1956=35) *12 Aquarius 56*, Latitude 35N04, Decl. 54N15, RA 299 05 28.

This hole in the Swan constellation was the first of the black hole family observed and defined. The X-ray eclipsing binary consumes the star HDE226868 and once shone as a star of about eight times the mass of the Sun. The eclipsing period is 5.6 days in length. This point holds most true to the Aquarian nature. It is often misunderstood and perceived almost in polarization of its nature. The individual must live with this, not in a concealing manner, but in an intentional display of self. Nine to fifteen months ahead of the current thinking trends, these people can act as barometers of human involvement. What they feel in advance affects the masses later. The political, economic and social implications suggest monumental altruistic proportions. Anyone connected to this point should be different. The message is: do not compare; above all do not protest. Resistance must run off the consciousness, allowing completely uninhibited reponses.

CYGNUS X-3 (3U2030+40) *27 Aquarius 53*, Latitude 40N47, Decl. 56N55, RA 307 38 15.

Cygnus X-3 completes the circuit of consciousness provoking black holes. This binary performs the X-ray eclipse in a short term cycle, merely 4.8 hours. This system is highly volatile with many catalogued eruptions. It suggests an extensive amount of talent. But until it deploys, it cannot be seen. The individual often feels their talent should be recognized in advance and often waits to be "discovered." It does not happen that way. They must push themselves, allowing for the full force of their talents and abstract ingenuity to manifest. Ahead of their time, a genius-like quality exists, often frustrating them into non-performance. It takes others a while to comprehend what they're all about. These people are some of the most abstract thinkers around and have little difficulty realizing four, five, or even more dimensions once they let go of their mental programming.

CONCLUSION

All of the points presented in this treatise refer to epoch 1950.0. An orb of four degrees can be applied for all aspects to these points. Obviously, a conjunction to a galactic point stands out as most significant. This is followed by squares and oppositions. Other aspects relate, yet in much more subtle ways. The results of trines, sextiles and minor aspects may be much more difficult to locate.

Well, that's that—a whirlwind tour of the galaxy, touching just a few of many documented points in the galactic domain. The precipice has been viewed. Soon the deeper implications of Galactic Astrology will jump out at you with the impact of a quantum leap.

Enjoy the plunge into the excitement of the unknown.

Myrna Lofthus

Myrna Lofthus, author of the book *The Spiritual Approach to Astrology*, graduated magna cum laude from Pacific Lutheran University and was listed in the 1955-1956 edition of *Who's Who Among Students in American Universities and Colleges*. After graduation she moved to the Seattle area. She is married and has a son, a daughter-in-law and two grandsons.

Edgar Cayce's writings originally sparked her interest in astrology. Additional studies on that subject, as well as different religions and philosophies and other metaphysical subjects (e.g. meditation, Tarot, numerology, dream analysis) helped formulate the basis of her spiritual approach to astrology. Myrna has taught self-awareness classes for twelve years. She is also a member of Astara, a Mystery School dedicated to teaching about the esoteric world. She has developed a new theory on the spiritual impact of Halley's Comet and a new interpretation of Nostradamus and related prophecies for current times, which are in unpublished booklets.

THE SPIRITUAL PROGRAMMING
WITHIN A NATAL CHART

Spiritual programming is a plan devised prior to birth for how we will use the astrological energies to try to make certain changes in our thoughts and emotional responses. The plan is implemented by the designated placements of the planets and signs in the natal chart. These placements show the attainments the soul has made in previous incarnations; they indicate the challenges that must be faced this lifetime in order to transform incorrect, but ingrained, thought patterns; and they help restore balance to the soul's karmic record. I have been continually amazed at the intricate interweaving of the planets, aspects, and zodiac signs which result in the creation of experiences that provide opportunities and/or impetus for the soul's growth. Through this programmed plan, the horoscope, we are helped in our efforts to achieve the next level of personal and spiritual growth.

First however, let me explain that spiritual programming involves the concept of reincarnation. This concept is a belief that our soul survives death and experiences many lifetimes. Numerous lifetimes allow our soul to: learn the balance of intellect and emotions, understand its relationship to the universe, and work toward the greater destiny obtainable only when the physical form has been transcended. Each lifetime adds to the soul's storehouse of knowledge and understanding.

Another principle related to reincarnation is the Law of Cause and Effect, also known as the Law of Karma. This law states that we are responsible for all of our actions and thoughts and are compensated for them through benefits and/or adversities. Our actions and emotional responses create a ripple effect, similar to that of a stone when it is cast into water. Eventually, the stone's ripples return to the point of origin. So too, do the ripples of our achievements and mistakes return to us. The soul learns from both beneficial and adverse events. Eventually these events present the opportunities and/or impetus for growth of the soul. This occurs even when there is no awareness of previous lifetimes.

To set the plan in motion, the patterns of the planets, aspects and signs are used. The signs have positive and negative expressions. The expression employed in a given lifetime depends upon free will. If we view life in a negative way, challenges can be perceived as obstacles which are difficult, if not impossible to overcome. You can be helped to understand the purpose behind the challenges through a study of your natal chart's spiritual programming. By perceiving that the positive energies within our chart can be applied to the obstacle/challenge, we may be better able to see it as a blessing that is being implemented in order to repay karma and/ or transform incorrect thought patterns. Furthermore, the use of these positive attributes will set in motion a transformation of the personality or assist one already in progress.

In studying the spiritual programming of a natal chart, seven main areas should be considered:

1. *Zodiac Signs of the Ascendant, Sun and Moon*
2. *Zodiac Signs on the House Cusps*
3. *Intercepted Signs*
4. *Moon's Nodes*
5. *Tone of the Chart*
6. *Aspects*
7. *Grand Trines, Grand Crosses, T-Squares, Yods*

SIGNS OF THE ASCENDANT, SUN AND MOON

The Ascendant (zodiac sign on the 1st House cusp) represents self-awareness, the form of the physical body, approach to life, and social personality. It depicts the way we present ourselves and how we appear to others. It also indicates the positive attributes the soul wishes to utilize in the development of these house affairs. By using the Ascendant's traits we conceal our emotionalism (Moon) and individuality (Sun). This social personality is commonly referred to as the "social mask."

While the Ascendant personifies the face we show to the world when we are in control, the Sun signifies our individuality, ego and our soul. It rules our pride, confidence, vitality, ambition, authority and personal determination. The positive traits of the Sun's sign are the attributes we wish to add to our character in this lifetime.

The Sun is composed of a core and three additional levels of gas. On a symbolic level, the core of the Sun corresponds to our soul. The three additional gas levels represent our individuality (ego) which is comprised of our conscious, subconscious and superconscious minds. The inner gas layer can be likened to the superconscious, the mind in the most direct contact with our soul. The middle layer, called photosphere, parallels the subconscious mind. This name is particularly apropros since we carry so many photographic memories in our minds. The outer layer symbolizes the conscious mind. The thinness of this gas layer serves as a reminder that our conscious mind has considerably less capacity to store knowledge and memories than our other two minds. Most of the energies of this layer, like the conscious mind's energies, are used to interact with the surrounding atmosphere. Occasionally, the Sun gathers a concentration of energy which can be visually seen as prominences, sun spots, and flares. This corresponds to our intense thoughts, actions and emotional responses, ranging from inspired to fanatical.

As the soul's light travels from the core through our three minds, its energy output becomes weakened. This power is decreased by lowered energy frequency as it passes through the substances of these minds, diffusion of light, and bombardment of negative thoughts, actions, and emotions. When we speak of needing to find the inner strength to face a crisis, we are asking for our soul to send a surge of power to sustain and inspire our conscious mind. As it passes through the superconscious mind, it is fortified by knowledge and understanding. The subconscious mind's memories and opinions will either interfere with or further strengthen the light emanating from the soul. When there is too much interference from traumas stored within the subconscious mind, the soul's light is distorted. Then the soul's quest to achieve this lifetime's spiritual programming may be distracted by negative thoughts and emotions, perpetuating a lack of initiative, fanaticism, desire for power, etc. But you can make an effort to control the negative memories and responses of the subconscious mind. By doing so, the soul's light can reach the conscious mind in sufficient force, so that the soul's aspiration for spiritual goals can be achieved.

The Sun symbolizes the individuality (soul), while the Moon represents the personality which encompasses our emotions, habits, moods, impulses, and sensitivities, brought forward from our most recent lifetimes through the help of the positive attributes of the Ascendant and the Sun.

The Moon has no light of its own and needs the Sun to bring it illumination. This reflection of the Sun's energy on the Moon symbolizes our personality's need (Moon) for the individuality (Sun) to bring it to light. The "dark side" of the Moon is the area that cannot be seen from earth. As the Moon rotates on its axis, it continually plunges different terrain into darkness while bringing other areas into the light. This rotation allows the Sun to shine on every part of the Moon's surface over a period of 27.3 days. The Moon's dark side can be compared to the negative emotions and thoughts within our conscious and subconscious minds and the light side to our positive thoughts and emotional responses. Like the Moon, when it is illuminated by the Sun, we use our soul's (Sun) energies to light our way through the labyrinths of our emotions, habits and traits. Thus, the illumination of the Moon by the Sun corresponds to the soul (Sun) illuminating the personality (Moon) in order to highlight both our negative and positive emotional thoughts and responses.

During our lifetime we continually express ourselves by bouncing back and forth between the three energies of the Ascendant, Sun and Moon. When the Sun and Ascendant signs are identical, we place double emphasis on cultivating the positive characteristics of that sign. If the Sun and Moon are in the same sign, we are inundated with both the positive and negative traits of that sign. This causes us through amplification to become aware of both the most and least desired qualities of the sign. With the Ascendant and Moon in the same sign, we automatically use the characteristics of the Moon personality as our social mask. Thus the prominent negative thoughts and emotions of this sign may be difficult to conceal. Whenever all three occupy the same sign, we develop the need to look at and use every possible aspect of that sign by giving ourselves fewer options with which to protect our egos.

In social situations and with people we do not know very well, we usually express the positive traits of the Ascendant sign. On the other hand, when we are in relaxed situations with people we know and trust, our Sun sign's positive characteristics combined with our social personality shine forth. The lunar personality is added when we are with people who create a strong emotional response within us.

When distress is encountered, we may be unable to maintain our social personality (Ascendant's positive attributes), and we can retreat into the negative traits of the Ascendant sign. If we cannot deal with the problem from this point of view, the next line of self-defense is the employment of the positive attributes of the Sun sign. With continued or severe distress, the positive characteristics of the Moon sign personality from past lifetimes are instinctively used. This may be followed by the use of the Moon sign's negative traits and emotional responses. At this point the ego will retreat no further and may either elect to continue the confrontation, using the Moon's negative characteristics or when physically possible depart from the scene.

Both positive and negative attributes of the Ascendant and Sun signs have different energy inputs. This should encourage us to question our diverse reactions to life and may lead to adjustment of the conditioned emotional responses of the Moon's negative characteristics. For example, with Aquarius rising, Sun in Pisces and Moon in Taurus, the social personality is friendly, helpful and tolerant. When with friends, positive Aquarian energies can be expressed along with the Piscean Sun's empathy, adaptability and unassuming disposition. Basically easy to get along with, this person can be stubborn and determined in a quiet manner. However, when under the stress of excess work, subjected to a negative or hostile environment and/or ineffectiveness of the traits of the Ascendant and Sun, they will retreat into conditioned emotional responses from former lifetimes. First, the positive Taurean Moon will be expressed as perseverance. Then, if the stressful situation continues, they may act out negative traits of Taurus such as irritability and stubbornness. Afterwards, they may wonder whatever happened to cause them to act so out of character.

Each lifetime attitude changes occur which affect the

personality. By incorporating the positive energies of the Ascendant, Sun, and Moon signs, we can accelerate and direct these changes. This phase of our spiritual programming can then be developed to its fullest potential, thereby hastening our personal and spiritual growth.

ZODIAC SIGNS ON THE HOUSE CUSPS

The signs on the House cusps indicate the energies we intend to apply to the respective house affairs and thought patterns from recent lifetimes that we desire to overcome. The following is a list of the signs (along with my keywords) and descriptions of what these signs reveal regarding recent past life incorrect attitudes and emotional responses, including examples of how the signs could affect changes in the current life.

ARIES - "Independence:"

In the Aries ruled house there is a need to think and act independently without allowing others to formulate our viewpoints and decisions. In the current life we fluctuate between being independent and once again relying upon someone else's ideas. Wherever Aries falls in the natal chart, it reveals that in recent lifetimes we have molded our actions, opinions, and emotional responses on other people's concepts or been influenced by authoritative figures in the house affairs. *Aries demands that we take a stand for our beliefs and live our lives in any manner which appeals to us.*

If for instance, Aries is on the 12th House cusp, we may have become dependent on others for sustenance (e.g. shelter, health care, spiritual insights). We may have studied under a guru, assuming that by being in the presence of a spiritual being, we too would be spiritually elevated. In a past life or in the interim between lifetimes, we learned that everyone must grow from within in order to attain spiritual development. Therefore, in the current life, we determine to become independent by developing our own spiritual concepts as to the meaning of life. Inner turmoil may be experienced because of wanting to discover the spiritual truths on our own, rather than gaining them under the guidance of a spiritual teacher. By recognizing this, we can take steps to effectively learn to listen to others but to formulate our own viewpoint.

TAURUS - "Productivity:"

Taurus denotes where we want physical results that can be seen, heard, tasted, touched, or smelled. This desire can lead to great productivity, but it may also lead to possessiveness of the people and affairs ruled by the house where Taurus is. In recent lifetimes there was very little incentive to work on the house affairs due to physical restrictions (e.g. lack of skill, a handicap), or others assuming our physical responsibilities against our will. *Taurus calls for us to be productive—to show the visible results of our labors. When we feel productive we begin to value ourselves, thereby gaining a sense of self-worth.*

The physical result of productivity is relatively easy to achieve in most of the houses. In the 10th the career can involve detailed work or a physical creation. Taurus on the 10th House cusp often depicts an excellent businessperson or architect. However, Taurus on the 12th cusp may create a dilemma. How can the physical senses see that life exists after death? Or how can we visually grasp a spiritual truth? In order to see results in 12th House affairs, it becomes imperative that our spiritual senses become tuned in psychically so that we can know the validity of spiritual truths.

GEMINI - "Curiosity:"

Gemini ruled houses are infused with intense curiosity, so that knowledge and experiences concerning them is continually sought. In the current life this curiosity can lead to greater insights but may also lead us to scatter our energies in too many directions without adequate control. Wherever Gemini is in the natal chart, it points out that in recent lifetimes we did not pursue these house affairs knowledgeably because of a lack of interest or the absence of available information and/or experiences. *Gemini stimulates our mind to seek out new knowledge and adventures which help us to grow mentally.*

Gemini on the 6th House cusp shows a need to experience a variety of work situations,—types, projects and/or environments. We need to look for intellectual excitement in the work area because in recent incarnations jobs were dull, routine, or the desired work was unavailable.

CANCER - "Nurturing:"

Wherever Cancer is found on the cusp, the nurturing energies are used to fulfill emotional yearnings in one or more of the house affairs, developing them to a point of strength and emotional satisfaction. In past lifetimes, we did not sufficiently work on the house areas because energies were channeled in other directions, or insecurities (from within or fostered by others) prevented nurturing of these concerns. However, instead of using the energies to develop new concepts, the pressures of life may cause us to divert into more familiar activities. *Cancer calls for us to apply our emotional nature in a constructive, sensitive manner toward a new endeavor.*

Cancer on the 11th House cusp suggests we were hampered by being goal oriented in a past lifetime, or had feelings of inferiority in developing friendships. As our lifetime progressed, loneliness may have surfaced, bringing the recognition of the value of friendship. In this life, we may experience emotional longing to form friendships, which we can nurture and which nurture us. If our overtures for friendship are rejected, we may turn our emotional nurturing to other house affairs such as goals and ambitions.

LEO - "Creativity:"

The Leo ruled house receives the full force of our creative power. (It is a focal point in the chart because the Sun rules Leo. Leonian energies create a need to alter our attitudes and responses to the house affairs. In turn, this becomes the key to changing actions in the other houses.) During recent lifetimes, obstacles to full participation in the Leo ruled house affairs may have been created due to fear of mental and emotional harassment, attitudes of superiority concerning the house affairs, or domination by others. Leo demands our very best creative efforts. Thus it provides the motivation to commit to these house affairs. If we do not respond, we may ignore the chance to interact in one or more of the house affairs even though we feel a sense of responsibility to them. *Leo forces us to recognize ourself and others as unique individuals with unique talents that should be used to enhance life.*

For example, Leo on the 7th cusp reveals that in recent lifetimes we may have had very little interaction with others in cooperative relationships because of a blockage, possibly due to the feeling of being dominated by others, or through our own desire to prevent mental and emotional harassment. We may have married, but close communication with the partner, as well as others, could have been limited. Because of Leo's need to interact with others, its greatest asset in the current life is the ability to overcome the barriers from the past.

VIRGO - "Analysis:"

The Virgo ruled house calls for us to analyze our handling of its activities. Unfortunately, all too often the analysis becomes criticism, directed either at ourselves or at the people ruled by the house. In recent lifetimes we may have had an aloof, detached attitude regarding these affairs because we used indifference as a form of self-protection after experiencing emotional pain when participating, or we expected others to take care of our needs. *Virgo calls for us to use analytical reasoning toward life's experiences and crises (both personal and with others) so that we may be better able to handle and understand them.*

Virgo on the 2nd House suggests an analytical attitude concerning the development of personal resources (money, possession, hidden talents, sense of self-worth). This could be a method of counteracting past desires and expectations of being taken care of by others. Or we may have adopted an emotionally detached attitude because our values and talents had been severely criticized. Virgo here can be helpful because it stimulates manual and mental dexterity which can aid in the development and obtainment of personal resources.

LIBRA - "Balance:"

The Libra ruled house reveals that thought patterns from recent lifetimes have been out of balance. The reasons are mental attitudes were extreme, being too weak or too aggressive, or we allowed others to intimidate us. This lifetime we need to achieve balance in our attitudes and emotional responses relating to the persons and affairs indicated by the house. The need to readjust attitudes or to be resolute, when necessary, becomes imperative. This time we may find ourselves trying so hard to achieve mental and emotional balance that we either end up sitting on the fence, incapable of making a decision, or we find ourselves displaying mental and/or emotional extremes. *Libra reveals our need to re-evaluate our personal viewpoints, as well as the other person's, before making a decision.*

With Libra on the 3rd House cusp the need is to be more resolute so situations which arise involving relatives and neighbors will force us to take a stand, even if it is contrary to the position they want us to take. The need is to learn to adjust, so we find that our extreme expectations of these people will be challenged. These confrontations may provide an opportunity to re-evaluate our viewpoints or risk losing contact with the people involved.

SCORPIO - "Involvement:"

Scorpio's vibrations bring a strong desire to concentrate energy toward only one house concern at a time, sometimes to the exclusion of all else, since Scorpio has difficulty maintaining an intensity of interest in more than one matter simultaneously. Because of this deep involvement, Scorpio's house placement indicates that in recent lifetimes there was a lack of personal commitment resulting in an inability to sustain the motivation and concentration needed to do the work, or a physical restraint by others. *Scorpio reveals our need to become deeply committed to a chosen endeavor.*

With Scorpio on the 9th House, we may feel an inner drive to achieve some form of higher education. Upon obtaining a degree, Scorpio energy may then be directed into traveling or a religious philosophy (other 9th House affairs). Regardless of the activity chosen, there is intense dedication to it. In recent lifetimes, or in the interims between, an interest may have been shown in these affairs and a committment made to concentrate energy toward future exploration.

SAGITTARIUS - "Expansion:"

There may be a tremendous urge this lifetime to expand through exploration and understanding of all the affairs ruled by the Sagittarian house. In recent lifetimes we felt restricted from totally experiencing these house activities because of personal prejudices, restraints inflicted by others' prejudices, or limited knowledge. In the current life, there is a desire for freedom to formulate personal viewpoints and ideas regarding the house affairs, through physical and mental exploration and interaction with the people ruled by the house. This could also lead to premature abandonment of interaction with house activities or people, if the desire for freedom is not controlled. *Sagittarius urges us to keep an open mind in order to allow inward and outward expansion through greater understanding.*

With Sagittarius on the 5th House, in a recent lifetime we may have been unable to explore our creative endeavors or to realize achievements through sporting events. This may have been due to being physically restricted because of other's prejudices, creating feelings of having missed out on an area of life that could have been fulfilling. In this life there is an urge to physically or vicariously investigate those house affairs as much as possible. Eventually, these creative endeavors and sports participation are narrowed down to a favorite few. These help in gaining a better understanding of our own capabilities and uniqueness as individuals and in realizing an inner fulfillment through participation with others.

CAPRICORN - "Discernment:"

Capricorn requires us to exercise discernment regarding its house affairs. In this life we may not perceive the overall picture because of the drive to excel, enmeshing us in the small details. We may feel compelled to improve and renovate the ideas we have brought forward from recent past lives because of incomplete evaluation and comprehension of the house affairs, or undeserved admiration and recognition from others, which was accepted as truth. This last reason can cause frustration and grief this lifetime if other people do not appreciate our efforts in these affairs. Recognition is not denied, but may come when least expected. The drive to improve and renovate these house activities can result in a feeling of being burdened, even though this may not be true. *Capricorn reminds us that we must work hard to achieve something for ourselves, regardless of the approval or lack of approval from others.*

With Capricorn on the 1st House cusp, we might yearn for recognition and praise for our life style, physical body, personal appearance, and social personality. In recent lives we may have been given compliments and admiration, receiving the impression that outer appearances rather than inner qualities were the true measure of identity. Now it is easy for us to become too involved in specific methods of improving the physical appearance of the body as opposed to the development of self-awareness.

AQUARIUS - "Reform:"

Aquarius demands that we reform our thought patterns and emotional responses regarding the house affairs where Aquarius is. Therefore sudden changes occur in order to break down any rigid ideas and viewpoints from past lifetimes. These changes can be constructive or destructive, depending upon how we view them. In recent lifetimes rigid thought patterns and emotional responses were created because of justification of actions and thoughts in order to avoid change, fanatical attitudes, or intellectual persuasion from others to adopt their narrow-minded concepts. *Aquarius asks us to determine what our goals and ambitions are and what incorrect attitudes and emotional responses we are willing to reform to achieve these.*

If Aquarius is on the 4th House cusp, we may have incarnated with preconceived ideas as to what would provide us and others with emotional security. In recent lifetimes the lack of emotional well-being was blamed on others in the home—the mother and/or because of the inferior quality of the home and its furnishings. This lifetime brings an emotional need for a close family unit or special type of home. If we cling to these assumptions, Aquarian energies will bring unexpected events in order to shock us out of them, such as damage to the home and its furnishings or family members being forced, by circumstances, to move away.

PISCES - "Faith:"

In the Pisces ruled house having faith in the self and our inner guidance is essential, since we experience emotional ups and downs and are easily swayed by other peoples' emotional appeals. Relying upon our intuitive abilities helps us perceive the motivations of others and gives trust in our ability to make the right decisions. In recent lifetimes we may have felt confusion regarding the appropriate attitudes and responses to be used toward these house affairs because of disillusionment, feelings of ill-use, or emotional persuasions of others, e.g. "If you loved me, you would . . . " This life, there may be vacillation in the manner we handle the house affairs and/or the people ruled by the house. *Pisces calls for us to develop our intuitive nature so that the karmic lessons and other experiences we attract can be better understood.*

Pisces on the 2nd House cusp, suggests having incarnated with contradictory viewpoints concerning how much each person should be required to contribute of their own personal resources (money, possessions, hidden talents, sense of self-worth) in a cooperative relationship. In recent incarnations we may have been inconsistent in our ideas and actions, possibly due to disillusionments or vulnerability to emotional appeals. Using Pisces' positive traits in these house affairs can unlock an intuitive knowing of how much of our personal resources we need to contribute.

INTERCEPTED SIGNS

An intercepted sign is one without a house cusp. It is contained within the house and the affairs relating to this sign may result in inner tension due to the inability to effectively utilize its energies. The interception of a sign indicates that this is the soul's second attempt to accomplish specific mental, physical, and emotional changes in those house affairs. By "locking up" the intercepted sign's energies, the positive attributes of the sign on the house cusp can be applied to the house affairs so that we can receive new insights regarding the intercepted sign's incorrect thoughts and emotional responses. These insights assist in the development of the intercepted sign's positive traits.

Help in revising the incorrect concepts, habits and actions of the intercepted sign is its utilization in the polar opposite house. It is natural for the energies of a sign on a house cusp to "leak through" to the opposite house. Even though intercepting a sign restricts the use of its power, its influence will still leak through to the opposite house. When the intercepted sign's incorrect attitudes fail to achieve the desired results and reactions in the opposing house affairs, we may be motivated to re-examine our incorrect thoughts and emotions. Use of new positive attitudes in this house becomes a key to unlocking the intercepted sign's positive use in its own house. The sign on the opposite house cusp is another key because this sign has different energies; it can help in dislodging incorrect mental and emotional responses. Thus an intercepted sign's forces can be unlocked by using the positive attributes of the sign on its house cusp, expressing the intercepted sign's energies (negative, then positive) in the affairs of its polar opposite house, or utilizing the positive attributes of the sign on the opposite house cusp.

Occasionally, two signs will be intercepted within the same house, indicating the possibility that one of these signs was intercepted in this same house in a previous incarnation. However, the needed attitude changes were not sufficiently made. This created the necessity of intercepting an additional sign, either the preceeding or succeeding one, for increased tension.

Pisces intercepted in the 1st House reveals the possibility of having incarnated with a hypersensitive and pessimistic approach to life. (Note: This is a different expression than having Pisces rising, which indicates the individual has incarnated with a confused attitude about life and 1st House affairs.) In order to control the Piscean hypersensitive approach to life, Aquarius on the Ascendant provides the person with an opportunity to reform this pattern. The humanitarian instincts and fixed quality inherent in Aquarius helps to overcome the Piscean withdrawal and vacillation tendencies. Unexpected and unusual events are also drawn into the life. These occurrences encourage a review of the personality and life style so that pessimism and supersensitivity can be conquered. By interacting in the opposite house (marriage, partnerships, other cooperative relationships), this individual could have numerous cooperative experiences with others whose conditioned responses of withdrawal or vacillation cause more difficulties. Since the experiences repeat, eventually the message is received that change is necessary. This change could break the destructive cycle of pessimistic and supersensitive attitudes. Additional help comes from the positive energies of Leo (optimism, affection, cheerfulness) on the 7th House cusp. Any new thoughts and emotional responses acquired can then be applied in the intercepted sign's own house affairs.

When Pisces is intercepted in the 1st House, its opposite sign, Virgo is intercepted in the 7th House. Virgo's interception indicates that the person may have incarnated with a skeptical attitude about their ability to achieve mental and emotional fulfillment in marriage, partnership and in other cooperative relationships. This is a result of lifetimes where too much emotional chaos or too many expectations of being taken care of by others was experienced. Thus, as a defense mechanism, the ego protected itself by adopting a suspicious attitude.

This is a difficult pattern to overcome. However, Leo

on the 7th cusp fosters a need to achieve something of value in these affairs. Leo's gregariousness and optimism help to counteract both Virgo's skepticism and Pisces' pessimism. (Note: Virgo on the 7th cusp indicates an incarnation with an analytical, detached, sometimes critical attitude. This is a different energy than skepticism. Virgo's analyzing ability on a house cusp assists in objectively viewing the house affairs.) The application of Virgo energy in the opposite house (self-awareness, physical body, approach to life) provides many occasions where a skeptical, aloof attitude can cause rejection by others. In turn, this rejection may aid the individual in becoming less cynical. Aquarius' positive power on the opposing house cusp brings additional challenges to Virgo's cynical attitude through friendliness and resourcefulness.

MOON'S NODES

The Nodes of the Moon are points created when the Moon's orbit intersects Earth's ecliptical plane (orbital pathway around the Sun). The North, or ascending Node (☊) is the point where the Moon intercepts the Earth's orbital pathway as it travels upwards from the Earth's southern hemisphere to its northern hemisphere. The South of descending Node (☋) is the point where the Moon intercepts the Earth's orbital pathway on its way down from Earth's northern hemisphere to the southern hemisphere. These intersecting lines are called the "Nodal Axes." The reflections of these Nodal Axes on the zodiac belt at the time of birth indicate the degree and minute of the natal North and South Nodes.

Just as gravity draws things downward, the South Node is the realm where we become enmeshed in activities because they are comfortable. Its house is where we have experienced karmic programming. These events may dispel our desire to maintain the same familiar routines in order that our mental and emotional energies might be channeled into North Node house affairs. The North Nodal house points out where we can make great strides in spiritual growth and where expansion of self can occur if enough mental, physical and emotional efforts are given to those house affairs. The North Node challenges us to gain spiritual insights. This requires work and resolution, but will eventually be rewarded by the North Node's positive sign characteristics flowing into all the other houses.

The Moon, representing emotional responses and habits, parallels the soul's descent into matter (physical form) and its longing to return to the celestial realms. This can be seen in the Moon's descent to the South Node (our physical nature/conditioned responses) and its ascension to the North Node (spiritual aspirations/new responses). A correlation can also be seen in this movement between hemispheres and the interaction of the Nodes in the chart. To arrive at a newer and greater vista, we must ascend, although climbing is hard work. It is less difficult to descend (lowering of the soul's vibratory frequency into physical form) or to remain with the physical. So to propel us into making the effort to climb toward spiritual growth (North Node) we must receive power and encouragement from the inner spirit. This in turn overcomes the urge to take the easier path with activities more familiar and easily achieved (South Node).

South Node

The South Nodal house designates the affairs where we have repeatedly responded in the same manner. We have walked this path so many times it has become a rut. Our limiting and ingrained emotional responses prevent the advancement of both personal and spiritual growth. Thus stress, setbacks and frustrations are experienced as we try to interact in these affairs in a familiar conditioned manner.

North Node

The North Node house is where we can gain insights to help adjust the conditioned and limiting responses and attitudes of the South Nodal house. By interacting in the North Node's house affairs, the mental and emotional energies can find a new direction and focus.

As we begin applying ourselves to the North Node house affairs, we experience strong feelings of insecurity. However, if we make the attempt, divine guidance is given. This will provide the inspiration needed to continue working on those house affairs regardless of the physical, emotional or mental stresses encountered. As each obstacle is overcome, we find a sense of purpose and a new approach to life, culminating in a deep fascination for these house affairs. The knowledge and insights gained through this house and sign foster the adoption of new approaches to the South Nodal house affairs.

Zodiac Signs of the Nodes

The signs the Nodes are placed in reveal attributes that require attention. Where the North Node is, the positive qualities need to be cultivated so that they can help in achieving growth in those house areas.

In previous lifetimes, in the South Node house, we used the positive characteristics of the South Node's sign. However in this life we are using these traits to create negative emotional responses because of the reactions of people ruled by the house. This in turn may cause us to express the negative characteristics of the South Node's sign. For example, with the South Node in Cancer in the 6th House, we may be industrious and sympathetic. But we, too often, do too much for others in the form of service, tending to stifle these people with attention. If a protest is made, we could feel rejected, giving rise to Cancer's negative expressions of depression and self-pity.

Aspects of Planets to Nodes

Trines and conjunctions (harmonious aspects) assist the energy of the Node while oppositions and squares (disharmonious aspects) indicate internal and external struggles. The following four aspects have the most effect on the Nodes.

Planets Trine the Nodes:

Planets that trine the Nodes seem to encourage and support the development and change in the Nodal house affairs. Both the energy and house affairs of the trining planets can be used to assist growth.

Planets Conjunct the South Node/Opposition the North Node:

Planets conjunct the South Node indicate that we have programmed the use of knowledge and talents from previous incarnations involving these planetary energies. Because this planet opposes the North Node, we must first gain insight through the affairs of the North Node house. Only then will the knowledge and talents of the planet be allowed to flow freely from the memory banks of the subconscious.

Planets Conjunct the North Node/Opposition the South Node:

Planets conjuncting the North Node enhance and unite their energies with those of the North Node in order to inspire or force us to work in the house affairs of the North Node. In order to set this in motion the opposition to the South Node activates resistance and crises from other people, causing internal and external stress. These people block our efforts to return to familiar attitudes regarding the South Node house affairs, thus forcing new and different experiences in the North Node house.

Planets Square the Nodes:

Planets squaring the Nodes indicate that we experience internal conflict in the Nodal and planet houses. In a previous incarnation some of the negative expressions of the squaring planet were used in the affairs of these houses. The need is to establish a balance between the house areas, planetary power, and the Nodes.

Aspects of Nodes to Other People's Planets:

When the Nodes form major aspects (trine, conjunction, opposition, square) to another person's planets, it indicates close karmic ties. When the South Node is harmoniously aspected, there is a drawing together for a mutually beneficial relationship because of having created good karma together in former lifetimes. Harmonious connections to the North Node indicate that the North Node person's ideas and viewpoints can be spiritually beneficial because they challenge the other person's attitudes and responses. The energy flows from the North Node individual to the person with the aspected planet; there is no perceivable effect on the North Node person.

Disharmonious connections to the South Node point out karmic difficulties to be ovecome with the South Node person owing an obligation to the other person. A disharmonious North Node contact suggests there may be a rejection of the North Node individual's ideas and viewpoints by the other person.

TONE OF THE CHART

The tone of the chart is the strongest single vibration in the horoscope since it represents the predominant element and quality. It is a compilation of the character traits and emotional responses being used in the current lifetime and affects all of the houses.

To determine the tone of the chart, count the planets in each quality and element. If there are several qualities with the same number of planets, add the Sun's quality a second time. If this has not broken the tie, add the Moon's quality again. If needed, add the quality of the Ascendant. However do not use the Moon or Ascendant if the Sun's quality breaks the tie. This same procedure is used in the case of an element tie.

Example:

Qualities			Elements		
Cardinal	= 4	Planets	Fire	= 2	Planets
Fixed	= 4	Planets	Earth	= 3	Planets
Mutable	= 2	Planets	Air	= 3	Planets
			Water	= 2	Planets

Sun in Aries
Moon in Cancer
Ascendant in Libra

To break the quality tie, the Sun in Aries (Cardinal) will promote the Cardinal Quality to 5. Thus the majority quality is Cardinal.

To break the element tie, the Sun in Aries (Fire) will promote the Fire Element to 3. There is now a three-way tie with Fire, Earth,and Air. By using the Moon in Cancer (Water) the Water element is 3. Now we have a four-way tie. By using the Ascendant in Libra (Air) the four-way tie is broken through the emphasis of the Air Element to 4. Thus the majority element is Air.

Since the quality is Cardinal and the Element is Air, the tone of the chart is Libra.

ASPECTS

If two planets are a designated number of degrees apart, it is called an aspect. This distance between planets as they "reflect" on the 360 degree zodiac belt, can be extremely important. Aspects create harmonious or inharmonious energies that aid us in accomplishing specific changes in emotional responses and attitudes. These aspect energies affect the planets, signs and houses involved.

Planets in aspect create an area of intense energy similar to the vortex which is formed by crossing two of Earth's meridian lines. Aspects set up a whirlwind of power. Depending on the type of aspect, this power can be difficult to control (inharmonious) or easily incorporated into the life (harmonious). Both reveal areas where time and attention should be focused.

In searching for the spiritual programming of a chart, examine only the major aspects. The harmonious aspects are: 1) conjunction of compatible planets such as Venus and the Moon, 2) sextile, 3) trine. The inharmonious aspects are: 1) conjunction of incompatible planets such as Mars and Neptune, 2) square, 3) inconjunct (quincunx), 4) opposition, 5) nonagen. Aspect orb is eight degrees except the nonagen (two degrees), the inconjunct (four degrees) and the sextile (six degrees). The closer the aspect is to the exact degree, the stronger the planetary effect of the combined energies.

Harmonious Aspects

Conjunction	0° - Power, Emphasis. Intensifies planetary energies.
Sextile	60° - Opportunity to productively use the energy of the planets.
Trine	120° - Ease, Harmony. Maximum benefit with minimum effort.

Inharmonious Aspects:

Conjunction	0° - Power, Emphasis. Intensifies planetary energies.
Square	90° - Obstacles, Stress. Internal conflict involving events and personal attitudes.
Inconjunct	150° - Discord, Stress. Adjustment needed.

Inharmonious Aspects, cont'd:

Opposition	180° - Awareness. Stress. Internal and external conflict involving other people. Need to compromise.
Nonagen	40° - Restriction. Self-imposed bondage.

Harmonious aspects indicate that many positive energies have been acknowledged by the consciousness. These planetary energies flow easily into and from your physical, mental, emotional and spiritual bodies.

Inharmonious aspects are the result of incorrect thought patterns and emotional responses from past lifetimes which activated the negative use of the planetary power. These aspects can be compared to the force of a hurricane, within which can be found a center of peace and harmony—"the eye." By searching for the "eye," you can achieve peace and harmony with the planetary and house affairs involved.

PAST LIFE MESSAGES OF PLANETARY ASPECTS

CONJUNCTION

The past life message of the conjunction depends on whether the planets have complementary energies. If compatible, in recent lifetimes the positive qualities were manifested. This lifetime the energies have been brought together in order to: 1) enhance each other's positive qualities, 2) unite their power. Goals can be achieved in the house involved.

Incompatible conjunctions: 1) help control and rechannel misused energies from past lifetimes, 2) provoke a review of interactions with house affairs and people ruled by the house. In former incarnations the planets may or may not have been adversely aspected.

SEXTILE

A sextile indicates that we have expressed many positive qualities of the planets. The sextiled planets' positive attributes are intensified. In our current life the sextile provides an opportunity to productively achieve some of the chart's programmed goals. However, to gain their full benefit we must employ time and effort in developing their maximum potential.

TRINE

Most of the positive qualities of the two trining planets were expressed in previous incarnations. Because of this, their energies are ingrained and operate on a subconscious level with some of their attributes and power flowing into your conscious mind. When planets are in trine their positive traits are heightened. We can develop the trine's full potential with a little time and effort. Basically trines represent and reward us for our disciplined efforts in recent incarnations.

SQUARE

In recent incarnations we resisted using the positive energy of the planets involved in the square because of: 1) apathy, 2) fear, 3) arrogance, 4) rebellion. Squares generate internal conflict involving events as well as our personal attitudes. Essentially we are locked "into a fight" with ourself as to how to express these planets. The conflict represents lessons that we have failed to learn in the past and now must face again.

INCONJUNCT (QUINCUNX)

Inconjuncts indicate that in recent lifetimes we made only partial adjustments in our thoughts, actions and emo-tions concerning the planets and houses they occupy. Complete adjustments are needed now to justify our reactions and responses in the houses and with the planets involved.

OPPOSITION

Opposing planets reveal that in recent incarnations we reacted in a contradictory manner. We used first the positive energies and then expressed the same energies negatively. In our current life, actions and desires that seemingly oppose us (real or imagined) create internal and external conflict involving other people. Others' character traits mirror the recent variety of ways we have used the two planets. This opposition causes a *subconscious* fear that the other person's attitudes and action may still be within us. The challenges we face are: 1) to recognize ourself in others, 2) to learn how to interact cooperatively with "challenging" people, compromising when necessary.

NONAGEN

A nonagen indicates that we feel temporary restriction in being able to fully use the energies of the house affairs where the planets are posited. Their full powers are withheld until later in life when, hopefully, maturity will help in correctly coping with: 1) karmic experiences relating to the house and planetary affairs, 2) the use of their energies. This self-imposed bondage usually manifests from thirty-eight to forty-two years of age, depending on the number of degrees between the planets. With a concerted effort toward soul growth, it is possible to release the nonagen earlier in life.

GRAND TRINES, GRAND CROSSES, T-SQUARES AND YODS

Grand Trines - Balance

A Grand Trine consists of three planets in mutually trining aspects. In most cases each planet will be in a different sign of the same Element (Fire, Earth, Air or Water). The majority Element will determine its type. Occasionally one of the planets will be in a different Element. This occurs only when planets are in very early or very late degrees of a sign.

If the odd planet is in the Element before the other two (i.e. one planet Water, two planets Fire) it acts as a "pusher" in motivating the use of the Grand Trine energies. When the odd planet is in the Element after the other two planets (i.e. one planet Earth and two planets Fire) it acts as an "outlet" for the use of the Grand Trine energies.

For example, a Grand Trine with planets at 4 degrees Aries and 2 degrees Sagittarius (Fire), with the "pusher" planet at 27 degrees Cancer, may indicate an entertainer (Aries) who would like to do something on a universal level (Sagittarius) with their talents. Cancer's need to nurture may then "push" us to find a way to feed the hungry (Water) through action (Fire) leading to benefits such as the "Live-Aid" for African Famine relief.

An example of an "outlet" Grand Trine is a planet at 28 degrees Taurus, one at 29 degrees Capricorn and a planet at 1 degree Libra. This indicates we may use our productive energies (Earth) to share through communication (Air). We could be drawn to the Peace Corps where our ability for detail work (Taurus) and organization (Capricorn) could be shared through teaching (Libra).

A Grand Trine indicates that disciplined efforts were initiated in previous incarnations concerning the planets and the houses occupied. In our current life, those efforts are rewarded by easy access to their combined planetary energies. Because the positive expression was absorbed on a subconscious level, then on a superconscious level, we are now easily able to draw this energy to our conscious mind. (Note: The energy of an ordinary trine is ingrained and operates from the subconscious only.) This creates a resistance to stress and confusion involving the house affairs of the planets. The traits of the three planets and their Elements can be further developed if we put time and effort into perfecting their potential. Without motivation from the conscious mind, a Grand Trine's potential and capabilities will never be fully realized.

When all three planets are in the same Element in the Grand Trine, the flow is at its highest expression and the Element represented shows the "predominant characteristic." Each Element sign has several positive attributes in common, the most common being the Grand Trine's "gifts." We will find that these are very effective tools for handling the Grand Trine's house affairs because they: 1) flow freely and easily from the subconscious and superconscious, 2) are inherent within the Element and/or in the signs, 3) indicate their conscientious development through disciplined efforts in recent incarnations.

When we have earned a Grand Trine, we can decide in which lifetime to activate it in order to achieve its greatest potential. A Grand Trine will not be recreated in the next incarnation if we have achieved its maximum potential, or misused its energies.

Grand Fire Trine: Active Energy

A Grand Fire Trine influences the abstract (theoretical) mind of the mental body, ruled by the superconscious. As a result the trine's energies flow through and operate from this area. Its predominant characteristic is intuition. Its gifts are enthusiasm and initiative. In order to gain understanding and insights, situations in all areas of life are pulled apart (mentally and/or physically) for closer examination. The Grand Fire Trine gives the willingness and motivation to examine, analyze and instinctively understand the individual parts of a situation and its relationship to the whole.

Grand Fire Trine Example
2nd House = Personal Resources (money, possessions, hidden talents, sense of self-worth)

6th House   = Work, Service, Health
10th House = Professional Career, Personal Achieve-
              ments

Dormant skills can be intuitively drawn from talents (2nd house) developed in former lifetimes, giving the ability to advance in work, career and business (6th and 10th houses). These capabilities are valuable assets. We can radiate enthusiasm and initiative in the work environment and develop our ability to perform and understand each task involved in creating a final product.

Grand Earth Trine: Productive Energy

A Grand Earth Trine influences the physical body by giving it the power to control and command the planetary and house energies represented. This results in high level physical drive. Its predominant characteristic is perception. The gifts are consistency and endurance. It gives the ability to develop physical techniques which are efficient, profitable and progressive.

Grand Earth Trine Example

1st House   = Self-Awareness, Physical Body, Approach
               to Life
6th House   = Work, Service, Health
10th House = Professional Career, Personal Achievements

Endurance and productivity are experienced toward life (1st house) and work (6th and 10th houses). The individual could devise efficient physical techniques that assist in the career (6th and 10th houses) and in the maintenance of their physical body's health (1st and 6th houses). These techniques can profit them through physical health, money, career advancements and/ or public acclaim.

Grand Air Trine: Mental Energy

This trine influences the concrete (reasoning) mind ruled by the conscious mind. We experience an easy flow through and operation from this area. Genius capabilities can be stimulated in the house affairs of the planets involved. The gifts of this Grand Trine are insight and vision. Its predominant characteristic is intelligence. Through visionary insights we are able to formulate many inspired ideas and projects. We can bring diversified components together in order to establish a harmonious unity. The Grand Air Trine gives the ability to unify divergent ideas and/or bring people together in order to create a harmonious oneness.

Grand Air Trine Example
5th House = Creative Self-Expression (children of body and mind)
9th House = Higher Education, Abstract Thoughts
12th House = Self-Undoing, Ultimate Understanding

Insights and visions can flow from the concrete (reasoning) mind toward creative endeavors (5th house), theoretical studies (9th house) and the mysteries of life (12th house). We are able to conceive of and gather creative ideas and/or bring people together harmoniously. We may be interested in and willing to investigate and try various suggestions, plans or themes in order to achieve unification.

Grand Water Trine: Psychic Energy

This Grand Trine influences the astral body, attuning it to emotional and environmental vibrations. The trine's energies flow through and operate from this body. Note: The astral body comprises the force field of our emotional substance—our lower desires and our higher aspirations. It is one of the seven bodies pertaining to three dimensional life. In appearance it is similar to the physical body but of a higher vibratory frequency. During sleep or astral projection meditations, this body departs the physical form in order to operate on the astral plane and gather pranic energy for the etheric body (the physical body's double). The interpenetration of the astral body with the physical/etheric bodies allows us to register sensation and emotion.

It remains connected to the physical body by means of a silver cord, which detaches upon death. When this occurs, the consciousness is totally transferred to the astral body.

The Grand Water Trine's predominant characteristic is mysticism. The gifts are sensitivity and flexibility of mind. It often bestows the ability to sense psychic impressions and to be creative in handling emotional crises.

Grand Water Trine Example

1st House = Self-Awareness, Physical Body, Approach to Life

6th House = Work, Service, Health

9th House = Higher Education, Abstract Thoughts

Psychic impressions can be transmitted from the astral body to the physical body (1st house) giving the ability to understand (9th house) and work (6th house) with the emanations coming from the places, people and objects in our lives. We are able to keep an open mind regarding different approaches to life (1st), working conditions (6th) and theoretical philosophies (9th).

Grand Crosses - Challenge

A Grand Cross is comprised of four planets, forming two oppositions and two squares. Tension and stress can be the motivating energies needed to break free from incorrect, but ingrained, thought patterns and emotional responses.

The type of Grand Cross is determined by the predominant quality (Mutable, Cardinal or Fixed). Usually the four planets are in the same quality, but occasionally one or two may be in a different quality. When that happens there is an emphasis involving the house affairs of the planets in the odd quality. As with the empty leg of a T-Square, we must expend extra time and effort on these house affairs in order to relieve the stress.

When two planets are in a different quality, we should first direct our power toward the initiating energies (Cardinal planets) and then to the adapting energies (Mutable planets). When Fixed planets are involved, the emphasis must be focused on the Mutable planets to stimulate flexibility or on the Cardinal planets to instigate activity, rather than on the rigidity of the Fixed planets.

Intense inner and outer conflict is created by a Grand Cross. With this configuration, we may often feel that our current life events are out of control and that the resulting turmoil is caused by others. In previous lifetimes we may have continually blamed others for our own difficulties, being unable to recognize or accept that we alone were and are responsible for our actions and experiences, both good and bad. The house affairs and planets have been mishandled and misunderstood so drastic action must be taken to dislodge conditioned and incorrect attitudes and emotional responses. The only way to gain peace of mind and secure a release from this cycle is by: 1) understanding the reason for the squares and oppositions, 2) examining our interaction with others relating to the houses involved, 3) transforming negative thought patterns and conditioned responses in the house areas, 4) recognizing that emotional security is achieved by changing the self, not others, 5) expressing unconditional love toward the house affairs and representative individuals.

If changes are not programmed, a Grand Cross in the next incarnation can become a more stressful configuration. When we fail to achieve the programmed changes, the intensified progression of stress continues as long as necessary and proceeds from Mutable to Cardinal to Fixed Grand Crosses, followed by Mutable, Cardinal and Fixed T-Squares. Sometimes a Cardinal Grand Cross and a Cardinal T-Square are repeated in the subsequent incarnation in order to accomplish the desired programmed action. There are also exceptions when a Mutable or Cardinal Grand Cross may become a Mutable T-Square, skipping the rest of the Grand Cross phases.

Mutable Grand Cross:

Blockage: Too changeable a nature

Outlet for Stress: Being decisive while still remaining adaptable

A Mutable Grand Cross is a warning by the soul to the conscious mind that decisiveness must be developed regarding the planets and house indicated. We have become too changeable with a desire to lean on others and to blame them for our difficulties. In a previous life, we may have felt controlled by outside conditions or people. This lifetime we may be prone to worries and negativity with a tendency to justify our thoughts and reactions. We must try to over come our vacillation by acting more decisively, thus lessening our stress.

The Mutable signs are associated with the arms, lungs, hips, intestines and feet. They suggest "movement" either of the extremities or of the digestive system in the body. A Mutable Grand Cross indicates there has been too much "movement" without adequate direction or personal control. It is imperative that we modify the "movements" of mind, body and emotions in order to correct past conditioned responses and attitudes regarding the house and planet areas involved.

If we continue to find it difficult to overcome our changeability, a Cardinal Grand Cross will be programmed for the subsequent incarnation. If we become too controlling, a Fixed Grand Cross may be instigated in our next life in order to forstall this tendency. A Mutable Grand Cross can be transcended when we stop justifying our actions and thoughts and recognize that we alone are responsible for the realities of our life.

Mutable Grand Cross Example

2nd House = Personal Resources (money, possessions, hidden talents, sense of self-worth)

5th House = Creative Self-Expression (children of the body and mind)

8th House = Joint Resources (sharing of personal resources in cooperative relationships),
Support from others
11th House = Friends, Goals

With a Mutable Cross in these houses, we must be
decisive in interacting in these areas. We may feel torn between the demands of our "children" (5th), of sharing in
cooperative relationships (8th), friends (11th) and our own
personal resources (2nd). You may tend to blame your
worries and stress on the behavior of others as well as your
own lack of personal resources.

Cardinal Grand Cross:
Blockage: Lack discipline of thoughts, action and
emotional responses
Outlet for Stress: Activity of a physical, emotional
and/or intellectual level

This Cross shows that decisiveness and the ability to
stop justifying responses were not successfully achieved in
the last reincarnation. It is necessary to apply more discipline in controlling incorrect actions relating to the planets
and houses involved.

The Cardinal signs are associated with the brain, stomach,
kidneys and gall bladder. All of these organs deal with digestion of thoughts, food and liquids. Digestion infers the necessity
for rethinking, mulling over and processing. By properly programming a Cardinal Grand Cross, the action initiating energies are highlighted. This creates experiences allowing for
rethinking conditioned responses. Situations challenge and
force us to function in crises. These varied experiences present opportunities to: 1) review our handling of previous
experiences, 2) observe other people's reactions to crises,
3) establish new viewpoints based on our own values.

It may be necessary to repeat this cycle in a subsequent
life when sufficient discipline has not been applied. But if
too much discipline/control is manifested, the cross pro-

gresses to the Fixed mode. A Cardinal Grand Cross can be transcended when we have transformed our incorrect reactions into constructive activity regarding the house affairs affected.

Cardinal Grand Cross Example

2nd House = Personal Resources (money, possessions, hidden talents, sense of self-worth)

5th House = Creative Self-Expression (children of the body and mind)

8th House = Joint Resources (sharing of personal resources in cooperative relationships), Support from others

With a Grand Cardinal Cross activating these houses, energy should be directed into developing personal resources (2nd) and creative talents (5th), sharing them in cooperative ventures (8th) and establishing mutual friends and goals (11th) with the support of others (8th). If we become actively involved in any of the house affairs (e.g. receiving backing from others, creative expression, community activity), we may discover that we are automatically disciplining our thoughts, actions and emotional responses.

Fixed Grand Cross:

Blockage: Abuse of power

Outlet for Stress: Anything that satisfies emotionally

This Cross suggests that in a recent incarnation discipline (Cardinal, or possible Mutable Grand Cross) was used incorrectly to control and/or manipulate. Power has come to represent emotional security. We might seek to control others rather than discipline ourselves because of a subconscious fear of emotional insecurity. Internal and external challenges can increase in intensity until we transform our attitudes and emotional responses involving the houses and planets.

The Fixed signs are associated with the heart, spinal column, body fluids, nose, bladder and thyroid gland. These represent the body's vitality, circulation, elimination and metabolism—the power circuits, and must be closely regulated to prevent abuse. A Fixed Grand Cross indicates that "power" has been misused in the previous lifetime under the Cardinal or Mutable Grand Cross. In this lifetime, we may experience heartache because our efforts toward controlling events are relatively unsuccessful. We can only achieve emotional security by becoming involved in something that satisfies on an emotional level. This too can deteriorate into further negativity such as terrorism which may provide a perverted form of emotional satisfaction but hinders spiritual growth.

If thought patterns are not significantly changed, the Fixed Grand Cross will evolve into a Mutable T-Square in the next lifetime. Because of its inflexible controlling nature, a Fixed Grand Cross is not repeated. It will be transcended when you have relinquished your emotional need to control or manipulate others.

Fixed Grand Cross Example

4th House = Personal Foundations (self-image and emotional security, Home

6th House = Work, Service, Health

10th House = Professional Career, Personal Achievements

12th House = Self-Undoing, Ultimate Understanding

With this Grand Cross, the need is to release the emotional desire to control people in our career environment (6th and 10th), those we are karmically programmed to serve (12th) and those in the home (4th). This can be accomplished through the pursuit of an emotionally rewarding career and/or a search for the meaning of life.

T-Squares - Imbalance

A T-Square consists of two planets in opposition both squared by a third planet. This configuration intensifies the separate planetary aspects. It emphasizes the unresolved

228 / Spiritual, Metaphysical & New Trends in Modern Astrology

issues or lessons from previous incarnations under the Grand Crosses. A planet is removed from the Grand Cross and the area of this missing planet is referred to as the empty leg of the T-Square. Isabel Hickey likened the T-Square to "a table with three legs instead of four." Symbolically it is like a three-legged table which is continually rocking. We always feel off-balance mentally and emotionally and are uncomfortably aware of our own vulnerability. When we attempt to blame events or other people for our difficulties, circumstances occur which reveal the fallacy of this viewpoint. The planet opposite the empty leg, the one squared by the other planets is in a position of great force, similar to an arrow waiting to release a stream of energy into the opposing house. Positive or negative, whether or not the arrow (energy) is released depends on us. If the energy is positive, new growth can be achieved in the empty house.

When one of the T-Square planets is in a different Quality, this planet's house affairs offer additional insight in overcoming the stress. This house often indicates where our greatest difficulties have occurred. If all the planets are in the same quality, equal emphasis is placed in all three houses.

When a transiting or progressed planet reaches the exact degree of the missing planet (directly opposite the squared planet), additional turmoil can be created. This planet issues a challenge or triggers a crisis which must be dealt with. The lessons are hammered home in the current life by not allowing us to feel emotional security.

The "outlets for stress" for the T-Squares are the same as for the Grand Crosses. So are the correlations to the parts of the body. The "blockages" are different, however. Other differences are the constant crises and feelings of emotional vulnerability that must be endured.

Mutable T-Square

Blockage: Mental and emotional imbalance
Outlet for Stress: Being decisive while still remaining
   adaptable

With this T-Square, we feel very vulnerable. To find relief, we may transfer control to others and submissively flow with the events and people in the environment. Through this method we hope to achieve emotional stability. Unfortunately we may overcompensate, so though achieving adaptability we also become indecisive. This can result in a loss of will to assume control of our own lives.

When we become too submissive, we can overcome this through the placement of a Cardinal T-Square in a subsequent incarnation. A Mutable T-Square can be transcended by achieving a mental and emotional balance between the previous lifetime's aggressiveness (Fixed Grand Cross) and the current life's submissiveness.

Mutable T-Square Example

2nd House = Personal Resources (money, possessions, hidden talents, sense of self-worth)
8th House = Joint Resources (sharing of personal resources in cooperative relationships), Support from others
10th House = Professional Career, Personal Achievements

Empty Leg
4th House = Personal Foundations (self-image and emotional security), Home

We need to balance our mental attitudes and emotional responses in the three occupied houses by developing better personal foundations (4th House - empty leg). This will help us flow more easily, but decisively. Strong inner foundations (4th) can also open the way for sharing personal and joint resources (2nd and 8th) through our careers (10th). Otherwise, we may feel we are at the whim of destiny and resignedly submit to trauma.

Cardinal T-Square

Blockage: Submissiveness
Outlet for Stress: Activity on a physical, emotional
        and/or intellectual level

This placement reveals that we have transcended our Mutable T-Square as well as the emotional need to control (Fixed Grand Cross) but instead of being assertive, we are too submissive. The Cardinal energy motivates us to search for answers and ideas to lessen our inner turmoil.

If we do not use our Cardinal energy to effectively deal with our submissiveness, the Cardinal T-Square will be repeated in the subsequent lifetime. But a Fixed T-Square will be programmed if the activities in this incarnation lead to wrong conclusions. A Cardinal T-Square can be transcended by overcoming submissiveness with discernment.

Cardinal T-Square Example

2nd House = Personal Resources (money, possessions, hidden talents, sense of self-worth)
6th House = Work, Service, Health
8th House = Joint Resources (sharing of personal resources in cooperative relationships), Support from others

Empty Leg

12th House = Self-Undoing, Ultimate Understanding

We must actively work on finding the answers to the mysteries and meaning of life (12th House - empty leg). Discovering a philosophy that answers our questions will allow us to use and share our former incarnation's talents (2nd) in our work, sevice (6th) and in cooperative relationships (8th). Until we find this philosophy, the pressures we experience from a lack of self esteem (2nd), from those we serve with at work (6th) and from sharing resources (8th) will continue to bring pain and a sense of futility.

Fixed T-Square

Blockage: Lack of discernment regarding answers in
   previous lifetime

Outlet for Stress: Anything that satisfies emotionally

This T-Square placement reveals that in a recent incarnation there was a failure to or disinterest in digesting the answers (Cardinal T-Square) and an inability to discern the truth. This configuration creates a deep determination to search for knowledge to break free from emotional and mental stress. Our intensity may be misinterpreted by others as a "power" drive, though actually it is a drive to find inner peace through emotional satisfaction.

A Fixed T-Square will be repeated in subsequent incarnations until it is transcended, although different planets may be implemented. We will transcend it when we transform incorrect mental attitudes and emotional responses and learn discernment in the houses involved.

Fixed T-Square Example

3rd House = Environment, Education, Communication
7th House = Cooperative Relationships, Partnerships
9th House = Higher Education, Abstract Thoughts
Empty Leg
1st House = Self-Awareness, Physical Body, Approach
   to Life

We need to work on establishing a better approach to life (1st house - empty leg) in order to find emotional and mental peace. In a previous lifetime we lacked the perception of truth from answers received through your communication with others (3rd and 7th). Until we know who we are and what kind of life style (1st House - empty leg) we want, we will experience unhappiness and frustration with those in our environment (3rd), in shared relationships (7th) and with philosophical concepts (9th).

YOD - Growth

A Yod is two planets in sextile, both inconjuncting a third. This pattern points out areas where we: 1) have been responsive to our higher self in previous lifetimes, but 2) are now hampered spiritually because of lack of attunement with that connection. The Yod is also called the "hand of God" and the "finger of destiny" and points the way to spiritual growth. In many ways it is a spiritual blessing because it encourages us to remember we are spiritual beings—that we have a greater mission in life than to be grounded in a three dimensional world. It can reveal areas in our life where thoughts and actions in the preceding lifetime were being directed toward the mundane, losing sight of the higher expressions of the planets and houses involved.

A Yod will be transcended if we connect the link to our higher self through meditation and prayer. We will be able to adjust incorrect thought patterns and emotional responses regarding the inconjunct planet and its house. The sextile planets show the opportunity areas.

A Yod gives dexterity and aptitude in the houses involved. It is especially powerful when transiting planets aspect it or conjunct the release point, which is halfway between the two sextiled planets. The progression or transit transforms the Yod into a "kite," giving it the ability to lift the higher levels of attitudes, actions and emotional re-sponses. We must make a concerted effort to change for if we fail to use the Yod's energy correctly, our previously achieved spiritual attunement regarding these planets and houses is lost.

Yod Example

3rd House = Environment, Communications, Education
8th House = Joint Resources (sharing of personal resources in cooperative relationships), Support of others

10th House = Professional Career, Personal
                Achievements

Pisces Moon in the 3rd
Leo Uranus in the 8th
Libra Jupiter in the 10th
    The focal point of this Yod is the Moon in the 3rd
House, showing the need to adjust emotionally to the many
changing environmental experiences. Sensitivity to the
environment (Moon in 3rd); intuitive insights (Moon in
Pisces); strong psychic feelings (Uranus in 8th); organizing
and leadership abilities (Uranus in Leo); congenial nature
(Jupiter in 10th); and diplomatic friendliness (Jupiter in
Libra) will enable us to assist siblings or others in our
neighborhood (3rd), in gaining support from them (8th)
and in career and personal achievements (10th).

But There is a Need For You To:
    Uranus sextile Jupiter: use this opportunity to tap our
psychic potential (Uranus) and inner wisdom (Jupiter) in
dealing with others in the neighborhood and work environments (3rd and 10th) and in our sharing in cooperative
relationships (8th House).

*And to Correct Errors in Thinking and Actions From Previous
Lifetimes Concerning:*
    Moon inconjunct Uranus: controlling sudden outbursts
of emotional anger during times of inner stress since hostile
words, once spoken or thought, are difficult to retract.
    Moon inconjunct Jupiter: overcoming feelings of in-
security.

Angel Thompson

Angel Thompson is an innovator, an astrologer with comprehensive experience in counseling and teaching, as well as in promoting astrology and new age metaphysics.

Currently she serves as President of Aquarius Workshops, Inc., a school of astrology and publisher of *Aspects*, a quarterly magazine.

Angel lectured for national groups such as AFAN, AFA, ISAR, NCGR, UAC, and regional astrological associations in more than 40 states. In 1984 and 1987, she was one of ten Americans invited to speak at the World Congress of Astrology in Switzerland.

Angel is Director of Cosmic Workshop, a new age astrological center. She is inventor of *Starcards—The Astrologer's Handeck*.

A co-founder of AFAN, she served on their steering committee for five years. She was one of the people responsible for organizing UAC '86.

Angel has travelled extensively to study and photograph celestial phenomena. Her photograph of a Solar Eclipse in Africa was featured on the cover of *Astronomy Magazine*, June, 1980. Her emphasis on ritual and ceremony comes from shamanistic experience with the American Indians.

TRANSFORMATIONAL ASTROLOGY

INTRODUCTION

From the beginning of time, mankind has had a meaningful and significant relationship with the Sun, the Moon, the planets and certain fixed stars. All of life's patterns from birth to death, and skills such as hunting and farming, were organized around the rising and setting of the stars.

This was a magical time when the world was populated with nymphs and fairies, gods and goddesses, spirits seen and unseen. Heaven and Earth were animated with spirit that influenced life's process, and there was no division between man and nature. There was harmony, because the individual participated in a dynamic relationship with the universe. This relationship was often expressed through imitation, for it was believed possible to acquire the power and skills of others by mirroring their appearance. Adorned in fur and feathers, assuming the posture, dancing the dance, all of nature was available to enhance and enrich man's concept of Self.

Astrology at this time was a living experience. Developed as a system to organize time, as well as to understand the intricate workings of destiny, the astrologer/priests were the translators, interpreting the messages of the gods to the people. It was easy to have a relationship with the stars and planets because they were a visible part of life. Everyone knew of the rising Sun, of the growing light of the Moon. Out of doors, enjoying a natural existence, astrology was alive and practiced as part of everyday routine.

Astrology provided themes for religious ceremonies which had a primary function in ancient cultures. Participation in ceremonies was a responsibility every citizen fulfilled. The shared focus and purpose connected all members of the community in unity, as well as enriching individual spirit by providing a sense of belonging and hope for the future.

Astrology was practiced as a matter of life. The phases of the Moon kept the time; Heaven and Earth were equally alive with spirit that influenced process. This aliveness was perceived through the senses, and experience gained through participation led to personal knowledge and growth.

Then came the Dark Ages. Technology and science divided the world into being and non-being, reality and fantasy, spirit and matter. The fairies and nymphs disappeared. One God replaced the concept of the multiple gods. Astrology was relegated to a dark and dusty past, while the old ways were forgotten. All personal relationship with the stars lost significance and we became separate and alone.

Now, again, this is changing. A shift in consciousness occurred in the last century, giving birth to a desire to re-create the original participatory relationship. Astrology is once again the key to the past and the future, but it is a new kind of astrology. No longer just a curious artifact from the past, this new form of astrology provides the information that can lead to awareness of self as well as a greater understanding of the universe.

HOW TO MAKE ASTROLOGY A LIVING EXPERIENCE

Transformational Astrology is a system I have developed over the last decade to make astrology a living experience. I use it 1) to teach astrology through expression and experience; 2) to create modern ritual and ceremony using celestial phenomena, such as New and Full Moons; and 3) to stimulate personal process that can lead to self-actualization.

My methodology was influenced by American Indian ritualistic philosophy, Zen and Tibetan Buddhism as well as Taoism and modern psychological systems. It includes astrology as performance, a form taken from religious theater to dramatize elements within the individual horoscope; experiential astrology, using art, music, writing and crafts to illustrate principles; and psychological games that awaken knowledge of process.

The synthesis of astrology, psychology and ceremony creates an expanded awareness of instinctive energy patterns. The exploration of these patterns can lead to an enrichment and involvement of life and expression that must be experienced to be understood.

THE ENERGY PATTERNS WITHIN

With its mathematical calculations and emphasis on observation, astrology is primarily a cerebral experience. But now science has taught us that the observed and the observer are one. Participation is the key to this new reality. Transformational Astrology enlivens the cerebral process, putting theories of the mind into sound, sight, and action. To understand how this works, we must look to the basics of astrology.

The zodiac is a series of stages through which all process must pass. All the signs, houses and planets are accorded equal status. The planets are not gods, but are metaphors for psychological processes inherent in all organisms and related to the urge to survive. The horoscope is a rich and full image with 12 signs, 12 houses and 10 planets. Each sign, house and planet maintains its identity yet has relationships with other signs and planets that can be harmonious as well as stressful. There are multifarious combinations that express all facets of response and stimuli, personality and behavior. In the personal horoscope some signs and planets have more or less emphasis. The planets and signs receiving the greatest emphasis determine specific charac-teristics and are more likely to be integrated into the overall personality pattern. Planets and signs with less emphasis, or in complicated patterns, are not as easily expressed or integrated.

The goal in life is to know the Self, to become fully aware of all the parts of our being, sensations, emotions, mind, and body, all working together with full awareness. Awareness means being able to choose how we respond at any given moment. Awareness means knowing the Self.

Astrology tends to encourage stereotypes. One can always explain bad behavior by quoting a Sun sign. ("I'm a Scorpio, that's why I'm suspicious.") It's easy to get stuck with a stereotype, as evidenced by the actor who only plays romantic roles. The trouble is that we are more than one character. We are complex - the producer, director and star in our own show. We play all the roles and each is appropriate at certain times and places. The task is to understand each archetypal energy and then learn how to express it at will. This means learning to be more of ourselves and being true to our instincts. Remember, we play all the parts. We are strong (Sun), sensitive (Moon), mental (Mercury), loving (Venus), physical (Mars), optimistic (Jupiter), conservative (Saturn), inventive (Uranus), imaginative (Neptune), and powerful (Pluto). We are all things; we "encompass the multitudes." At any given moment, we have a full range of qualities with which to meet life's challenges. To be able to call on appropriate behavior has great benefits. Why should the Moon/emotions balance the books when Mercury/ mind can do a better job. Can we call on Libra during negotiations, or Aries for an adventure? We can act like any sign or planet when it suits our needs if we are aware and skilled at behavior modification.

When we learn to play all the parts of the horoscope,

we free ourselves from the limited perception of stereo-types, be it race, religion, sex or Sun sign. By expanding awareness to include all parts of our character, we actualize the full potential of our being and develop a range of expression and behavior that contributes to adaptability and thus to survival.

THE METHOD AND TECHNIQUE

How do we learn to play all the parts? This was a question that took many years to answer. Over countless class sessions, group meetings, discussions with other experiential astrologers and personal study, one thing became very clear—learning is accelerated when participation is included with traditional teaching. The challenge was to provide the atmosphere and structure wherein we could interact with each other and experience astrology as a living form.

Over the years, with the help of other astrologers and counselors, I developed techniques that 1) helped to explain astrological principles; 2) awakened others to their own psychological dynamics; and 3) created modern astrological ceremonies.

Astrological ideas are taught through mini-lectures, storytelling and demonstrations. Personal process is explored through playing games, participating in dialogues and scenarios, and sharing experience and feelings. Gathering in a circle recalls a ceremonial form and gives rise to non-specific religious feelings that can lead to changing awareness. The exercises sometimes combine all three, merging together much as romance, engagement and wedding inevitably lead to marriage—a synthesis from which emerges a new form.

HOW TO START: SPACE AND DIRECTION

Where are you? Here I am! Each moment is unique and can be measured in time and space and then analyzed.

We make a direct connection to time by aligning ourselves with the planetary energies of the moment. Cast a chart for the time the session begins. Indicate or mark the four directions in the room—North, South, East and West. Show where the planets might be in terms of the room's orientation to the directional points. For example, Jupiter might be in the West while Venus is in the East. To experience the expansive, optimistic energy of Jupiter, sit in the West. To feel more loving or pleasant, sit in the East with Venus. Different feelings arise from being in different spaces.

The emphasis on space and direction is connected to the study of geomancy, location astrology and feng shui, the Chinese art of placement—all designed to analyze the relationship of life's fortunes through the directional markings of the compass. Awareness of directional energy is fundamental to developing a relationship with nature and the cosmos.

"SPEEDREADING"

The traditional model found the teacher at the front of the room while the students sat quietly taking notes and not interrupting. This was fine for the teacher's ego but over and over, students complained that they weren't learning, that the ideas weren't becoming part of them.

I have always encouraged comments and questions from students and expanded this natural tendency by asking each person, in turn, to comment on a subject. Naturally, self-consciousness stopped some of the students. I found that by requiring a quick answer, an instinctive response was made. The students didn't have time to mentally formulate a response and the answer came from body sensations and instincts. The benefit is that self-consciousness breaks down and innate knowledge is given a natural expression. I call this "speedreading" and have used it to teach every part of the horoscope. For example, I ask for keywords for the Sun. Each person, in rapid succession says a word—hot, warm, fiery, summer, picnics, father, strict, light, fire, etc. No comments or corrections are made. It is as acceptable to repeat words as to have an inappropriate response. If a person gets stuck for a response, I just say "pass" and keep up the very quick rhythm. By requiring a quick response, everyone participates. Once a thought is vocalized or a behavior acted out, it is known in the heart as well as the head, and the performance can be repeated at will. Students often comment that they didn't know they knew so much. It is amazing how much we do know. It's just a matter of learning to express this knowledge.

CIRCLES

As a way to introduce the idea of ceremonies to modern astrologers, I begin by forming circles, inspired by the American Indian rituals. Forming circles is basic to human nature. Since tribal times when people gathered around an open fire, sharing warmth, the circle has been a natural expression of unity and wholeness. There is no hierarchy, no front or back. Everyone is equal and comes together out of shared purpose. Gathering in a circle focuses energy. I always take my place in the circle because it is important for the facilitator to be part of the group. Either move the chairs or ask that the group stand in a circle.

The circle can be formed according to the position of any natal planet. I use Sun signs because everyone knows their birth date and can find the appropriate spot. For those who know the position of the planets in their chart, Moon or Mercury signs are also effective.

In Sun sign order, everyone states their sign in rapid succession, "I am Aries, I am Taurus, I am Gemini," and so on. Then go around the circle again and each is asked to make a sound like the animal representing their sign. Leo often roars like a lion, Taurus may moo like a bull, while

Scorpio often hisses. Each sign can then imitate the posture appropriate to the sign, or all take turns walking like each of the signs. Opposing signs can meet in the center, imitate each other and trade places. The circle can be rotated so that Aries stands in Taurus's space and Taurus in Gemini's space. Significant learning takes place afterwards when participants report their experience. Aries feels tied down in the Taurus space, Taurus feels more free in the Gemini space, and so on.

MUSIC

Music is an important part of any experience. It is a universal language and an effective way of controlling the environment. It covers outside noise and sets the mood (quiet music to calm, rousing music to awaken). Singing is a good way to build unity and I always start and end a circle session with a song. I use simple melodies and short sentences, my favorite being—"I am a circle, I'm healing you. You are a circle, you are healing me. Unite us. Be one. Unite us. Be as one." When sung three times in succession, it can be a moving experience. Even when working in a foreign country where the group was primarily German speaking, and the words had to be translated, there was no problem with interacting.

It is possible to compose music of the moment, based on the position of the planets for any given time. Tapes of astrological music of historical events are available and this is a good non-verbal way to examine the connection between astrology and music.

I create "elemental music" by dividing the room into four element groups based on the Sun sign. The Fire signs clap their hands, the Earth signs stamp their feet, Water signs hum and Air signs say "light, light, light." I get a good rhythm going and then everyone plays their part while we march around the room, singing and making our own music.

GUIDED IMAGERY

Guided imagery is a good way to help break stereotypes. First, put the group into a meditative space with eyes closed, breathing slowly and regularly. Then slowly, describe a scenario. Subjects might—become another sex or race; become a tree; climb a mountain to find a good luck stone; return to childhood dreams; travel to the stars; or become a multi-faceted crystal. The guided imagery should take about 15 minutes and participants are always guided back to the present time and space. This is very relaxing and serves as a stimulus to the imagination. If the belief system can be suspended for just a few minutes, all kinds of new thoughts and ideas have room to enter.

I use fairy tales and stories to illustrate ideas and they have a similar effect to guided imagery. Stories fit unconscious content into conscious fantasy, which in turn enables us to deal with that unconscious content. Fairy tales offer new dimensions that are difficult to discover on one's own. Even more important, the form and structure of the fairy tale suggests images which can give better direction and an expanded awareness of personal potential.

I like to use some of the many myths known about the planets, as well as childhood favorites such as "Pluto and Persephone" to illustrate the process of transformation; "Phaeton and the Chariot of the Sun," while discussing pride and will; "The Three Little Pigs," when talking about the Earth signs; and "Peter Pan," to illustrate the complex of the puer eternus.

PHYSICAL CONNECTIONS

Astrology is the most powerful tool available for understanding human nature. When we learn something, it is in the mind. When we know something, it is in the heart and in the body. Each sign and planet has a physical counterpart in the body. Transformational Astrology attempts to connect the body with the mind through exercises designed to help recognize the association in the body.

As a warm-up, I lead the group through a series of movements, each one connecting with a part of the body. This can be simple or complicated depending on the mood. There are many variations. Basically, it is an emphasis on each part of the body in turn. A simple version might be: Aries, hands on head; Taurus, hands on throat; Gemini, arms extended; Cancer, arms cradled in front of stomach; Leo, hands on heart; Virgo, hands rubbing intestinal area; Libra, arms extended like a balance; Scorpio, touching the genitals; Sagittarius, stroking the thighs; Capricorn, knees bent, hands lowered to the knees; Aquarius, ankles together; Pisces, feet together, arms together in a wavy motion like a fish. Performed in sequence, these movements form a tai-chi of astrology. All parts of the body receive attention; focused breathing helps to release accumulated thoughts and to calm the mind. There are many variations to these movements and the participants become creative and inventive once the basic form is demonstrated.

ASTRODRAMA AND VOICE DIALOGUE

Dramatizing the planets is not new. All religious theater from ancient Greeks to modern Moslems act out the adventures of the gods and goddesses. A cast of characters portrays the planets using suitable costumes, action and dialogue. A story is told, the music swells, the drama unfolds. This is entertaining, as well as educational. Modern astrodrama expanded this method to include acting out the individual horoscope, as well as the archetypes, thus combining astrology as performance with psychodrama techniques. A person plays the role of one planet in his or her chart. Another person plays a different planet in that chart. The teacher gives a theme; a diaglogue is established between the two planets. The individual and the audience get to see and hear how the two planets work. This is very effective for illustrating the many internal conflicts we all experience.

This technique was further expanded into a method called "voice dialogue" in which one person takes both parts, switching back and forth, essentially talking to himself. For example, the point of study is a Sun/Saturn opposition. The facilitator sets the scene by giving a theme. Sun and Saturn will discuss whether they stay home and work, or whether they take time off to go to the movies. Both planets have definite needs that may be in conflict with each other. Both planets need full expression. If one urge is sacrificed for the sake of the other, internal pressure, frustration and conflict are the result. The person must learn to identify the needs of both planets, then negotiate and compromise with Self in order to fulfill both needs. A compromise is reached after sufficient discussion. The person would go to the movies, fulfilling the urge of the Sun, but would skip lunch the next day to do the required work, fulfilling the need of Saturn. Both planetary urges are satisfied. The conflict is resolved. Major learning has taken place. We have seen and heard the planets in action; we have worked out the conflict. The challenge has been met.

It is important to remember that every planet in the horoscope must and will have expression. It is just a matter of finding the appropriate time and place for the expression.

Astrodrama and voice dialogue are very effective for studying all parts of the horoscope. The results are always different because the responses are spontaneous.

MIRRORS AND COUPLES AND QUARTETS

Wherever we go, there we are. We are always meeting ourselves when we meet others. Good and bad qualities are reflected in others, and the things we like or dislike in others, in most cases, are qualities we ourselves have.

Unfulfilled expectations and disappointments greet

the belief that we are all the same. To be aware of how we are different adds to our awareness of Self.

We all want to have loving relationships by trusting others, but feelings of love and trust cannot be manufactured. To do so only creates dishonesty in behavior. However, honesty is a quality that can be chosen. Even if we cannot choose to like or dislike another, we can choose to be honest about our feelings. When we are honest, we may not like it, but we trust them. This is of great benefit in open communication.

It is human nature to trust someone who appears to be like we are. When we are able to mirror the speech and behavior of others, we have an effective tool for building confidence. This can be learned by working in pairs.

Form the group into couples. Each is identified as "A" or "B." For a few minutes, they talk to each other, working on such themes as "I feel powerful when I . . . " "I feel weak when I . . . " "I notice we're different because . . . " Other exercises could be non-verbal, each person mirroring the facial expression or body language of the other. Pair work is good for experiencing ourselves through others. It is a good way to examine aspects of the horoscope and it teaches open communication and risk-taking. Pair work also has the benefit of allowing participants to interact with each other, thus developing social contacts and inspiring new methods of behavior.

Working in groups of four is also effective. Divide the participants into four groups based on Sun sign elements. Each group has five minutes to prepare a report that expresses how the Sun behaves in that element. The theme might be pride. Each element group reports. Fire Suns feel pride in their ability to lead, and Earth Suns in their ability to get the job done. Water Suns feel pride in their sensitivity, and Air Suns in their ability to reason and communicate. Afterwards, the entire group discusses the differences and similarities, and again, participation facilitates learning.

Another exercise is to form into groups of four people. Each person in the quartet chooses an element to portray. Now for two minutes each person talks in the mode appropriate to that element. For example, Air might gossip and chat; Water might speak softly; Earth is practical and questioning; Fire is high-spirited. After each person has a chance to talk in their chosen element, they should switch places and adopt a different mode. This is repeated for four rounds until each person has behaved like each element. It is a lot of fun even though at times it sounds like a "tower of babble."

WRITING/ARTS AND CRAFTS

Writing, drawing, painting and collage are all good non-verbal ways to reach unconscious content. Participants can make a planetary notebook, each page devoted to a sign or planet, and can list keywords, images or sentences to help identify how a planet or sign works. For example, the Sun page might have key words like bright, fiery, purposeful, sentences to complete such as "I shine when I . . . " and images of powerful explosions, stars, sunsets, etc.

Writing short essays is also very revealing. Themes might be—Moon—I remember mama; Jupiter—my most embarrassing moment; or Saturn—my greatest lesson. The essays may be read aloud to the group and discussed, noticing the similarities and differences.

Drawing is a simple experience that works to break self-consciousness and false expectations. All the paper, pencils, crayons, etc., are placed in the center of the room and everyone takes what they want. Give a theme. Draw all Suns or Moons. Use all circles or triangles. Compose pictures with all the shapes. The drawings are shared; comments are made. Sometimes interpretations emerge, sometimes silent viewing is best. Everyone benefits from art and this teaches that art is a quality within each of us.

It is fun to make masks. Popsicle sticks and paper plates, bits of ribbon, glitter and colors make interesting masks in a short time. Once again, adorned in fur and feathers, we can imagine the astrology of the ancients, mirroring the images of the gods and goddesses. A mask of Jupiter does help when a task of Jupiter is at hand.

Another good art exercise is to have the entire group work on a collage or mural, using the solar system, the rites of spring, or the birth of Venus as a theme. Displaying the art is inspiring to others, encouraging the recognition that this is something all of us can do.

GROUP GAMES

I use group games to illustrate archetypal principles. Each person works alone but with shared purpose and common goals. For Jupiter, I have everyone blow up a balloon with the "hot air" of opinions that prevent full expression of being. A key word describing the opinion is written on the balloon with a marking pen. Then, at a given time, either I surprise them by popping the balloons, or I allow them to pop their own. It's interesting to see how attached one becomes to his own "hot air."

The "Secrets" game is played in adjunct to the study of the planet Pluto. It usually brings intensity to the already complex subject of transformation. Everyone writes their deepest secret on a piece of paper. All the papers are put into a bowl. Each person picks someone else's secret and then all the secrets are read aloud. It is amazing how the skeletons in the closet lose their significance when read by someone else. Of course, no one knows which secret belongs to whom so it is very safe. This same idea can be used to explore the greatest fear when studying the planet Saturn.

I save this exercise for last. It is taken from the American Indian tradition and called the "Give Away." Each person writes on a piece of paper some gift they will give away. "I give you a smile; I give you peace of mind; I give you laughter." These are some of the gifts. Everyone exchanges papers and all receive a wonderful gift illustrating the principle of "as you give, so shall you receive."

CONCLUSION

As mentioned earlier, there is no end to the inventive techniques and games that can be developed by the teacher and the group. The inspiration and focus is always available by casting a horoscope for the moment the session begins. This automatically shows what planetary energies are manifesting, and these planets can serve as a stimuli to imagination and purpose.

I have given some examples of the techniques used in the practice of Transformational Astrology. By no way are they complete. The instructions are sparse because this is meant to serve as an introduction rather than as a working outline.

Transformational Astrology can be done alone for self-cultivation or used for groups from 2 to 200, 1) to teach astrological principles through expression and experience; 2) to awaken awareness of personal process; and 3) to create modern ceremonies using traditional astrological forms.

For the student of astrology, this offers a new and lively experience that deepens and accelerates learning. For the professional astrologer it provides a framework that can lead to greater understanding between client and counselor, teacher and student. For those on the path of self-actualization, it offers new skills useful in expanding awareness and integrating all parts of being, as well as opportunities to develop open and honest communication with others.

With Transformational Astrology, we can learn to

expand the knowledge of all parts of our being, to actualize the full potential of destiny and character. We can learn a broad range of expression and response that contributes to adaptability, and thus to survival.

Once again, we have found a personal relationship with the stars. They are in us, with us, and part of us. We can walk with nature as we expand our vision of a greater universe. Once again, astrology is a living experience.

My advice to the world: Make everything you do a creative expression of yourself.

I want to give special thanks to Jeff Jawer, the inventor of Astrodrama. Many of the ideas that led to the development of Transformational Astrology spring directly from playing and working with Jeff.

> Between the Dream
> And the Dreamer
> Lies the Vision
>
> Between Time
> And Space
> Is the Instant
>
> In an Instant
> I am Whole
> In the Wholeness
> I am One
>
> Dreaming the Dream
> Of the Dreamer
> I am Home.
>
> Angel

STAY IN TOUCH

On the following pages you will find listed, with their current prices, some of the books and tapes now available on related subjects. Your book dealer stocks most of these, and will stock new titles in the Llewellyn series as they become available. We urge your patronage.

However, to obtain our full catalog, to keep informed of new titles as they are released and to benefit from informative articles and helpful news, you are invited to write for our bi-monthly news magazine/catalog. A sample copy is free, and it will continue coming to you at no cost as long as you are an active mail customer. Or you may keep it coming for a full year with a donation of just $2.00 in U.S.A. ($7.00 for Canada & Mexico, $20.00 overseas, first class mail). Many bookstores also have *The Llewellyn New Times* available to their customers. Ask for it.

Stay in touch! In *The Llewellyn New Times'* pages you will find news and reviews of new books, tapes and services, announcements of meetings and seminars, articles helpful to our readers, news of authors, advertising of products and services, special money-making opportunities, and much more.

The Llewellyn New Times
P.O. Box 64383-Dept. 380, St. Paul, MN 55164-0383, U.S.A.

• • •

TO ORDER BOOKS AND TAPES

If your book dealer does not have the books and tapes described on the following pages readily available, you may order them direct from the publisher by sending full price in U.S. funds, plus $1.00 for handling and 50¢ each book or item for postage within the United States; outside USA surface mail add $1.50 per item postage and $1.00 per order for handling. Outside USA air mail add $7.00 per item postage and $1.00 per order for handling. MN residents add 6% sales tax.

FOR GROUP STUDY AND PURCHASE

Because there is a great deal of interest in group discussion and study of the subject matter of this book, we feel that we should encourage the adoption and use of this particular book by such groups by offering a special "quantity" price to group leaders or "agents".

Our Special Quantity Price for a minimum order of five copies of *Spiritual, Metaphysical & New Trends in Modern Astrology* is $29.85 Cash-With-Order. This price includes postage and handling within the United States. Minnesota residents must add 6% sales tax. For additional quantities, please order in multiples of five. For Canadian and foreign orders, add postage and handling charges as above. Credit Card (VISA, MasterCard, American Express, Diners' Club) Orders are accepted. Charge Card Orders only may be phoned free ($15.00 minimum order) within the U.S.A. by dialing 1-800-THE MOON (in Canada call: 1-800-FOR-SELF). Customer Service calls dial 1-612-291-1970. Mail Orders to:

LLEWELLYN PUBLICATIONS
P.O. Box 64383-Dept. 380 / St. Paul, MN 55164-0383, U.S.A.

PLUTO: The Evolutionary Journey of the Soul
by Jeff Green
If you have ever asked "Why am I here?" or "What are my lessons?" then this book will help you to objectively learn the answers from an astrological point of view. Green shows you how the planet Pluto relates to the evolutionary and karmic lessons in this life and how past lives can be understood through the position of Pluto in your chart.

Beyond presenting key principles and ideas about the nature of the evolutionary journey of the Soul, this book supplies practical, concise and specific astrological methods and techniques that pinpoint the answers to the above questions. If you are a professional counselor or astrologer, this book is indispensible to your practice. The reader who studies this material carefully and applies it to his or her own chart will discover an objective vehicle to uncover the essence of his or her own state of being. The understanding that this promotes can help you cooperate with, instead of resist, the evolutionary and karmic lessons in your life.

Green describes the position of Pluto through all of the signs and houses, explains the aspects and transits of Pluto, discusses Pluto in aspect to the Moon's Nodes, and gives sample charts and readings. It is the most complete look at this "new" planet ever.

0-87542-296-9, 6 x 9, 360 pages, softcover. $12.95

ARCHETYPES OF THE ZODIAC
by Kathleen Burt
The horoscope is probably the most unique tool for personal growth you can ever have. This book is intended to help you understand how the energies within your horoscope manifest. Once you are aware of how your chart operates on an instinctual level, you can then work consciously with it to remove any obstacles to your growth.

The technique offered in this book is based upon the incorporation of the esoteric rulers of the signs and the integration of their polar opposites. This technique has been very successful in helping the client or reader modify existing negative energies in a horoscope so as to improve the quality of his or her life and the understanding of his or her psyche.

There is special focus in this huge comprehensive volume on the myths for each sign. Some signs may have as many as *four different myths* coming from all parts of the world. All are discussed by the author. There is also emphasis on the Jungian Archetypes involved with each sign.

This book has a depth often surprising to the readers of popular astrology books. It has a clarity of expression seldom found in books of the esoteric tradition. It is very easy to understand, even if you know nothing of Jungian philosophy or of mythology. It is intriguing, exciting and very helpful for all levels of astrologers.

0-87542-08805, 592 pages, 6 x 9, 24 illus., softcover $12.95

URANUS: Freedom From the Known
by Jeff Green
This book deals primarily with the archetypal correlations of the planet Uranus to human psychology and behavior to anatomy/physiology and the chakra system, and to metaphysical and cosmic laws. Uranus' relationship to Saturn, from an individual and collective point of view, is also discussed.

The text of this book comes intact in style and tone from an intensive workshop held in Toronto. You will feel as if you are a part of that workshop.

In reading *Uranus* you will discover how to naturally liberate yourself from all of your conditioning patterns, patterns that were determined by the "internal" and "external" environment. Every person has a natural way to actualize this liberation. This natural way is examined by use of the natal chart and from a developmental point of view.

The 48-year sociopolitical cycle of Uranus and Saturn is discussed extensively, as is the relationship between Uranus, Saturn and Neptune. With this historical perspective, you can see what lies ahead in 1988, a very important year.

0-87542-297-7, 192 pages, 5¼ x 8, softcover $7.95

CHIRON
by Barbara Hand Clow
This new astrology book is about the most recently discovered planet, Chiron. This little-known planet was first sighted in 1977. It has an eccentric orbit, on a 50-51 year cycle between Saturn and Uranus. It brought farsightedness into astrology because Chiron is the *bridge to the outer planets*, Neptune and Pluto, from the inner ones.

This is the most important astrological book yet about Chiron! Chiron presents exciting new insights on astrology. The small but influential planet of Chiron reveals *how* the New Age Initiation will affect each one of us. Chiron is an Initiator, an Alchemist, a Healer, and a Spiritual Guide.

For those who are astrologers, *Chiron has more information than any other book about this planet, which was first sighted in 1977.*
   • *Learn why* Chiron rules Virgo and the Sixth House.
   • Have the necessary information about Chiron in each house, in each sign, and how the aspects affect each person's chart.

The influences of Chiron are an important new factor in understanding capabilities and potentials which we all have. Chiron rules: Healing with the hands, Healing with crystals, Initiation and Alchemy and Alteration of the body by Mind and Spirit. Chiron also rules Cartomancy and the Tarot reader. As such it is an especially vital resource for everyone who uses the Tarot.

0-87542-094-X, approx. 300 pages, 6 x 9, charts $9.95

OPTIMUM CHILD
by Gloria Star

This is a brand new approach to the subject of astrology as applied to children. Not much has been written on developmental astrology, and this book fills a gap that has needed filling for years. There is enough basic material for the novice astrologer to easily determine the needs of his or her child (or children). All it takes is the natal chart. A brief table of where the planets were when your child was born is included in the book so that even if you don't have a chart on your child, you can find out enough to fully develop his or her potentials.

In *Optimum Child* you will find a thorough look at the planets, houses, rising signs, aspects and transits. Each section includes physical, mental and emotional activities and needs that this child would best respond to. It is the most comprehensive book yet on child astrology. This one is definitely not for children only. Every parent and professional astrologer should read it thoroughly. You should use it and help your child develop those talents and potentials inherent in what is shown within the natal chart.

0-87542-740-5, 360 pages, 6 x 9, softcover   **$9.95**

SIGNS OF THE TIMES
by Stan Barker

With remarkable accuracy, Barker predicts political and social events from now until the next century, based on Neptune's current transit through Capricorn.

In this book the author predicted:
- The popularity of Ronald Reagan
- The popularity of the Bill Cosby Show
- The U.S. involvement in Central America
- The Space Shuttle disaster

And you can too!

Stan Barker discovered that the planet Neptune astrologically indicates the direction of America. Here, he shows how the position of Neptune against the Zodiac has always indicated U.S. involvement in wars, depressions and politics. More than that, the *Neptune Factor* also shows very clearly how the transits of Neptune indicate: our morals; architecture; fashion, popular music, movies, and books; and our economic trends.

While this book is valuable for astrologers, it is not just for experts in that field—*even if you know nothing about astrology, you will fully understand this book!* This is because everything is fully and clearly explained. Explanations show how the Neptune Factor has affected America since Columbus, and how Neptune affects our country when it is in any particular sign. From this, the future is easy to determine.

Neptune entered a new sign in 1984, and will be in that sign until 1998. Will you be ready for this period and beyond? Get *The Signs of the Times* and be prepared!

0-87542-030-3, 320 pages   **$9.95**